THE

TRANS-PACIFIC PARTNERSHIP AND CANADA

THE
TRANS-PACIFIC PARTNERSHIP AND CANADA

A CITIZEN'S GUIDE

EDITED BY SCOTT SINCLAIR
AND STUART TREW

JAMES LORIMER & COMPANY LTD., PUBLISHERS
TORONTO

James Lorimer & Company Ltd., Publishers acknowledges the support of the
Ontario Arts Council (OAC), an agency of the Government of Ontario, which
in 2015–16 funded 1,676 individual artists and 1,125 organizations in 209
communities across Ontario for a total of $50.5 million. We acknowledge the
support of the Canada Council for the Arts, which last year invested $153 million
to bring the arts to Canadians throughout the country. This project has been
made possible in part by the Government of Canada and with the support of the
Ontario Media Development Corporation.

Cover design: Adam Hartling
Cover image: Shutterstock

Library and Archives Canada Cataloguing in Publication

The Trans-Pacific Partnership and Canada : a citizen's guide / edited by
Scott Sinclair, Stuart Trew

Includes bibliographical references and index.
Issued in print and electronic formats.

ISBN 978-1-4594-1180-7 (paperback).--ISBN 978-1-4594-1181-4 (epub)

1. Trans-Pacific Strategic Economic Partnership Agreement (2005).
2. Free trade--Canada. 3. Free trade--Pacific Area. 4. Foreign trade
regulation--Canada. 5. Foreign trade regulation--Pacific Area. 6. Canada--
Commerce--Pacific Area. 7. Pacific Area--Commerce--Canada. 8. Canada--
Foreign economic relations--Pacific Area. 9. Pacific Area--Foreign
economic relations--Canada. I. Sinclair, Scott, editor II. Trew, Stuart,
editor

HF2570.7.T73 2016   382'.911823   C2016-902685-X
                                                        C2016-902686-8

James Lorimer & Company Ltd., Publishers
117 Peter Street, Suite 304
Toronto, ON, Canada
M5V 0M3
www.lorimer.ca

Printed and bound in Canada.

CONTENTS

INTRODUCING THE TPP

Scott Sinclair and Stuart Trew

One of the last acts of Stephen Harper's Conservative government in 2015 was to clinch the Trans-Pacific Partnership (TPP) agreement at a final negotiating round in Atlanta, Georgia. For two years, the prime minister had promised Canadians he would only sign the twelve-country trade deal if it were in Canada's best interests to do so. Lo and behold, it was, "without any doubt whatsoever, in the best interests of the Canadian economy," said Harper on October 5. "Ten years from now, I predict with 100 per cent certainty, people are looking back, they will say if we've got in it, they'll say that was a great thing. And if we haven't, they'll say that was a terrible error."[1]

Two weeks later, the Conservative government was voted out of office in an election that was widely billed as a referendum on Harper's vision and priorities for Canada.[2] The TPP, on the other hand, would live on, handing the incoming Liberal government a contentious file and potentially saddling Canadians with a controversial legacy that could endure long after other Harper-era policies have been discarded. Whether the TPP actually comes into force will be determined largely by U.S. domestic politics. However, the Canadian people and their new government still have the power to decide whether Canada should be part of it.

There are very good reasons, many of them outlined in this book, why Canada should walk away from the TPP. Interestingly, the public might even prefer it. In June 2016, on the eve of a North American leaders' summit in Ottawa, an important public opinion poll showed that Canadians were sharply divided over that TPP template — the North American Free Trade Agreement (NAFTA).[3] Only one-quarter of respondents said Canada has benefited from NAFTA since it was adopted, while more than a third think it should be renegotiated or exited immediately. In the wake of the stunning UK Brexit vote and rising opposition to free-trade agreements in the U.S., such results must be disquieting for Canada's free-trade champions.

Once the bitter, existential debate over the Canada–U.S. Free Trade Agreement and NAFTA receded, Canadian governments of all political stripes acted as if the virtues of unfettered markets and corporate-led globalization were a settled issue. Canada's business and political leaders have wholeheartedly embraced free trade as part of a broader neoliberal ideology that favours deregulation, privatization and austerity; most tend to view the TPP as just another step in an inexorable, irreversible progression.[4] For years, the Canadian public appeared largely willing to defer to leaders and orthodox economic experts on how best to manage trade and investment liberalization. But today there is no clear consensus on this issue, as the recent polling indicates. Undoubtedly, this situation will be further shaken up by the growing public backlash in the U.S. and the EU (Canada's major trading partners) to ever-deeper globalization and more intrusive trade and investment treaties.

A growing body of economic research now confirms what blue-collar workers and marginalized groups in the developing and developed worlds know from experience: intensified international trade and laissez-faire globalization, even if they are not the only causes, have contributed to job insecurity and stagnant living standards for a good many people.[5] Authorities including economists Joseph Stiglitz and Thomas Piketty have analyzed how the benefits of trade and globalization have gone almost exclusively to the very wealthy and that this is fuelling inequality.[6] They are not arguing to turn back the clock on globalization or to retreat within national borders, but that these disturbing social trends lend urgency to the task of building a more humane, sustainable and inclusive global economy. Efforts to expose and check the extreme corporate ambitions that drive the TPP and similar treaties, and to democratize and rebalance trade rules and treaty negotiations, are also essential.

As the analyses in this volume attest, the scope of modern trade and investment treaties has become unreasonably broad with serious implications for democratic decision-making. At the urging of corporate lobbyists, these "external constitutions" are constantly colonizing new areas of policy and regulation only peripherally related to trade.[7] In fact, the main thrust of the progressive critique of the current free-trade agenda is that most of what is being pursued under the guise of agreements like the TPP is not about trade at all. Instead, these treaties have become convenient and effective tools to help multinational corporations pursue unpopular legislative and regulatory changes, including longer patent and copyright protections for brand-name drugs, music, films and books, or special rights for foreign investors to challenge environmental and public health regulations. These corporate victories are achieved through the back door of secretive negotiations rather than openly through the democratic process or domestic courts.

A "Made-in-America" agreement

Most political and news commentary on modern trade agreements overlooks their antidemocratic foundation. There is also startlingly little discussion in the media on the fact the TPP is an overtly U.S.-driven and -dominated initiative, designed to bolster that country's corporate and strategic ambitions. As the United States Trade Representative (USTR) boasts in its branding material for the agreement, the TPP is truly "made-in-America." That is not to say the majority of U.S. citizens and workers will benefit. On the contrary, the TPP is simply the latest in a series of U.S. free-trade deals that have subjected American workers to intensified globalization and international competition, resulting in job losses, growing inequality and downward pressure on wages.

The TPP negotiations began, for all intents and purposes, in 2008, when the U.S. signalled its interest in joining a little-known and relatively insignificant trade pact between four small Pacific Rim nations: New Zealand, Chile, Brunei and Singapore. In the same year, Australia, Peru and Vietnam also expressed interest in being part of the talks. The U.S. formally joined the process in 2009, a year before Malaysia. The first major negotiating round among the nine earliest members was held in

November 2010. Canada and Mexico were admitted in 2012, followed later that year by Japan, bringing the TPP up to its current level of twelve countries.

The TPP aims to create binding rules on everything from regulatory policies, drug patents and copyrights to how state-owned enterprises can and cannot operate. In practical terms, this means aligning other countries' standards, intellectual property rights regimes and other business norms with those in the U.S., as far as possible. But while the TPP is frequently portrayed as a unified free-trade area comprising 40 per cent of global GDP, it is really a hub-and-spoke arrangement with the U.S. at its centre.

At U.S. insistence, the TPP does not include the most-favoured-nation (MFN) treatment for goods that is a staple of multilateral trade treaties. Under MFN, the best tariff treatment given to goods from any member country is automatically extended to goods from any other ("Favour one, favour all"). The U.S. calculated it could get better deals by negotiating individually with each TPP member without MFN. The result is that even on the core issue of market access for goods, the TPP is a complicated grab bag of bilateral arrangements rather than a true free-trade zone.[8] Similarly, while the final TPP agreement encroached seriously on other countries' regulatory autonomy in U.S. priority areas, it accommodated U.S. domestic sensitivities around government procurement (where "Buy American" laws were untouched), transparency on drug pricing (Medicaid and Medicare were carved out) and temporary movement of workers (where the U.S. made no commitments).

U.S. dominance of the TPP process is also reflected in the detailed terms of entry it negotiated with Canada and Mexico, and subsequently Japan, as discussed in more detail below. If the TPP is ratified, the U.S. will continue to play this vetting role, determining which additional countries will be admitted and on what terms. Moreover, under domestic law the U.S. administration must affirm (certify) that any original TPP member is in full compliance before the treaty can come into force.[9] This gives the U.S. government another lever to shape the internal affairs of TPP member countries to the advantage of U.S.-based multinational corporations.

Initially, the agreement was pitched by U.S. officials as open to China's eventual membership — as long as the country's leadership was prepared to accept a "high-standards" agreement. But since the 2012 entry of Japan to the TPP, led by hawkish Prime Minister Shinzö Abe, and with growing Congressional opposition in Washington, the pact is more frequently portrayed by the administration as a strategy to contain China. "If we don't write the rules for free trade around the world, guess what, China will," said President Obama. "And they'll write those rules in a way that gives Chinese workers and Chinese businesses the upper hand."[10] The TPP has become the second prong of the Obama administration's "pivot to Asia" — the commercial counterpart to a stepped-up U.S. military presence in the region.[11]

Security concerns, growing tension over conflicting territorial claims in the South China Sea, and China's increasing military capabilities have stoked fears among its closest neighbours. This helps explain why even poor Asian countries such as Vietnam are willing to accept disadvantageous rules ill-suited to countries at that level of development.[12] To Vietnam, Brunei and Malaysia, moving under the TPP umbrella carries an implicit promise of U.S. protection, which makes other concessions more palatable.

What are the trade benefits for Canada?

Canada is largely peripheral to broader U.S. geopolitical goals in the Asia-Pacific. The biggest TPP impacts in this country will be of a commercial and regulatory nature, and not in the positive way proponents of the agreement would have us believe.

As John Jacobs explains in Chapter 1, claims the TPP will generate significant trade benefits for Canada are unfounded. The reasons for this are straightforward. Canada already has tariff-free access to most of the TPP region. In fact, exports to TPP countries with which Canada does not have an FTA represent only 3 per cent of the country's total exports (see Figure 1 on page 29). At the same time, 7 per cent of Canadian imports come from these countries. Canada mainly exports unprocessed and semiprocessed goods, while importing mostly manufactured and higher-value-added products.

Since Canada imports more than it exports, and these imports currently face higher tariff protection than the exports, tariff elimination under the TPP will worsen Canada's existing trade deficits with non-FTA countries in the TPP region. It will also deepen Canada's dependence on natural resource exports at the expense of its manufacturing sector. While certain industries such as beef, oilseeds and pork will see new opportunities from tariff liberalization — though, as now, in competition with U.S. exporters — others will be worse off. Dairy, automotive and other manufacturing sectors will experience negative impacts from Canada's ratification of the TPP. The overall impact on the trade balance and the quality of Canada's exports will most likely be negative.

These sobering conclusions are broadly consistent with other studies that have attempted to estimate the impacts on Canada of tariff elimination under the TPP. A Tufts University study projects a tiny one-time boost to the Canadian economy of 0.28 per cent of GDP by the year 2025.[13] Moreover, the Tufts study predicts 58,000 job losses in Canada and increased income inequality since most of the gains from trade flow to wealthy corporations and investors rather than to workers. Most recently, a study by the C.D. Howe Institute predicts a gain of just 0.056 per cent to Canadian GDP by the year 2025 and only 0.068 per cent by 2035.[14] Perhaps more importantly, the C.D. Howe study predicts a loss to the Canadian economy of only 0.026 per cent of GDP (just over $900 million by their calculation) by the year 2035 if the TPP goes ahead *without* Canada. Although some sectors will be disadvantaged, other key sectors including the auto industry will actually be *better off* if Canada stays out of the agreement. The argument that Canada cannot afford to miss out on the TPP, which Harper so emphatically made in October 2015, is not supported by macroeconomic forecasts.

Far beyond trade

If the trade gains are minute from Canada's participation in the TPP, the costs to democracy and the regulatory capacity of government are high. A key theme of this book is that the TPP is about far more than trade. In fact, only a handful of the agreement's thirty chapters address traditional barriers to the free movement of goods between nations. With tariffs and import quotas already small globally, the focus of newer, more expansive treaties like the TPP has turned to so-called non-tariff barriers, the most important of which are regulations. Citizens should be aware of the threats this free trade "mission creep" poses to democratic governance in the public interest.

As Nobel Prize–winning economist Joseph Stiglitz has pointed out, "Huge multinational corporations complain that inconsistent regulations make business costly. But most of the regulations, even if they are imperfect, are there for a reason: to protect workers, consumers, the economy and the environment."[15] The chapters in this book examine several of the key provisions in the TPP that directly interfere with the critical regulatory role of government. Our goal is to explain, in straightforward language, how the agreement could have serious and potentially irreversible negative impacts on public policy in the following areas.

Health care and the cost of medicines

The contributions from Scott Sinclair (Chapter 2) and Joel Lexchin (Chapter 3) explore the implications of the TPP for public health care and drug costs resulting from the agreement's provisions on intellectual property, services and investment. Canada already has an industry-friendly system for protecting pharmaceutical patents, reflected in our paying the fourth-highest drug costs per capita among OECD countries.[16] Meanwhile, research and development in Canada's pharmaceutical sector has fallen to historic lows.[17] The TPP will worsen this situation by extending patents to account for supposed regulatory delays in approving drugs for sale, driving up costs to our domestic health system while inflicting great harm internationally. As Doctors Without Borders and others have passionately argued, these changes will cost lives in the poorer TPP countries and in other developing nations as the treaty is expanded.

Lexchin, an emergency room physician and one of Canada's foremost drug experts, points out where the TPP creates new opportunities for U.S. and Japanese drug companies to comment on, review and appeal Canadian regulatory decisions. This could adversely affect drug approvals and safety if it encourages faster regulatory approvals of medicines, as evidence suggests this leads to a higher incidence warnings and withdrawals. Sinclair, a former trade official and the Canadian Centre for Policy Alternatives (CCPA)'s trade policy expert, explores how expanded investor rights threaten stronger public health regulation and make preserving and extending Canada's publicly funded, universal health-care system more difficult and costly. A fought-for carve-out of tobacco control measures from the TPP's controversial investor–state dispute settlement process (more on this below) implicitly recognizes the threat these rights pose to other forms of regulation: government controls on transfats, sugary drinks and legalized marijuana, for example, are left exposed to corporate lawsuits. As Sinclair explains, the TPP's financial services chapter also makes it easier for foreign insurers to challenge the expansion of public health insurance into new areas such as pharmacare or dental care.

Environmental and labour protections

The U.S. and Canadian governments have touted the TPP as the most progressive trade deal ever, with the White House asserting that "tough, fully-enforceable standards will protect workers' rights and the environment for the first time in history."[18] The analyses by Jacqueline Wilson (Chapter 4) and Laura Macdonald and Angella MacEwen (Chapter 5) cast serious doubt on this claim, which is further discredited by the scale of opposition to the TPP from U.S. labour and environmental organizations.[19]

"[T]he TPP at best represents the status quo for environmental protection, and will not offer any safeguard against environmentally destructive provisions found elsewhere in the agreement," concludes Wilson, an environmental lawyer at the Canadian Environmental Law Association. This is because the environment chapter's language is generally weak and unenforceable, "climate change" is never mentioned anywhere in the agreement, and TPP governments are given broad discretion to decide whether and how to address environmental issues. Furthermore, as these weak disciplines only apply to central governments (an important oversight in federal states like Canada), the TPP's dispute mechanisms are unlikely to be enforced for environmental protection and provide little room for public participation, and the additional public complaint mechanisms are ineffective.

Similarly, MacEwen, an economist with the Canadian Labour Congress, and Macdonald, a political scientist and Latin American specialist at Carleton University, find little in the TPP's labour chapter that might impede the "race to the bottom" in wages and labour protections that accompanied the free-trade era.[20] The chapter contains positive, aspirational language related to workers' rights, but like its environmental counterpart it fails to provide meaningful, enforceable safeguards. For example, Chapter 19 recognizes the need for minimum wages, defined hours of work, and occupational health and safety standards. But the TPP's labour protections only apply if the alleged violations can be shown to involve a "sustained or recurring course of action or inaction in a manner affecting trade or investment between the parties." Otherwise, TPP governments are free to ignore their labour obligations. Contrasted with the powerful rights and dispute process given foreign investors, the relatively toothless protections afforded to labour rights and environmental policy space merely confirms their second-rate status in the minds of the TPP's architects and proponents.

Movement of migrant workers

Enshrining the right of employers to move certain categories of workers across borders on a temporary basis, without going through the usual immigration process, is one of the more surprising features of modern trade treaties. A so-called temporary entry system already exists under NAFTA and several other Canadian free-trade agreements, but the regime would be significantly expanded if the TPP comes into force.

As CCPA researcher Hadrian Mertins-Kirkwood explores in Chapter 6, Canada's temporary entry commitments in the TPP cover a wider range of occupations and sectors than NAFTA, and for the first time the system would be extended to countries such as Australia and Japan. While there are benefits to some workers from easier access to jobs in other countries, these arrangements are not risk free. The TPP prohibits countries from applying any form of economic needs test or numerical quotas in industries or employment sectors where they have made temporary entry commitments. For example, the labour market impact assessments required under Canada's controversial Temporary Foreign Worker

Program (TFWP) would run afoul of these limitations. The effect of the TPP's temporary entry chapter would be to allow Canadian employers to hire migrant workers in covered sectors even in parts of the country where unemployment is high and qualified local workers are available.

Had this chapter been negotiated up front with labour participation it would look much different, but it was never meant to be for workers primarily. The TPP's temporary-entry system, like the TFWP, is designed to give *employers* greater labour market flexibility. Making matters more urgent, while the Canadian program can be reformed, the temporary-entry system in the TPP cannot easily be altered after ratification. Unfortunately, neither system actually addresses the long-term needs of the Canadian labour market. As Mertins-Kirkwood argues, if local workers are available, it seems natural they should be hired first, and if there are genuine labour and skill shortages that only migrant workers can fill, these workers should be offered pathways to permanent residency in Canada. The TPP fails to advance either goal.

Investor rights

In Chapter 7, Gus Van Harten analyzes one of the most contentious features of the TPP and similar agreements going back to NAFTA. The investor–state dispute settlement (ISDS) mechanism gives foreign investors the right to seek compensation (sue for damages) when they believe government laws, regulations and other decisions have interfered with their private interests in ways that violate one or another investment treaty to which the country is a party. "Nothing like these rights exists for other actors in international law, whether they are other foreign nationals, domestic investors or citizens," writes Van Harten, a respected expert in international law. This is true "even in the most extreme situations of mistreatment."

Since the 1990s, recourse by investors to ISDS has soared from virtually no known cases to about seventy cases annually today.[21] Canada has been sued thirty-nine times under NAFTA's ISDS process, nearly always by U.S. investors, and has paid over $190 million in compensation in known awards or settlements. This record makes Canada the most-sued developed country in the world. NAFTA lawsuits have challenged a broad range of laws, regulations and policies, including measures related to public health, environmental protection and resource management. In some circumstances the threat of an ISDS claim has deterred Canadian governments from adopting polices or introducing new public services. At the same time, Canadian companies are lodging more and more cases internationally against environmental or resource management decisions in countries where they have prominent energy and mining interests.

Van Harten explains how the TPP's arbitration process to protect foreign investors, which entrenches and expands the NAFTA model on which it is based, contradicts the basic principles of judicial independence and fair process. Moreover, as his research shows, the foreign investors that have benefited financially from the rights in agreements such as the TPP have overwhelmingly been large companies and very wealthy individuals.[22] Expanding and enshrining such investor privileges carries major risks for voters and taxpayers in all TPP countries, with no compelling evidence of a corresponding benefit for the public.

Van Harten concludes the threats in the ISDS system, to democracy, sovereignty and the rule of law, are reason enough to reject the TPP. U.S. environmentalists, horrified by TransCanada's US$15-billion NAFTA lawsuit against the Obama administration's decision not to approve the controversial Keystone XL tar sands pipeline, have tended to agree and are now catalyzed against the TPP and other similar agreements, including the parallel Canadian and U.S. free-trade agreements with the European Union (CETA and TTIP).[23]

Cultural diversity

Just as labour rights and the environment are not sufficiently safeguarded in the TPP, Canada has further diluted protections for cultural diversity and national cultural policy — contrary to its international obligations and in ways that will affect Canada's artists and other cultural workers.

In Chapter 8 of this book, Alexandre Maltais discusses how the TPP turns away from values enshrined in the 2005 UNESCO convention on cultural diversity, and toward the notion that culture is merely a commodity like any other. Maltais, a former consultant with the United Nations Conference on Trade and Development (UNCTAD), explains that TPP countries have agreed to a conditional and quite limited general exception for culture and cultural policy based on U.S. government preferences influenced by the powerful entertainment industry. While Canada secured some more robust country-specific cultural reservations from market opening (liberalization) requirements in the TPP, these are considerably weakened with respect to promoting Canadian content and regulating online access to audiovisual goods and services. Maltais warns that the TPP, if ratified, would be a set-back for Canadian and international advocates of cultural diversity.

It is also far from clear whether the partial and fragmented cultural exclusions the Canadian government settled for in the TPP can be relied on to adequately safeguard Canadian cultural identity and industries in the future. In general we can say the narrower and more specific Canada's cultural protections become in agreements like the TPP, the more diffi-cult it will be for current and future governments to craft nationally and regionally appropriate cultural policy. This should raise flags for anyone engaged in discussions about how to adjust Canada's telecommunica-tions, broadcasting and other cultural legislation for the digital age.

Copyright
In Chapter 9, Michael Geist, one of Canada's most knowledgeable and incisive critics of the TPP, examines the implications of its copyright pro-visions. As anticipated early on in the negotiations, the TPP dramatically alters the balance between the interests of copyright and other intellec-tual property rights holders and the users of the goods and services those companies offer. These draconian changes have drawn fire from diverse quarters, ranging from former Research In Motion co-CEO Jim Balsillie — who argues the TPP will hobble the development of a knowledge-based economy in Canada — to the country's research librarians, who are concerned about the threat posed "to the way knowledge is shared and culture is preserved."[24]

As Geist explains, the forced extension of the copyright term on books, films, audio recordings and other goods will ensure no new works enter the Canadian public domain for twenty years after the TPP is implemented, with the main financial beneficiaries being foreign rights holders in the enter-tainment, film and music industries. By requiring laws to criminalize the circumvention of "digital locks," which allow copyright holders to encrypt software in computerized devices, the TPP will upset the compromises underlying Canada's 2012 copyright legislation — one of the few enlightened policy achievements of the Harper Conservatives' decade in power.

Postal services and state-owned enterprises

The restrictions in the TPP on the activities and funding of state-owned enterprises are yet another of the agreement's unusual features. These provisions, instigated and driven by the U.S., are ostensibly aimed at state-owned companies that allegedly compete unfairly with the private sector in postcommunist societies such as Vietnam and China. In Chapter 10, Daniel Sheppard and Louis Century, lawyers at Goldblatt Partners, provide a compelling case study that warns how corporate interests in the U.S. might take advantage of these novel provisions to undermine an iconic Canadian public-sector rival.

The multinational courier industry has for some time taken advantage of free-trade agreements to challenge Canada Post and other public postal services around the world. These efforts include a failed investor–state lawsuit from UPS against the Canadian government under NAFTA. The TPP contains a surprising number of rules targeting postal services that were inserted at the request of U.S. industry lobbies. Sheppard and Century suggest these intrusive provisions should concern anyone who wishes to see Canada maintain a viable, universal public postal service across the country.

While, the TPP does not require the outright privatization of Canada Post, or insist its monopoly over letter mail services be ended, the agreement would increase the risk of future trade challenges from corporations or member states unhappy with Canada's policy choices in the area of postal services. It is a tragedy, the authors note, that these risks could have been avoided had the Canadian government included better protections for postal services as some other TPP countries did.

A flawed negotiating process, a delayed consultation

The bigger tragedy is that the TPP would certainly not have taken the shape it did had it been negotiated differently. Modern free-trade agreements are products of a deeply flawed process that fails to respect basic democratic norms of openness, accountability and adequate public participation. The TPP process offers a prime example of this failure, especially so in the case of Canada.

Canada was accepted into the TPP negotiations quite late in the game, in 2012, after two years of heavy lobbying by the Harper government. The Department of Foreign Affairs and International Trade (now Global Affairs Canada) at first balked at the onerous demands coming from the USTR. But the file was eventually taken over by the prime minister's chief of staff, Nigel Wright, who was dispatched to Washington to secure Canada's entry, apparently at any cost.[25]

Without seeing any of the agreement up to that point, the Harper government agreed to accept all negotiating texts on which the nine current members had already reached consensus (e.g., "closed" chapters), and said it would not reopen any already agreed upon text in chapters that were still being negotiated. Canada also pledged it would not block consensus on an issue if it were the lone dissenting voice. By acceding to these restrictions on the ability to negotiate freely, the Harper government clearly telegraphed its desperation to the Obama administration, further undermining Canada's position.

By agreeing to close the deal in Atlanta in October 2015, right in the middle of the federal election campaign, the Harper government flouted basic precepts of parliamentary democracy. Constitutional convention dictates that "caretaker governments" should refrain from taking major policy decisions between the time one parliament is dissolved and another constituted after an election. If a decision point is unavoidable, the "caretaker" government is obliged to fully consult with opposition leaders on the appropriate steps to take. This did not happen. Instead, the Conservative government, struggling to cling to power, eagerly dropped the TPP bombshell into the final weeks of an election campaign it would ultimately lose. This disruptive, antidemocratic move locked Canada into a deal the Obama administration and other TPP parties now insist cannot be altered.

For opponents of the deal, Harper's manoeuvre added insult to injury. The entire TPP process was already at that point characterized by extreme secrecy and undue corporate influence. Only cleared advisors, overwhelmingly from the corporate sector and bound by strict nondisclosure agreements, had access to parts of the negotiating text. Also unusual for a major trade deal was that, except for a few chapters, the full text was never leaked — despite a US$100,000 bounty offer from WikiLeaks. The text was classified on national security grounds so those caught sharing it could face criminal charges. All the negotiating documents, except for the final text itself, remain classified until "four years from entry into force of the TPP agreement or, if no agreement enters into force, four years from the close of the negotiations."

Most Canadians, including unions, non-governmental organizations and independent experts, had few opportunities to be involved in formative discussions shaping the TPP agreement. Meanwhile, in February 2016, Perrin Beatty, president and CEO of the Canadian Chamber of Commerce, told a House of Commons trade committee: "We met with the negotiators periodically, probably as many as ten times throughout the course of the negotiations, so we received briefings. They responded to questions that we had. We were in touch from time to time with the minister as well, directly, and with his office, so that we were kept apprised broadly of the direction in which things were going."[26] (In contrast, the TPP text was not made available to the public in draft until November 2015.)

In early 2016, the newly elected Liberal government declared the agreement would be impossible to change. During the election campaign, the Liberals had embraced free trade and the TPP, but only in principle. Decrying the secrecy of the Harper government's approach, and sensing growing public unease with the Asia-Pacific pact, they also promised to "hold a full and open public debate" if elected. The decision to sign the treaty in New Zealand in February 2016 largely undermined this promise, though, as Trade Minister Chrystia Freeland has stressed, signing does not equal ratification. Consultations have gone ahead and, at time of writing, the government continues to say it has not yet made up its mind regarding whether Canada should ratify the TPP.

The promised public debate and cross-country hearings have so far come up short of anyone's definition of meaningful public participation.

A pre-study of the TPP by the parliamentary trade committee was confined largely to pro-TPP business groups. Subsequent hearings have been rushed, with presentations by key witnesses such as Perry Bellegarde, national chief of the Assembly of First Nations, and Jim Keon of the Canadian Generic Pharmaceutical Association cut short in a way unbefitting of what the government calls a "very important consultation process."[27]

Prospects and prognosis

Despite this rocky start to the Canadian consultations, there were some positive signs in the summer of 2016. The public was invited to submit written comments to the parliamentary trade committee and thousands grasped the chance to be heard. Also, despite pressure for an earlier decision on the TPP from elements of the business community and the Conservative opposition, the committee has prudently decided to delay its report on the agreement until early 2017, after U.S. elections are over and a new U.S. administration has taken office. Both the Democratic and Republican candidates, Hillary Clinton and Donald Trump, have stated their opposition to the TPP as negotiated. This makes U.S. ratification far from certain, especially since both houses of Congress must either approve or reject the deal without amendments.

At this point, the Obama administration views the lame-duck session of Congress (which occurs after the U.S. elections but before the term of the newly elected Congress begins) as its best chance to push through TPP ratification before a new president takes office. But it may still shy away from such a provocative initiative for fear of losing the vote. The most probable scenario is that the new U.S. president rejects the agreement in its current form and seeks to reopen negotiations, which could unravel the deal, especially since the narrow July 2016 electoral victory for the ruling coalition in Australia threatens parliamentary support for ratification in that country. Depending on how much political capital the new U.S. administration wants to wager on the TPP, other participating countries should expect pressure for even more concessions.

Despite her misgivings heading into the election, Clinton previously supported the TPP, even referring to it as a "gold standard" agreement.[28]

As Secretary of State, she was one of the key architects of the U.S. pivot to Asia.[29] And in July 2016, Clinton's supporters on the Democratic platform committee defeated an attempt by Bernie Sanders's followers to have the party clearly oppose ratifying the TPP. A Trump victory would, to say the least, have unpredictable consequences for the TPP and Canada–U.S. relations. Evidently the Republican candidate intends to put "America First," or at least his version of America. Even the TPP may not be a sufficiently capacious vessel for such raw egoism and naked ambition.

Canadians and their government need to prepare for either eventuality: U.S. ratification in the lame-duck session or, as appears more likely, a renewed push from the incoming U.S. administration to renegotiate the already imbalanced deal. Whoever becomes the next president, U.S. pressure for renegotiation can hardly be expected to improve the deal from a public interest perspective.

A regressive agreement that ignores current challenges

As the contributions to this book illustrate, the TPP is highly illegitimate in terms of how it was negotiated and the substance of the agreement is unfair, one-sided and intensely biased toward U.S. political and corporate interests. Left holding the short end of the stick are other TPP countries, including Canada, and the majority of citizens throughout the entire region, including in the U.S. It is, as many critics have argued, an agreement of and for the one per cent.

Former New Zealand Trade Minister Tim Groser, a driving force behind the TPP, spoke of the "ugly compromises" needed to complete the agreement, which he compared to eating dead rats: "And when we say ugly, we mean ugly from each perspective — it doesn't mean 'I've got to swallow a dead rat and you're swallowing foie gras.' It means both of us are swallowing dead rats on three or four issues to get this deal across the line."[30] This is not just a metaphor for the unpleasant but necessary steps countries must take to ensure greater prosperity. For Groser and other free-trade advocates these ugly concessions are ends in themselves.

The very purpose of a treaty such as the TPP is to coerce governments into making legislative and regulatory changes that most politicians would not normally entertain or be able to justify in open democratic debate before their own citizens. Many progressives would welcome policy handcuffs like this if they were part of a global environmental treaty for reversing climate change. In the case of the TPP we get the opposite: more restraints on environmental protection measures in the interest of freeing capital and investment. The commitments trade negotiators make behind closed doors (and governments sign off on afterwards) lock in a myopic and increasingly embattled neoliberal orthodoxy — small government, big finance, weak regulation and a preference for privatized service delivery — that prevents future progressive governments from changing course without great political and financial costs.

From a Canadian perspective, how better to explain entrenching ISDS when Canada is already the most-sued developed country in the world? How better to explain extending monopoly patent protections when we already pay too much for prescription drugs while brand-name drug companies invest so little in Canadian R&D? How better to explain pigeonholing Canada as a seller of raw and semiprocessed goods while acceding to U.S. and industry demands on copyright, trade secrets and digital rights that dig us further into this hole? How better to explain locking in the future privatization of public services, down to even the local level, through so-called standstill and ratchet clauses that prevent the remunicipalization of privatized services such as sanitation or transit?

The significant public opposition to the TPP in the U.S. from across the political spectrum is a sign that the ideology driving the TPP and other expansive trade and investment agreements is close to exhausting its reserves of legitimacy. Canadians and their political leaders would be wise to pay attention. At the same time, it would be highly imprudent, and more than a bit irresponsible, for progressive voices to sit back and expect the TPP to meet its demise in U.S. domestic politics.

Collectively, the contributions to this book set out a strong case against Canadian ratification of the TPP, providing a critical guide for citizens as they weigh the treaty's costs against its stated benefits. Criticism of the self-interested corporate agenda embodied in the TPP is neither anti-trade nor protectionist. It is simply drawing an obvious conclusion. A project defined overwhelmingly by the commercial aims and interests of U.S.

multinational businesses — from Big Pharma to Hollywood to the powerful fossil-fuel and extractives industry — cannot be assumed to advance the broader public interest within any of the TPP countries.

Despite its pretensions to be a progressive, twenty-first-century agreement, the vision of society the TPP offers is deeply regressive, mean-spirited and incompatible with meeting the more important global challenges facing humanity. The way it is currently written, the TPP can only worsen today's inequality of wealth and power, as shown in this book's chapters on investment, intellectual property and labour. Likewise, the agreement will strip governments of the tools they need to address climate change — an existential threat that will require more, and more assertive, government intervention and regulation.[31] Extreme investor rights agreements like the TPP are relics of an era when market fundamentalism — the belief in the virtues of fully liberalized markets — was the prevailing political wisdom. Experience tells us it is time to move on.

CHAPTER 1
Will the TPP be Good for Canadian Trade?

John Jacobs

The Trans-Pacific Partnership (TPP) is billed as a "twenty-first-century trade agreement" that will boost growth and expand trade between the twelve participating Asia-Pacific nations. The U.S. government has been open about the role it believes the TPP will play in containing the economic ambitions of China, and perhaps Brazil, Russia and India, the other "BRIC" nations. "The rules of the road are up for grabs in Asia," says the United States Trade Representative (USTR), the arm of the U.S. administration responsible for negotiating free-trade deals. "If we don't pass this agreement and write those rules, competitors will set weak rules of the road, threatening American jobs and workers while undermining U.S. leadership in Asia."[1]

As explored elsewhere in this book, the "rules of the road" in the TPP include a wide range of constraints on the policy flexibility of governments in areas such as finance, environmental protection, cultural promotion, intellectual property rights, public services and public health regulation, etc. This has been the agenda of free-trade agreements for some time, as tariffs are at all-time lows globally. Still, it is a useful exercise to test the assertions of TPP proponents that benefits will automatically flow from the removal of remaining tariffs.[2]

This chapter attempts to do just that — to assess the likely qualitative and quantitative impact of tariff removal on Canadian trade with countries not covered by existing free-trade agreements (i.e., excluding countries where tariffs have largely been eliminated already). We can conclude from this research that, despite the potential for the TPP to have a minimally positive effect on some Canadian exports, the agreement will very likely undermine Canada's trade balance, as well as our ability to generate employment and expand activity in the manufacturing and high-tech sectors. The TPP could therefore prove to be a significant obstacle to the federal government's commitment to diversify the Canadian economy beyond its current reliance on extraction and exports of primary goods.[3]

Canada-TPP trade by the numbers

According to proponents of the TPP, the agreement's tariff removal schedule will provide significant benefits to the Canadian economy, giving exporters preferential access to almost 40 per cent of world trade and 800 million potential consumers.[4] It is true the combined market share of TPP countries currently accounts for 36 per cent of global GDP (it was 52 per cent in 2000), but much of Canada's existing access to that market (76 per cent of GDP within the TPP region) is already tariff free (see Table 1).[5] It is a vast overstatement to say the TPP grants Canada new access to fast-growing Pacific Rim economies.

Exports to TPP countries account for a significant portion (81 per cent) of Canada's total exports (see Table 2), though 94.6 per cent of this trade is with the United States and covered by the North American Free Trade Agreement (NAFTA). When we add the other TPP countries with which Canada already has tariff-free access — Mexico, Chile and Peru (through FTAs), and Singapore, which does not apply tariffs on imports — we see 96.8 per cent of Canadian exports to the TPP region face no tariff barriers (see Figure 1).[6] The remaining 3.2 per cent of Canada's current regional exports go to prospective TPP countries where some tariffs still apply (i.e., where there is no FTA in place), but these account for only 2.8 per cent of Canada's total exports to the world.

Proponents also claim the TPP will provide access to 800 million consumers, but here, too, Canada already has preferential access to 66 per cent (538 million) of them. The difference between preferential access to 76 per cent of TPP country GDP and 66 per cent of consumers in

Table 1: TPP GDP, Population and GDP per Capita (2014)

	GDP ($US millions)	% of TPP GDP	Population (thousands)	Pop. as % of TPP	GDP per Capita ($US)
Australia	1,474,849	5.2%	23,622	2.9%	62,414
Brunei	14,971	0.1%	417	0.1%	35,376
Japan	4,586,748	16.3%	126,795	15.5%	36,116
Malaysia	326,113	1.2%	29,902	3.7%	10,803
New Zealand	202,169	0.7%	4,495	0.6%	44,420
Viet Nam	186,599	0.7%	92,423	11.3%	2,016
TPP (non-FTA)	**6,791,450**	**24.1%**	**277,655**	**34.0%**	**24,460**
Canada	1,786,670	6.3%	35,544	4.4%	50,294
Chile	258,358	0.9%	17,763	2.2%	14,537
Mexico	1,279,305	4.5%	125,386	15.4%	10,334
Peru	201,251	0.7%	30,973	3.8%	6,541
Singapore	301,193	1.1%	5,507	0.7%	54,593
United States	17,526,951	62.3%	323,241	39.6%	53,702
TPP (Tariff-free)	**21,353,728**	**75.9%**	**538,413**	**66.0%**	**39,660**
TPP Total	**28,145,178**		**816,068**		**34,403**

Sources: GDP & GDP per capita, UNCTADstat; population UNCTADstat and Statistics Canada; author's calculations.

the region is accounted for by the relatively lower income of more populous countries such as Vietnam and Malaysia, where per capita GDP is $2,016 and $10,803, respectively (the TPP average is $34,400). Table 1 shows that per-capita GDP — an indicator of purchasing power — is 38 per cent lower in TPP countries where Canada has no FTA than in its current FTA partners, throwing cold water on the idea that simply adding more potential consumers will automatically benefit Canadian exporters.

Figure 1: Canada-TPP trade

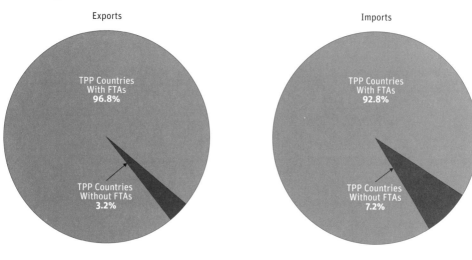

Source: Industry Canada Trade Data Online

Canada-TPP trade balance

For some time, Canada's positive global trade balance has depended on a healthy trade surplus with the U.S. while our deficit has grown with the rest of the world (see Figure 2). In 2009, in the wake of the Great Recession, Canada posted its first global trade deficit in recent history. Since then, Canada has had trade deficits in three of the past six years[7] and posted a record-high trade deficit in 2015.[8]

The trend toward increased trade deficits is also evident in Canada's trade balance with TPP countries (see Table 2 for 2015 data). When trade with the U.S. is removed from the equation, Canada has an overall trade deficit with TPP countries and enjoys surpluses only with Australia, Singapore and Brunei, which together account for a marginal 0.7 per cent of Canada's trade in the TPP zone. Canada imports significantly more from non-FTA TPP countries than it exports to them, leading to persistent trade deficits that reached a total of $11.3 billion in 2015 (see Table 2). In effect, Canada imported $1.83 of goods for every $1 it exported to non-FTA countries participating in the TPP. These trade deficits are indicative of Canada's imbalanced trade with the region: they represent

Figure 2: Canadian Trade Balance

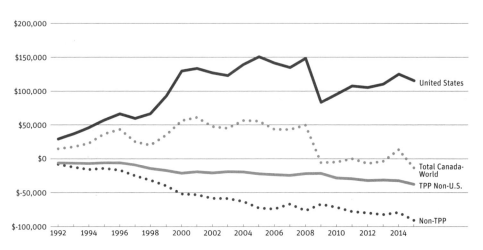

lost production opportunities and jobs for the Canadian economy, as a disproportionate quantity of products purchased in Canada are produced, and generate jobs, elsewhere.

The TPP would not correct this imbalance, and will likely worsen it, since a smaller portion of Canada's exports (3.2 per cent) would become tariff-free than imports (7.2 per cent). To the degree that lowering tariffs increases trade in both directions, we should therefore expect Canada's imports to grow more than exports to TPP countries not already covered by an FTA. This is consistent with Canada's experience under other free-trade agreements and is contributing to growing trade deficits with most countries other than the United States.[9]

Table 2: Canada - TPP: Exports, Imports & Trade Balance (2015)					
($ CAN millions)					
Canada's TPP Negotiating Partners	Canadian Exports	% Canadian TPP Exports	Imports to Canada	% Canadian TPP Imports	Trade Balance
United States	400,306	94.5%	284,945	82.3%	115,361
Japan	9,755	2.3%	14,765	4.3%	-5,010
Mexico	6,574	1.6%	31,156	9.0%	-24,581
Australia	1,890	0.4%	1,680	0.5%	210
Singapore	1,507	0.4%	954	0.3%	553

Chile	791	0.2%	1,854	0.5%	-1,063
Malaysia	790	0.2%	2,637	0.8%	-1,847
Peru	858	0.2%	3,260	0.9%	-2,402
Vietnam	653	0.2%	4,089	1.2%	-3,436
New Zealand	475	0.1%	683	0.2%	-208
Brunei	3	0.0%	4	0.0%	-1
Total TPP	423,601		346,027		77,575
TPP without US	23,295	5.5%	61,082	17.7%	-37,786
TPP FTA	**410,036**	**96.8%**	**321,215**	**92.8%**	**88,822**
TPP non-FTA	**13,565**	**3.2%**	**24,812**	**7.2%**	**(11,247)**
	Exports		Imports		
Total Cdn Global Trade	521,922		535,156		-13,234
TPP % Cdn Total Trade		81.2%		64.7%	
TPP Without US (% of Cdn. Global Trade)		4.5%		11.4%	
Source: Industry Canada Trade Data Online, author's calculations.					
Singapore is included in the TPP FTA category given its 0.0% average tariffs on imports.					

Composition of Canada's TPP trade

Canada's trade with TPP countries not currently covered by a FTA exemplifies our general reliance on exporting primary commodities and importing more advanced manufactured goods. As we see in Table 3, about 90 per cent of Canada's top twenty-five exports to these countries are primary or barely processed commodities, with the top five (copper, seeds, pork, coal and lumber) making up 54 per cent of the value in this category. Most of these exports (72 per cent) are destined for Japan (see Table 2). Oilseeds, pork and wheat account for a greater portion of Canada's exports to TPP countries not covered by FTAs (36 per cent of the top twenty-five exports) when compared to Canada's global exports, which are dominated by petroleum (46 per cent of the top twenty-five) and transportation products (34 per cent of the top twenty-five).[10] Exports of nonrenewable resources, such as coal, copper, gold, iron and aluminum, nonetheless make up a large portion (35 per cent of the top twenty-five) of Canada's exports to the TPP FTA countries.

Table 3: Canada–TPP Trade (non-FTA countries) by Product (Top twenty-five, HS4 product codes, 2015, $CAD millions)

(Australia, Brunei, Japan, Malaysia, New Zealand, Vietnam; Singapore is not included in Canadian Exports as it does not apply tariffs. Canadian Imports include Singapore as Canada does apply tariffs to imports from Singapore)

Primary or Basically Processed Products highlighted.

Canadian Exports		Canadian Imports	
Category (HS4)	Value ($m)	Category (HS4)	Value ($m)
2603 - Copper ores	1,118	8703 - Automobiles	3,208
1205 - Rape or Colza Seeds	1,058	8708 - Motor Vehicle Parts	1,520
0203 - Meat of Swine	977	8483 - Transmission Shafts and Cranks, Bearing	1,143
2701 - Coal	969	8517 - Telephone Sets	1,067
4407 - Lumber	893	8443 - Printing Machinery	757
1001 - Wheat	648	8429 - Earth moving vehicles	626
1201 - Soya Beans	468	8542 - Electronic Integrated Circuits	455
4703 - Chemical Woodpulp	388	4011 - New Pneumatic Tires of Rubber	436
3004 - Medications	362	8471 - Magnetic/Optical Readers	380
3104 - Fertilizers	342	8803 - Parts of Helicopters, Airplanes	378
2601 - Iron Ores	335	9403 - Furniture	341
8802 - Helicopters, Airplanes and Spacecraft	208	2204 - Grape Wines	336
0306 - Seafood	180	0202 - Meat of Bovine Animals - Frozen	327
8803 - Parts of Helicopters, Airplanes	140	8525 - Audio - visual Transmission Cameras	259
4403 - Wood in The Rough	139	3004 - Medicaments	217
8411 - Turbo-Jets, Turbo-Propellers, Turbines	130	7112 - Waste and Scrap of Precious Metals	217
2503 - Sulfur	126	8544 - Wire, Conductors, Optical Fibre Cables	206
1107 - Malt	110	6403 - Shoes, Boots, Sandals and Slippers	201

7601 - Unwrought Aluminum	110	9018 - Medical Instruments / Appliances	188
0303 - Frozen Fish (Excl. Fish Fillets)	99	8701 - Tractors	184
8483 - Transmission Shafts and Parts	94	0204 - Meat of Lamb, Sheep and Goats	182
7504 - Nickel Powders and Flakes	87	2844 - Uranium	147
8105 - Cobalt and Articles Thereof	86	7318 - Screws, Bolts, Nuts, Rivets, etc.	145
7502 - Unwrought Nickel	77	8504 - Electrical Transformers & Converters	142
0713 - Leguminous Vegetables	66	8413 - Pumps For Liquids; Liquid Elevators	140
Top 25 exports total	9,211	Top 25 exports total	13,203
Primary Commodities top 25	8,277	Primary Commodities top 25	872
# of primary products (of 25)	21	# of primary products (of 25)	4
Share of Top 25 Total Value	89.9%	Share of Top 25 Total Value	6.6%

Note: Primary Commodities, Standard International Trade Classification (SITC 0 + 1 + 2 + 3 + 4 + 68 + 667+ 971)

Source: Industry Canada Trade Data Online

In the same table, we can see that Canada's imports from TPP countries not covered by an existing FTA (non-FTA) are 93 per cent composed of more sophisticated manufactured goods. Japan alone accounts for 65 per cent of Canadian imports from the TPP (non-FTA) economies, a large portion of this trade (36 per cent of the top twenty-five products) generated by the auto industry (24 per cent autos, 12 per cent auto parts). Also in the top five imports to Canada are transmission and drivetrain parts, telephone sets and printing machinery.

Not only is Canada–TPP trade imbalanced in a quantitative sense, in that it produces steady trade deficits, but it is also qualitatively so, with exports dominated by resources, and imports by more highly processed manufactured goods. This pattern is indicative of Canada's integration into the international economy, which is increasingly characterized by an expansion of primary commodity exports and a decline in manufactured exports (see Table 4). Overall, Canada's global exports as a portion of

GDP declined from 40 per cent in 2000 to 32 per cent in 2014.[11] Between 2000 and 2014, manufactured goods declined from 64 per cent to 46 per cent of total exports. The export of primary commodities (unprocessed and minimally processed goods) increased from 30 per cent to more than 50 per cent of total exports over the same period.

Table 4: Sectoral Composition of Goods Exports (percentage of total exports)									
	Food		Agricultural raw materials		Fuels		Ores and metals		Manufactures	
	2000	2014	2000	2014	2000	2014	2000	2014	2000	2014
Canada	6.4	10.8	6.2	4.1	13.2	28.1	4.4	7.0	63.8	46.4
High income	6.1	9.2	1.7	1.6	11	10.6	2.8	3.9	73.6	70.1
Euro area	7.8	9.8	1.5	1.4	3.2	6.6	2.2	2.6	79.4	76.5
East Asia & Pacific	7.1	5.3	1.7	1	6.2	4.6	2.1	1.8	82.4	87.1
World	6.9	9.4	1.8	1.6	12	10.7	3.0	4.0	72.4	70.6

Note: Merchandise export shares may not sum to 100 per cent because of unclassified trade.

Source: World Bank Development Indicators

While many high-income economies have seen a decline in manufacturing as a portion of total exports, we can see from Table 4 that Canada's experience is disproportionate. Meanwhile, East Asian and Pacific TPP economies have grown their share from 82 per cent to 87 per cent, often by specializing in high-tech industries. The shift in Canadian exports is partially accounted for by the commodity price boom of the 2000s, which increased the total value of primary exports relative to nonprimary exports. But as Figure 3 indicates, since about 2005, Canadian manufactured exports have stagnated in absolute, not just relative, terms. Between 2000 and 2014, primary commodity exports increased by 189 per cent and manufactured goods by 20 per cent. The World Bank's export volume index (an indicator of the quantity of units traded) shows that while the value of Canada's exports increased by 66 per cent between 2000 and 2013, the volume of exports

Figure 3: Canadian Global Exports

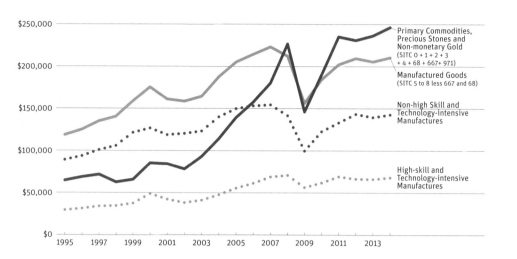

declined by 4 per cent. In other words, we have been exporting less but the products have been, until recently, worth more.[12] During the same period, Canadian import volumes increased by 40 per cent and the import values increased by 94 per cent, indicating that Canada's exports have not kept pace with the increase in imports as measured by volume *and* value.[13]

Canada–TPP tariff rates

While applied tariffs are already low by historical standards, the removal of Canadian tariffs in several strategic sectors could undermine Canada's advanced manufacturing sectors and prospects for economic diversification. The average applied tariff rates of TPP countries are all below 5 per cent except for those of Malaysia and Vietnam, reflecting their positions as developing countries making use of tariffs to support emerging manufacturing sectors. Malaysia and Vietnam account for 1.7 per cent of total GDP in the TPP region and will not provide game-changing market opportunities for Canada. Singapore does not apply tariffs, and for the remaining traders (without Malaysia and Vietnam) rates are very low. For the most part, Australia has the highest tariffs within this group, indicating some potential opportunities for Canadian exports when these come down. But here, and in general, the potential benefits of tariff removal must also take into account the comparatively higher transportation costs faced by Canadian exporters relative to those of other Asia-Pacific TPP partners.

Table 5: TPP (Non-FTA) Most-Favoured-Nation Applied Tariffs as % of the value of product imported "simple average of simple average" and weighted averages, nonagricultural goods, 2015 (%)

Product Category		Manufactured goods, ores and metals	Ores and metals	Manufactured goods	Chemical products	Machinery and transport equipment	Other manufactured goods
Australia	Average	3.2	1.24	3.33	1.68	2.85	4.19
	Weighted	2.91	1.49	2.93	1.58	3.26	3.18
Brunei	Average	1.85	0.0	1.9	0.45	3.72	1.43
	Weighted	1.54	0.0	1.54	0.37	1.85	1.09
Canada	Average	2.37	0.01	2.52	0.62	1.2	3.86
	Weighted	1.97	0.02	2.04	1.07	2.32	2.11
Japan	Average	2.33	1.23	2.4	2.64	0.03	3.33
	Weighted	0.86	0.11	0.98	1.1	0.0	2.32
Malaysia	Average	5.91	2.7	6.11	2.56	4.52	8.32
	Weighted	4.45	2.45	4.67	3.35	3.77	8.51
New Zealand	Average	2.42	0.81	2.51	0.74	2.86	3.04
	Weighted	2.67	0.99	2.71	1.58	3.12	2.4
Singapore	Average	0.0	0.0	0.0	0.0	0.0	0.0
	Weighted	0.0	0.0	0.0	0.0	0.0	0.0
Vietnam	Average	8.38	1.7	8.74	3.05	6.03	12.2
	Weighted	4.14	0.63	4.38	3.07	3.22	7.07
Avg. non-Canada	Average	3.44	1.10	3.57	1.59	2.86	4.64
	Weighted	2.37	0.65	2.04	1.16	2.06	2.25
Average Not Including Malaysia and Vietnam	Average	1.96	0.66	2.03	1.10	1.89	2.40
	Weighted	1.60	0.52	1.63	0.93	1.65	1.80

Source: UNCTADstat

Notes: In simple average of simple average, "the same weight is given to all products, without taking into account how much the products are traded." In calculating weighted average, "more weight is given to products with larger import flows."[14]

Canada tends to apply higher average tariffs on imports of processed ores and metals, manufactured goods and "other manufactured goods" than the TPP average when Malaysia and Vietnam are excluded (see Table 5). This could indicate some small advantages for TPP exporters to Canada, but overall the differences between applied tariff rates are minimal. Lowering or removing tariffs via the TPP could have indirect consequences for Canada's exports to the U.S., which would become less competitive relative to goods from TPP countries with lower production costs. This could, in turn, lead to a significant shifting of production away from North America generally, contributing to downward pressure on wages and employment in Canada and across the TPP zone.[15]

Canada–Japan trade

Japan is by far the largest economy among TPP countries with which Canada has no FTA, accounting for 68 per cent of GDP and 72 per cent of Canadian exports to this group. Japan is a major global exporter of advanced manufactured goods, and the lowering or removal of tariffs on trade with Japan will have a far greater economic impact on Canada than trade liberalization with any of the other non-FTA TPP countries. The tariff-free portion of agricultural imports are similar for Canada (51 per cent) and Japan (47 per cent), but the WTO tariff profiles indicate that, with the exception of dairy products, Japan is more protective of its agriculture sector than Canada is.[16] It is possible there would be an increase in exports of Canadian agricultural products such as grains, oilseeds and pork as Japanese tariffs are reduced through the TPP.[17]

The situation is quite different outside of agriculture: 83 per cent of Canada's nonagricultural exports to Japan already face no tariffs, while the same can be said of 69 per cent of imports from Japan. Canada's new export opportunities are therefore less relative to Japan in that Japanese exporters could benefit from tariff reductions on a further 31 per cent of its current exports compared to 17 per cent for Canadian exporters.[18]

Table 6: Canada and Japan, Advanced Manufacturing Import Tariffs						
	Canada			Japan		
Product Group	% product groups tariff free	Avg. applied duties (%)	Maximum tariffs (%)	% product groups tariff free	Avg. applied duties (%)	Maximum tariff (%)
Non-electrical machinery	93	0.4	9	100	0	0
Electrical machinery	83	1.1	9	98	0.1	5
Transport equipment	41	5.8	25	100	0	0

Source: WTO Tariff profiles, Canada, Japan

Canada's tariffs on imports of advanced manufactured goods, such as electrical and nonelectrical machinery and transportation equipment, are higher than Japanese tariffs for these product groups (see Table 6). For example, Canada applies an average tariff rate of 5.8 per cent on 59 per cent of transportation equipment product groups, whereas Canadian transportation exports to Japan are not tariffed. Upon tariff removal, the cost of Japanese transportation exports to Canada could be reduced by 5.8 per cent on average, whereas the cost of Canadian transportation exports to Japan would not be affected. Given that Japan has no tariffs on most advanced manufactured imports, Canadian manufacturing firms have little to gain from the TPP. Conversely, Japanese exporters will benefit from tariff reductions on an average of 27 per cent of the advanced manufacturing product groups imported to Canada.[19] Consequently, the removal of tariffs on Canada–Japan trade could exacerbate Canada's current trade trajectory described above (i.e., toward the export of primary commodities and the decline in manufacturing exports).

Challenges of resource-driven exports

The main opportunities for Canadian exports generated by tariff elimination under the TPP appear to be in the provision of raw materials to be processed and transformed offshore, and possibly reimported to

Figure 4: Canada's TPP Trade Balance by Sector

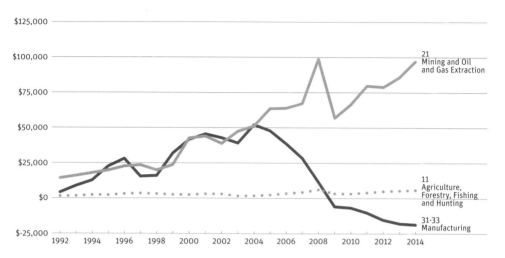

Source: Industry Canada Trade Data Online

Canada as value-added manufactured goods. This imbalanced trade can be seen in Canada's sectoral trade balances with TPP negotiating countries, as expressed in Figure 4, but it is also reflective of Canadian trade patterns in other parts of the world outside the U.S.

Exports from high-tech industries can play a leading role in facilitating innovation and productivity increases in the Canadian economy. But, as we saw in Figure 3, Canada's high-skilled and high-tech manufactured exports have declined as a portion of total goods exports, from 18.7 per cent in 2000 to 14.9 per cent in 2014, and high-tech exports are not keeping pace with growth in the Canadian economy, declining from a high of 6.6 per cent of GDP in 2000 to 3.8 per cent in 2014.[20] These findings are confirmed by OECD reports that show Canada is a laggard in terms of business investment in research and development, and that we have a comparative disadvantage in high-technology and medium-high-technology manufacturing, but a comparative advantage in low and medium-low manufacturing.[21]

The TPP would curtail Canada's ability to reverse this trend. Partly it would do this by removing important sector-development policy tools that have historically proven successful in the transition to a more diversified economy and the production and export of value-added high-tech products in advanced economies. We have seen this with respect to tariffs applied in support of strategic sectors. But, like other free-trade and investment agreements since NAFTA, the TPP also prohibits an extensive list of performance requirements (technology transfers, domestic content or employment quotas, etc.) that states might reasonably wish to attach to foreign investment in nonrenewable resource extraction.[22] The TPP procurement and state-owned enterprises chapters further limit the use of public spending and federal crown corporations to bolster local development.

These and other industrial policies, which violate free-trade orthodoxy, have been instrumental in enabling economies to move up the value chain in the context of economic globalization, as in the rapid industrialization of the East Asian economies.[23] China is successfully using strategic interventions to move from being a low-cost producer of labour-intensive exports into producing high-tech value-added products such as heavy construction machinery and aircraft.[24] Developed economies have also been contemplating sectoral development strategies as they seek to lift themselves out of the economic stagnation that has followed from the Great Recession.[25]

Some employment implications

Canada's increasing reliance on primary commodities for its goods exports could impact employment creation prospects. Statistics Canada has noted that, in the 2000s, the extractives sector experienced the "longest and strongest cycle for resources in postwar history," which generated record levels of investment, doubled profits and "lifted the stock market to record heights," but the sector has "not been a large source of jobs for Canadians."[26] Indeed, employment in the resource sector has been in decline as a portion of total employment in Canada — from 10 per cent in 1990 to approximately 7 per cent during the commodity price boom in 2007.[27] This is partly due to employment growth in the service sector, but it is also indicative of the increasing capital-intensity of the extractives industries.[28]

Table 7 provides several measures of job creation associated with the mining, oil and gas and manufacturing industries. Manufacturing is more employment-intensive than the extractive industries, providing more jobs as a portion of GDP, exports and value-added production. This stands to reason, given the high level of capital investment required to explore for, extract and bring to market mineral deposits. The extractives industries tend to pay higher wages on average, but offer far fewer employment opportunities.[29] Statistics Canada's value-added exports data to 2011 (most recent for this data set) show that manufacturing exports generated 612,000 direct value-added jobs (40 per cent of all value-added export jobs) compared to 61,000 jobs (4 per cent of export jobs) generated by mining and oil and gas industries, and 68,000 by crop and animal production (Table 7).[30] Add indirect jobs and we see manufacturing employs 1,321,700, mining and oil and gas employs 276,700, while crop and animal production employs 128,700.[31] When indirect jobs are considered, the portion of value-added jobs in the extractives industries more than doubles (from 4 per cent to 9 per cent), but this is still less than one-quarter of the portion of value-added jobs created by the manufacturing sector. Agricultural production is more labour-intensive and produces a disproportionate number of jobs relative to its contribution to exports.

Table 7: Employment Intensity of Manufacturing and Mining and Oil and Gas

Industry	Goods Producing Industries (2014)		Jobs per $1 billion Exports (2014)	Value -added Exports (2011)		
	% of GDP	% of Employment		% of Exports	% of Jobs	% Direct & Indirect Jobs
Manufacturing	36%	52%	4668	52%	40%	45%
Mining & Oil & Gas	27%	8%	1525	21%	4%	9%
Crop & Animal Production				3%	4%	4%

Sources: Statistics Canada (Tables 379-0031, 281-0024, 381-0032), Industry Canada Trade Data Online & author's calculations

Note: Comparable data for percentage of GDP, percentage of employment and jobs per $1-billion exports is not readily available.

The composition of Canadian primary commodity exports to the TPP non-FTA countries is (roughly) evenly divided between the renewable natural resource sectors (36 per cent of top twenty-five exports: agriculture, forestry and fishing) and the nonrenewable extractives industries (35 per cent of top twenty-five), whereas Canada's global trade is dominated by extractives.[32] As noted above, tariff reduction in the TPP could provide opportunities for increased agricultural exports, but the impact on employment is likely to be small. The employment potential of increases in seed and pork exports must be weighed against the job losses following from increased Canadian dairy imports resulting from the TPP, and the aforementioned impacts on Canadian manufacturing.[33]

In general, however, we can say that Canada is increasing exports of goods produced via resource extraction (low employment intensity) and imports of manufactured products (high employment intensity). In effect, Canada is exporting goods that create relatively few domestic jobs and importing goods that create more jobs elsewhere. This could account for some of the decline in manufacturing employment over the past decade, and points to long-term challenges for job-creation strategies and achieving full employment in Canada. The prioritization of resource extraction and export by the previous Conservative government can be seen as having sidelined job-creating, value-adding and productivity-enhancing industries.

TPP would harm Canadian auto industry

A 2016 CCPA study by Queen's University and Automotive Policy Research Centre researchers John Holmes and Jeffrey Carey found the Trans-Pacific Partnership (TPP) will negatively impact the Canadian automotive industry, undermining the competitiveness of assembly and small and medium-sized auto parts plants. Holmes calls the TPP "a game-changer for the global automotive industry" because of how it "will significantly affect decisions regarding what, where, and how automotive products will be produced within the wider TPP region, with Canada getting the short end of the stick."

The TPP's automotive provisions and rules, which take up over 600 pages of the agreement, are complex, especially regarding so-called rules of origin

(ROO) and regional content-value (RCV). According to Holmes and Carey, these rules will affect the Canadian auto industry in the following ways:

- The TPP's ROO and RCV requirements will have a much greater impact on the automotive industry in Canada than the removal of tariffs per se. The TPP sets RCVs at between 35 and 45 per cent depending on the automotive product. This is the minimum content in the product that must originate in the TPP zone to receive preferential (or tariff-free) treatment under the agreement — significantly lower than NAFTA's RCV of 62.5%. Furthermore, "complex products" like car engines can contain up to 10 per cent "non originating" material (parts produced outside the TPP zone) and still qualify for tariff-free treatment.

- Growth in Canadian vehicle exports to markets outside North America will be limited at best, because only two TPP countries with commercially significant markets, Malaysia and Vietnam, still have high import tariffs on automotive products. Barriers to the Japanese market are all non-tariff-based, such as unique safety and environmental regulations, high auto-related taxes, complex rules affecting car dealerships and domestic consumer preferences for locally made vehicles.

- Phasing out Canada's 6.1% auto tariff (on vehicles imported from outside North America), on the other hand, will make foreign-produced vehicles more competitive in the domestic market. To the extent this has a negative impact on domestic vehicle production it will, in turn, affect Canada's important domestic auto parts sector.

- The very great difference between U.S. and Canada in tariff phaseout periods on imported vehicles from Japan — five years in steps for Canada; twenty-five years beginning in year twenty for the U.S. — could favour Japanese automakers locating new assembly investment and reinvestment in the U.S. rather than Canada.

- Small and medium-sized Canadian parts makers will face increased competitive pressure from parts produced in low-cost non-TPP countries due to the weaker rules of origin for both vehicles and parts. Suppliers furthest from the assembler in the supply chain and producing discrete parts for components such as engines, suspension and brake systems will be most vulnerable. These same rules will provide new growth opportunities outside of Canada for Canadian-based global parts makers (i.e., supply chains may be changed, with a net job loss in Canada, as global parts manufacturers shift production to other TPP countries or even outside the TPP zone).

Assessing the potential impact of these complex rules on the Canadian automotive industry is complicated by the fact the industry is so highly integrated with U.S. production, and so dependent on the U.S. market for the sale of both finished vehicles and automotive parts. Consequently, one must be mindful not only of the direct impact of the TPP on Canadian automotive production, but also the indirect effect caused by changes to U.S. production levels.

While undoubtedly there will be winners and losers from TPP-influenced industry restructuring, assert Holmes and Carey in their report, the automotive provisions in the agreement, if implemented, will have overall negative consequences for automotive production and employment in Canada.

Reliance on the export of primary commodities also contributes to exchange-rate volatility and vulnerability as increases in commodity prices put upward pressure on the Canadian dollar. This volatility creates challenges for other exports. For example, a strong Canadian dollar increases the cost of manufactured goods for foreign buyers and thereby, as in the case of the commodity price boom of the 2000s, contributes to a decrease in non-resource-sector exports, as well as job losses. Between 2001 and 2014, the Canadian economy lost 493,000 manufacturing jobs.[34] The inevitable decline in commodity prices from the record highs of the 2000s has also had adverse effects on economic growth and public finances, as evident from the fiscal challenges the federal and several provincial governments are currently facing.[35]

Conclusion

The following chapters describe the broad impacts the TPP would have in a number of policy areas only loosely, if at all, related to trade. This chapter simply examines the potential impacts of tariff reduction in the TPP on the Canadian economy, which has been a major selling point for proponents of the agreement. Far from automatically benefiting workers and consumers, it appears the TPP will entrench Canada's reliance on low-employment-intensity and lower-value primary commodity exports. The potential for the TPP to open up opportunities in certain sectors, such as pork and seed exports, must be assessed against the expected increased imports of dairy products from the U.S., New Zealand and Australia, the likely increase in tariff-free imports of advanced manufactured products from Japan, and of non-advanced manufactured goods from lower-cost jurisdictions such as Malaysia and Vietnam. Finally, the TPP will remove many of the tools governments might reasonably use to foster the growth of innovation-driven exports. Given the current government's stated objective of diversifying the Canadian economy, ratifying the TPP would appear to be a long step in the wrong direction.

CHAPTER 2
The TPP and Health Care

Scott Sinclair

With refreshing clarity, the prime minister's mandate letter to the new health minister, issued shortly after the 2015 federal election, stated the "overarching goal will be to strengthen our publicly funded universal health-care system and ensure that it adapts to new challenges."[1] The Trans-Pacific Partnership will frustrate this objective. While Canada's public health-care system is partially shielded from the commercializing pressures of the TPP, overall the treaty will weaken that system, undermine health regulation and obstruct efforts to renew and expand public health care in the face of new challenges.

For example, Canadians already pay too much for prescription drugs and the TPP will worsen this situation by extending patents and impeding cost-saving measures. Research clearly shows that extending monopoly protection and boosting brand-name drug company profits in hopes of generating higher levels of research and development (R&D), and more innovative medicines, has been a failure. The TPP will burden the Canadian health-care system with higher drug costs while sabotaging efforts to find a better balance between needed innovation and the affordability of medicines.

The TPP also includes strong foreign investor protections and a highly controversial investor–state dispute settlement (ISDS) mechanism that threaten stronger public health regulation and make preserving and extending our publicly funded, universal health-care system, for example through publicly insured pharmacare, more difficult and costly. Recognizing the threat this might pose to tobacco control measures, anti-smoking groups fought for and won a novel carve-out from the TPP's investment chapter rules, but even this will be of limited use to Canada, as explored below.

Finally, this chapter will review a range of other TPP provisions affecting health, including those governing cross-border trade in ser-vices, temporary entry of professionals and public-private partnerships. In most of these areas the new impacts of the TPP on our health-care system will be marginal or in line with Canada's existing trade and investment treaty obligations (e.g., in NAFTA). But that does not mean these provisions are totally harmless, as flaws found in previous trade and investment agreements are repeated, while some new aspects are raising concerns.

The TPP and drug costs

Without doubt, the TPP's single biggest direct impact on the Canadian health-care system will be to increase drug costs as a result of extending patents. Canada already has an industry-friendly system of intellectual property protection for pharmaceutical patent holders. This is reflected in the high prices Canadians pay for prescription drugs. Per capita, drug costs in Canada are the third-highest among countries in the Organization for Economic Cooperation and Development (OECD).[2] According to recent OECD data, Canadians pay an average of US$713 annually for pharmaceuticals, significantly higher than the OECD aver-age of US$515.[3]

The TPP will further increase these costs by requiring the federal gov-ernment to extend the term of patents to account for supposed regula-tory delays. Specifically with respect to patented drugs, TPP parties must "make available an adjustment of the patent term to compensate the patent owner for unreasonable curtailment of the effective patent term as a result of the marketing approval process."[4] The TPP does not specify precisely how countries must meet this obligation, leaving some flexibil-ity to define national patent term restoration systems. Canadian officials have indicated the federal government will meet this obligation through

Figure 5: R&D Spending vs. Drug Costs in Canada

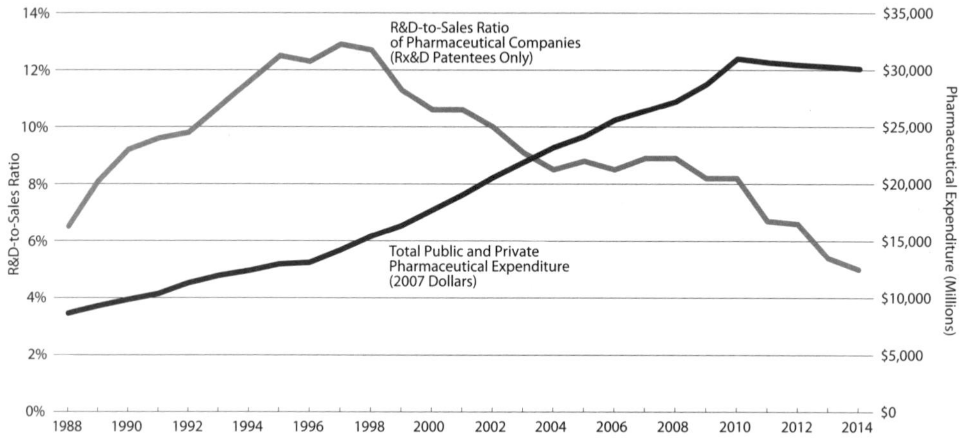

Source: PMPRB 2014 Annual Report, Table 16; Canadian Institute for Health Information, "National Health Expenditure Trends, 1975-2015: Complete data tables," Table G.14.1.

the so-called *sui generis* patent extension system required by the signed but not yet ratified Canada–European Union Comprehensive Economic and Trade Agreement (CETA).

It should be stressed that when the previous federal government insisted the TPP would require no changes to Canada's *existing* intellectual property regime for drugs, it was already including the *future* changes Canada would have to make to comply with CETA. Ratification of the pact with the EU, initialled by the federal government and European Commission in late 2013, was still, in the autumn of 2016, in question over strong public opposition in Europe. By agreeing to the TPP system of patent term restoration, the federal government concedes that our drug costs will rise, whether CETA goes ahead or not.

The TPP and CETA requirements for patent term restoration are roughly equivalent. Under its proposed *sui generis* approach, Canada plans to limit the patent term adjustment to a maximum of two years. Carleton University professor Marc-André Gagnon estimates that if the patent term restoration system required by the TPP were implemented in Canada today it would increase the average market exclusivity for patented drugs by 287 days.[5] By further delaying the availability of cheaper generic medicines, this would result in an annual cost increase of $636 million, or 5 per cent of the annual cost of patented drugs in Canada.[6] Provinces have demanded compensation for the fiscal impacts of these changes — costs the Harper government claimed, in a technical summary of CETA, it was "prepared to address."[7] Yet even if the new Liberal government were to abide by this vague pledge, it simply means that Canadian taxpayers would pay at the federal rather than the provincial level in order to boost the profits of the brand-name pharmaceutical industry. People paying for their drugs out of pocket or through private insurance will be hit twice — through higher drug costs *and* an increase in their federal taxes (or reduced public services).

Despite claims to the contrary by brand-name manufacturers, higher drug costs are unlikely to be offset by increased R&D expenditures in Canada. Since 2003, Canadian brand-name manufacturers have consistently failed to meet previous pledges to invest 10 per cent of their sales revenues in researching and developing new products. According to the latest data from the Patented Medicine Prices Review Board (PMPRB), the R&D-to-sales ratio of the brand-name pharmaceutical industry fell to 5 per cent in 2014. This is its lowest level since the PMPRB began collecting data in 1988.[8] In fact, data collected by the PMPRB totally dispels the argument that providing stronger patent protection will spur higher pharmaceutical investment in Canada. The PMPRB report notes that several comparable OECD countries, "which have patented drug prices that are, on average, substantially less than prices in Canada, have achieved R&D-to-sales ratios well above those in Canada." Furthermore, it observes, "[a]lthough price levels are often cited as an important policy lever for attracting R&D, the data has not supported this link domestically or internationally."[9] The most recent PMPRB annual report emphasizes that the patent restoration system envisaged under CETA: "will require amendments to the Patent Act to provide pharmaceutical patentees with up to two years of additional market exclusivity. Such a change would come at a time of high drug prices and record low R&D, causing some to question the effectiveness of the PMPRB and whether a policy balance conceived over twenty-five years ago continues to serve its intended purpose."[10]

Even in the U.S., which has led the charge for more industry-friendly patent protection in the TPP, there was outrage over a proposed tax-avoiding merger between the U.S.-based multinational Pfizer and the smaller European firm Allergan.[11] By shifting its headquarters to Ireland, Pfizer planned to garner a windfall in profits by reducing its corporate income tax rate. With many asking why the U.S. government should champion the cause of a company that refuses to accept its fair share of taxes, this aggressive manoeuvre spilled over into the congressional debate on the TPP. Pfizer and Allergan called the deal off in April 2016.

In the developing world, access-to-medicine advocates, such as Médecins Sans Frontières/Doctors Without Borders (MSF), have strongly decried the adverse impacts of the TPP on drug costs and the affordability of life-saving medicines. MSF concludes that, "although the text has improved over the initial demands, the TPP will still go down in history as the worst trade agreement for access to medicines in developing countries."[12] The group's continuing concerns include the TPP requirements for patent term restoration, provisions that facilitate "evergreening" (the practice of patenting new uses or formulations to extend monopoly protection for drugs whose patents are about to expire) in developing countries, and the requirement for up to eight years of data protection and market exclusivity for biologic drugs. With the exception of the previously discussed patent term extensions, such provisions are generally in line with Canada's existing drug patent regulations. But the hardships that would be inflicted on the poor, the sick, and already strained public coffers in developing countries such as Vietnam and Malaysia are reason enough for Canadians to reject such "abusive" intellectual property (IP) provisions.[13] What's more, by establishing a new high-water mark for corporate-friendly IP protections, the treaty sets a terrible precedent for future agreements involving developing countries. By accepting the TPP approach to intellectual property and pharmaceuticals, the Canadian government would fail citizens in developing countries and diminish its standing in the developing world.

Extended patent terms would clearly be the most directly harmful impact of the TPP's intellectual property rights chapter. Accepting the patent extensions required by the TPP would increase costs to consumers and patients at home and abroad, reward broken promises by the brand-name pharmaceutical industry, perpetuate a failed approach to consumer protection and industrial policy, and diminish Canada's standing globally. The TPP could also have adverse effects on the criteria that Canada uses to decide on drug safety and effectiveness, how it approves or does not approve new drugs for marketing, post-market surveillance and inspection, the listing of drugs on public formularies and how individual drugs are priced in the future, as discussed by Joel Lexchin in the next chapter.

Investor rights and investor–state dispute settlement

The TPP investment chapter is essentially modelled on NAFTA's Chapter 11 and its modifications in subsequent U.S. bilateral investment treaties. Notably, the deal contains an investor–state dispute settlement (ISDS) mechanism that enables foreign investors to sue governments for violating the treaty's broadly worded investment protections. Such claims bypass the domestic courts and are adjudicated by largely unaccountable arbitration tribunals. While the tribunals cannot directly overturn a government measure, they can order financial compensation. Such monetary awards are fully enforceable in the domestic courts of any TPP country, and they can act as a deterrent to introducing public interest regulations that may draw ISDS challenges from foreign investors.

There are some minor interpretive glosses in the TPP to the basic investment treaty obligations regarding minimum standards of treatment, national treatment and indirect expropriation that aim to curb some of the most problematic interpretations of these provisions by

51

arbitral tribunals. There is also a partial carve-out for tobacco control measures. But on the whole, the chapter heavily reflects the traditional U.S. approach of creating strong investor rights that apply to both established and planned investments, with only minimal or weak exceptions for government regulation in the text itself.[14] This compels governments to rely on country-specific reservations to protect vital public interest regulations and public services, even in critical areas such as health.

A major concern about ISDS and TPP-style investor protections is that they effectively lock in privatization. For example, once foreign investors become established in a health sector previously insured or delivered exclusively through the public system, investor–state compensation claims make it costly to reverse course and return these services to the public health-care system. A closely related concern is that ISDS interferes with the expansion of public health insurance into areas currently insured by private providers. The prospect of incurring potentially large compensation costs, determined by a private tribunal outside the reach of domestic courts and legislature, can put a chill on the expansion of public health insurance into new areas such as pharmacare. Investor–state litigation creates uncertainty and potential liabilities for the taxpayer, and can tip the political balance in favour of foreign commercial interests opposed to expanding a public health-care system. The TPP actually makes such claims more likely to succeed by allowing financial services providers, such as health insurance companies, to launch investor–state claims alleging violations of the minimum-standards-of-treatment (MST) obligations, something that is not permitted under previous Canadian trade and investment agreements.[15] These provisions have been rightly criticized as a "strikingly flexible catch-all standard," allowing arbitrators to impose their own preferences and prejudices in a dispute.[16] The MST obligation is the most frequently invoked by investors in investor–state arbitration claims.[17]

These are not abstract or hypothetical concerns. In Europe, foreign investors have used investment treaties to challenge reversals of privatization in public health insurance systems. In at least two instances they succeeded. In 1999, a Dutch-based insurance firm, Eureko, acquired a 30 per cent stake in Poland's national health insurance provider. In 2001, the Polish finance ministry announced it intended to issue more shares to private companies, a move that would have allowed Eureko to acquire a majority stake. The planned privatization generated considerable political controversy and was subsequently cancelled by the Polish government. Eureko then sued Poland under a Netherlands–Poland bilateral investment treaty (BIT). In 2005, the investor–state tribunal ruled two-to-one in Eureko's favour, asserting the cancelled shares offering violated investor protections in the BIT. The Polish government eventually settled the dispute for an estimated US$1.6 billion.

Slovakia similarly experimented with health insurance privatization in 2006–07. A newly elected government then took steps to reverse this policy.[18] A Dutch holding company, Achmea, which owned an insurer that had entered the Slovakian market, launched a pair of investor–state claims against Slovakia under the Netherlands–Czechoslovakia BIT. In the first case, the company was awarded 22.1 million euros after the tribunal decided the regulatory requirement to reinvest profits in the health insurance system (rather than transferring them as dividends to investors), and restrictions on the transfer of insurance portfolios, violated the fair-and-equitable-treatment (FET) provisions of the investment treaty. The Slovak government, even though backed by the European Commission, was unsuccessful in having that monetary award set aside in the European courts.[19] A second, even more aggressive claim by the same investor attempted to persuade a tribunal to take pre-emptive action against the Slovak government to stop the establishment of a single-payer public health insurance system. The Slovak government won that case, although the tribunal's ruling emphasized Achmea would be able to bring a claim for damages if the government proceeds with a public health insurance plan that harms the company's investments.[20]

Canada's health-care reservations do not in any way protect against challenges under the articles dealing with expropriation or minimum standards of treatment (equivalent to the fair-and-equitable-treatment provision in European investment treaties). These TPP provisions apply with full force to the Canadian health-care system. An expansion of Canadian public health insurance or a reversal of future privatization at any level of government would therefore be vulnerable to investor claims similar to those experienced by Eastern European governments. The TPP not only fails to redress these serious flaws in the ISDS process, it expands their application. By covering foreign investors from more countries (including Japan, which is home to approximately 2.5 per cent of Canadian foreign direct investment), the TPP significantly increases the likelihood of future claims. If ratified in its current form, the TPP would also greatly complicate future efforts to reform investment protections and ISDS, since adjustments to the treaty would require reaching consensus among twelve governments, a far more difficult undertaking than in NAFTA where three countries need to agree.[21]

The TPP and public health regulation

The number of investor–state claims is burgeoning worldwide.[22] Increasingly they involve challenges to public health regulation. Among the most notorious of these are cases brought by tobacco giant Philip Morris against plain-packaging laws in Australia and health warnings on packages in Uruguay.[23] (An arbitration tribunal tossed out the case against Australia on procedural grounds, not the merits of the company's arguments; Uruguay won the second case in July 2016.) Canada is also the target in a high-profile investor–state challenge by U.S. pharmaceutical firm Eli Lilly, which is seeking $500 million for the invalidation of two of its extended patents by the Canadian courts.

The TPP investment chapter contains no general exception insulating health regulatory measures from ISDS. This contrasts with other chapters of the TPP, such as those covering trade in services (Chapter 10) and trade in goods (Chapter 1), where governments can invoke a general exception, like the one in the General Agreement on Tariffs and Trade (GATT), to defend measures *necessary* to protect health that would otherwise be inconsistent with the TPP obligations.[24] While such exceptions are difficult for governments to argue successfully, it is still alarming that the TPP chapter with the most powerful provisions and the most intrusive dispute settlement mechanism should lack such a basic safeguard. Instead, the investment chapter contains cynical language, in Article 9.16, which states: "Nothing in this Chapter shall be construed to prevent a Party from adopting, maintaining or enforcing any measure *otherwise consistent with this Chapter* that it considers appropriate to ensure that investment activity in its territory is undertaken in a manner sensitive to environmental, health or other regulatory objectives (emphasis added)." As many analysts have noted, this wording is circular and self-negating.[25] If a health measure is consistent with the chapter, it would not need protection. If it is inconsistent, this wording provides no defence. The article is little more than window dressing, leaving health and other regulatory measures exposed to investor–state challenge.

Chapter 29 of the TPP does, however, include a more meaningful exclusion for tobacco control measures that permits a TPP member to deny foreign investors the right to bring an investor–state claim against measures to control or discourage smoking.[26] If Canada proceeds with plain packaging, as pledged in the prime minister's 2015 mandate letter to the health minister, it could use this exclusion to disallow investor–state claims under the TPP.[27] If the TPP comes into effect, Canada should certainly take advantage of this opt-out to protect future plain-packaging regulation. But it must be stressed that plain-packaging laws would still be exposed to state-to-state challenges under the TPP (i.e., the U.S. government could launch a dispute on behalf of its tobacco industry). Moreover, the U.S. tobacco industry could bring an investor–state claim on its own behalf against Canadian plain-packaging laws by using NAFTA's ISDS mechanism. In this sense, the TPP carve-out provides greater protection against ISDS claims to countries such as Australia, whose pre-existing free-trade agreement with the U.S. does not include ISDS, than to Canada.

The TPP tobacco exception is a positive step for tobacco control regulation that makes it harder for multinational tobacco firms to make an ISDS claim. But at a deeper level the specific carve-out for tobacco implicitly highlights the broader threats posed by the TPP and ISDS. The very need for such a tobacco carve-out recognizes that ISDS poses a threat to health regulation. And if tobacco requires a carve-out, why have other critical areas of health regulation been left exposed to ISDS? For example, nothing would prevent foreign investors from bringing investor–state claims challenging new regulations restricting the commercial marketing of unhealthy food and beverages to children, tougher regulations to eliminate trans fats in processed foods, or restrictions governing the sale of legalized marijuana.[28]

During the TPP negotiations, there were other, more robust options on the table to protect health regulation from investor–state claims. Malaysia, for example, consistently advocated a full carve-out for tobacco control measures that would have protected them from all challenges, investor–state or government-to-government. Dozens of health groups from many TPP countries, including the American Public Health Association, the American Medical Association, the American Cancer Society and the National Association of Attorneys General, endorsed Malaysia's approach.[29] The Australian government also proposed that government measures that are "manifestly non-discriminatory and for legitimate public welfare objectives, such as public health, safety and the environment," should not be subject to investor–state claims. Unfortunately, neither of these sensible proposals survived the cut and thrust of negotiations. Clearly, the weak protection for public health in the TPP is neither an accident nor an oversight. It is an accurate reflection of the priorities of the U.S. government and corporate lobbies who deliberately placed investor rights over public interest regulation, including measures to protect public health.

Cross-border trade in services

Chapter 10 of the TPP governs cross-border trade in services. As with other parts of the agreement it reflects a bias toward commercial rights at the potential expense of the public good, including public health. The chapter's key obligations include the following:

- *National Treatment* — no government may discriminate in favour of local service suppliers;

- *Most-Favoured-Nation Treatment* — the best treatment given to any foreign service supplier must be extended to all foreign services or suppliers;

- *Market Access* — governments cannot limit the number of service suppliers in a sector or require services to be delivered through a specific type of legal entity (such as not-for-profits); and

- *Local Presence* — governments are prohibited from requiring foreign service providers (e.g., of telemedicine) to be resident in a jurisdiction in order to supply the service.

These obligations, with their emphasis on globalizing and commercializing services, run counter to fundamental principles of the Canadian medicare system. In principle, Canada's public sector health insurance monopoly, and the strict regulations around who can provide health-care services to Canadians and on what terms, contradict many of these provisions.[30] In practice, however, these TPP obligations are subject to reservations, or country-specific exceptions, that each party has the opportunity to negotiate for the protection of vital interests such as health care.

In the TPP, as in previous trade and investment treaties, Canada relies on two key reservations to protect its public health-care system. These exemptions shield government measures in the health sector from some, but not all, of the TPP's investment and services obligations. The first of these, Annex I, includes a general reservation that allows Canadian provincial and local governments to maintain all their existing nonconforming measures, including those in the health sector. The Annex I reservation applies against national treatment (Articles 9.4 and 10.3), most-favoured-nation treatment (Articles 9.5 and 10.4), market access (Article 10.5), local presence (Article 10.6), performance requirements (Article 9.10) and senior management and boards of directors (Article 9.11).[31] Under the terms of the Annex I reservation any "existing, non-conforming measures" are bound, meaning they can only be amended to make them more TPP-consistent. As the United States Trade Representative's summary of the TPP services chapter explains, "In listing a measure in Annex I, the country commits to a 'standstill,' which ensures that the measure will not become more restrictive in the future, as well as a 'ratchet,' which means that if the measure is amended in the future to become less restrictive, the new, more favorable treatment will set the benchmark for the standstill requirement."[32] Accordingly, if a nonconforming measure is rescinded or amended it cannot later be restored by a future government.

Canada also negotiated a second reservation that excludes the Canadian health-care sector from only some provisions of the TPP's investment and services chapters. The Annex II reservation is unbound. This means it protects existing nonconforming measures and, in addition, allows Canadian governments to take new measures that would otherwise be TPP-inconsistent. The reservation, however, stipulates that any such measures must be related to health to the extent that it is "a social service established or maintained for a public purpose."[33] These terms are undefined and have been subject to sharply differing interpretations by the U.S. and Canadian governments.[34] The TPP Annex II reservation is virtually identical to its NAFTA counterpart, but it is stronger in one respect: it applies against the most-favoured-nation treatment clause of the TPP investment chapter.[35] This means that in the sectors excluded by the reservation, investors from all TPP parties would not automatically be entitled to the best treatment Canada provides to investors from other countries (e.g., European investors under CETA if the Canada–EU deal is ratified).[36]

These two reservations — Annexes I and II — are vital in ensuring Canadian governments at all levels have the ability to maintain existing health measures and to adopt new health measures that would otherwise be inconsistent with the TPP. But, like reservations under previous trade and investment treaties, they are also incomplete and flawed. Significantly, the Annex II reservation does not clearly exclude so-called ancillary health services such as food services, cleaning services, maintenance services, computer and data management services, hospital administration and other support services that are critical to the health-care system. Where such services are contracted out or privatized, attempts to re-reregulate or to return them to the public sector could be exposed to legal challenge under the TPP and other trade and investment agreements.

The limited scope of Canada's Annex II reservation can be illustrated through a recent controversy over testing for registered nurses' certification. Nurses' unions have expressed serious concerns over the decision by Canadian nursing regulatory bodies to move implementation of the Computerized Adaptive Testing (CAT) exam for registered nurses to the National Council of State Boards of Nursing (NCSBN), a U.S. body. These include testing geared to U.S. rather than Canadian nursing practice, inadequate translation and lack of preparatory materials in French, higher rates of failure following the adoption of the U.S. exam, and concerns over the privacy of nurses' personal data becoming subject to intrusive U.S. security laws such as the *USA PATRIOT Act*. Canada's Annex II reservation only excludes measures related to "public training." The NCSBN is a private, not-for-profit organization. Consequently, measures regulating the testing and training services provided by this U.S. service provider would fall outside the scope of the Annex II reservation.[37] If provincial governments or the regulatory bodies move to address nurses' concerns, complaints by the U.S. service provider could result in a government-to-government or investor–state dispute under NAFTA or the TPP. In addition, the TPP chapter on e-commerce prohibits requirements to store data, including personal information, locally. Efforts to address the privacy concerns related to nursing candidates' personal information by requiring that such data be stored securely within Canada could be disallowed by these TPP e-commerce rules.[38]

The TPP also includes a new NAFTA-plus mechanism for applying pressure around reserved, otherwise nonconforming measures at the provincial level. The agreement states: "If a Party considers that a non-conforming measure applied by a regional level of government of another Party, as referred to in subparagraph 1(a)(ii), creates a material impediment to the cross-border supply of services in relation to the former Party, it may request consultations with regard to that measure. These Parties shall enter into consultations with a view to exchanging information on the operation of the measure and to considering whether further steps are necessary and appropriate."[39] Such consultations provide a direct channel for pressuring Canadian provincial governments to amend or rescind reserved measures in any sector, including health.

The TPP also contains new, unique provisions restricting nondiscriminatory domestic regulation. Much of them apply on a "best endeavours" basis. The binding part requires that each signatory country "shall ensure that all measures of general application affecting trade in services are administered in a reasonable, objective and impartial manner." These terms are undefined, leaving trade tribunals considerable discretion in interpretation. Fortunately, the TPP domestic regulation obligations do not apply to health services to the extent that these are reserved from national-treatment and market-access obligations under Canada's Annex I and Annex II.[40]

Overall, the TPP trade-in-services provisions largely preserve the status quo with respect to Canada's health-care services and trade treaties. The Canadian reservations are essential, but still leave certain areas of the health-care system exposed. In failing to fully exclude Canada's health-care system, the trade-in-services provisions repeat the mistakes made in previous agreements, including NAFTA.

Temporary entry of health professionals

Like most Canadian FTAs, the TPP includes a chapter on the temporary entry of business persons that allows certain types of workers from TPP countries to enter other TPP countries on a temporary basis without going through the usual immigration process (see Chapter 6 of this book).[41] There have been impacts with this process in the past for the health sector. In the 1990s, for example, thousands of Canadian nurses used NAFTA's temporary entry provisions to move to the United States to work, and many still do today.[42] NAFTA's rules for "professionals" allow an unlimited number of nurses to migrate between Canada, the United States and Mexico on a temporary basis. Other health-related occupations covered by NAFTA include dentists, pharmacists, psychologists and medical technologists.[43]

The TPP is unlikely to have a similar impact because the scope of the temporary-entry provisions in the health sector are far more limited. In the category of "professionals," which is of greatest concern, Canada has excluded "all health, education, and social services occupations and related occupations" for each TPP country that would otherwise be covered. That means Canada offers no new access to health professionals in the TPP other than that provided under existing agreements or programs. Most TPP countries make similar exceptions, but there are some apparent variations. Australia and Brunei have not listed any sectoral reservations for professionals in their annexes to Chapter 12, so presumably all health services are covered. Malaysia has explicitly offered access for occupations in the category of "specialized medical services." Mexico offers access to all "technician professionals in health," which includes nurses, pharmacists and physiotherapists, although these professions are already covered for Canadians under NAFTA. The potential access to Australia for Canadian health professionals may be most significant, although it is unlikely to rival the access that NAFTA affords to Canadian health workers in the United States. Australia has clarified that all potential TPP "professionals" require employer sponsorship and must meet the "domestic standard" in Australia for their profession, which is subject to interpretation.

Like previous agreements, the TPP also gives temporary-entry rights in the category of intra-corporate transferees (ICTs). There are no sectoral restrictions for ICTs in the TPP and the rules are essentially the same for all TPP countries. In theory, this category could be used by private, multinational health services firms to move some health workers into and out of Canada from certain TPP countries. The firm would need to have a presence in both countries and the worker would need to qualify as a "specialist," defined as "an employee possessing specialized knowledge of the company's products or services and their application in international markets, or an advanced level of expertise or knowledge of the company's processes and procedures." Since this definition is subject to interpretation by immigration agents it is impossible to say at this point exactly which occupations might be covered. It appears unlikely that the ICT provisions will facilitate meaningful numbers of health workers into or out of Canada, although these rules may gain significance if more aspects of the health system are privatized.

Public-private partnerships

Despite their serious shortcomings and negative track record, public-private partnerships (P3s) are increasingly used as an alternative to direct government provision and/or conventional government procurement of services. The investment chapter of the TPP contains provisions that would allow foreign investors to submit an investor–state claim on the grounds that a government has breached "investment authorisations" or "investment agreements."[44] It should be stressed that these provisions enable international investment arbitration tribunals to adjudicate not only breaches of investment treaties, but also disputes regarding the investment agreement itself. This is the case even if the P3 contract obliges the parties to use other forms of dispute resolution.

It is astonishing that Canada would agree to rules that allow the private party in a P3 to disregard contractually agreed-upon dispute resolution provisions and bypass the domestic courts in favour of investor–state arbitration under the TPP. Investor–state arbitration is a very lengthy, complex, and costly procedure for resolving disputes. Even more troubling is the fact that arbitration tribunals tend to exhibit a pro-investor bias at the expense of the public and taxpayer interests, and fail to exercise the judicial restraint typically shown by domestic and international courts in similar contexts.[45]

These draconian rules would apply to new P3s at the federal level in Canada. In defining investment agreements, the TPP investment chapter includes typical public-private partnerships such as those between a central government and an investor to "supply services on behalf of the Party for consumption by the general public for: power generation or distribution, water treatment or distribution, telecommunications, or other similar services supplied on behalf of the Party for consumption by the general public."[46] A footnote to this definition explains: "For the avoidance of doubt, this subparagraph does not cover correctional services, *healthcare services*, education services, childcare services, welfare services or other similar social services (emphasis added)."[47]

While this clarification certainly excludes core health-care services that might be provided through P3s, it does not clearly exclude services such as maintenance, computer and data management services, administration and other health-care support services. Indeed, even if a future P3 contract attempted to exclude such matters as related to health care it would be futile. Since the TPP gives foreign investors the right to bypass the dispute resolution mechanisms specified in the P3 agreement, sensitive decisions about the scope of the loosely worded exclusion for health-care services would be made by investor arbitration panels that are beyond the reach of domestic law and the courts.

The transparency annex and drug pricing

Another aspect of the TPP that raises health-related concerns is Annex 26-A, entitled "Transparency and Procedural Fairness for Pharmaceutical Products and Medical Devices." The annex does not cover the direct procurement of drugs (e.g., those medicines used in hospitals). But its purpose, as Dr. Deborah Gleeson notes, is "to discipline national pricing and reimbursement schemes for pharmaceutical products and medical devices."[48] Throughout the TPP talks, the U.S. government and brand-name pharmaceutical lobbyists targeted New Zealand's government agency Pharmac, which does an exemplary job of controlling drug costs. Pharmac negotiates with both brand-name and generic companies over the costs of drugs that it approves for use in the country's health-care system. As a result, New Zealand's per-capita drug costs are among the lowest in the OECD. In the TPP's transparency annex, the U.S. pursued new rights for brand-name companies to contest the decisions of public drug agencies and tilt the playing field toward "market-based" pricing, increasing costs to governments and the health-care system.

New Zealand and Australia strongly resisted this push, and the final wording of the annex has been considerably watered down from the initial U.S. proposal that was leaked in 2011.[49] The annex is still generally biased in favour of commercial interests and against those of taxpayers and consumers. Initially, the restrictions apply only to the four TPP countries that already operate "national healthcare programs" regarding the reimbursement and pricing of drugs. These are Japan, the U.S., Australia and New Zealand. The annex specifies, "Canada does not currently operate a national healthcare programme within the scope of this Annex."[50] Nevertheless, Canada bowed to U.S. pressure to prospectively cover federal health-care authorities. Consequently, if Canada develops a future national health-care program covering drug pricing and reimbursement it will come under pressure to comply with the transparency annex.

While most drugs in the Canadian public health-care system are purchased by or have the costs reimbursed by provincial governments, the federal government pays the cost of medications for Aboriginal peoples, the military and some other groups. Encumbering the federal government in its future ability to get the best therapeutic value for taxpayers' money when it pays for medicines sets a bad precedent. The TPP transparency annex could also hamper Ottawa's future ability to co-operate effectively with provincial and territorial governments in joint measures to make drugs more affordable.

Conclusion

As a legal advisor to the 2002 Romanow Commission on the Future of Health Care in Canada observed, if the NAFTA investor protection provisions "and the accompanying investor–state dispute settlement mechanism procedures had existed in the 1960s, the public health system in its present form would never have come into existence."[51] The commission, after extensive study, recommended that in all future trade treaties Canada should seek a full exclusion for health care that makes "explicit allowance for both maintaining and expanding publicly insured, financed and delivered health care." The TPP safeguards for health do not come anywhere close to attaining this essential goal. Instead, the TPP would result in increased drug costs — a significant burden Canada's medicare system simply can't afford. The TPP also aims to expand the already controversial rights of foreign investors to challenge health regulation, lock in privatization and impede the future expansion of Canada's public health insurance. The treaty's only innovative, beneficial public health safeguard — the partial carve-out for tobacco control — actually serves to underline the broader risks to health regulation.

While strong international trade is critical to Canada's economic success it should not, and need not, come at the expense of our public health system. Indeed, international trade barriers are already so low that imposing unnecessary costs and unpredictable risks on the Canadian health-care system in exchange for improved market access is a very poor bargain. The increased burden on taxpayers and consumers from higher drug costs alone would likely exceed the full savings to Canadian consumers from the TPP's elimination of tariffs on imports into Canada, undercutting one of the chief arguments for liberalized trade. Moreover, the extension of patents in the TPP's intellectual property chapter, and the agreement's ISDS process, will erode the democratic authority of Canadian governments to renew and expand Canada's most important social program. While health care is better protected from TPP restrictions than many other sectors, the TPP can still be expected to deepen corporate influence over health-care systems in Canada and the other partnering countries.

CHAPTER 3
The TPP and Regulation of Medicines in Canada

Joel Lexchin

As discussed elsewhere in this book, though the impact of the Trans-Pacific Partnership (TPP) on trade flows (imports and exports of goods and services) will be, for the most part, minimal, the deal would place many new constraints on government policy in areas not strictly related to trade.[1] One of these areas is how governments regulate the pharmaceutical sector and set prices for medicines — two issues of importance mainly for U.S. and Japanese brand-name drug companies. The changes proposed in the TPP will have costs for public and private purchasers of pharmaceutical products. In particular, the agreement will restrict future policy options in these areas in ways that benefit brand-name producers over consumers and the broader public interest.

This chapter examines the possible effects a ratified TPP will have on how Canada regulates medicines and how much the country spends paying for them. Among the thirty chapters in the TPP, five contain language specifically related to medicines in the following ways:

- The chapter on technical barriers to trade (Chapter 8) contains clauses on transparency, regulatory harmonization and acceptable marketing approval processes that further entrench the views of foreign governments — and by proxy their pharmaceutical sectors — in federal medicines policy, with no guarantee that harmonization will be upward (to the highest standards) and no additional requirements on Canadian manufacturers to be open about public inspections of their facilities.

- The chapter on intellectual property rights (Chapter 18) contains additional monopoly rights for brand-name pharmaceutical companies in the form of extended patent terms, while locking in Canada's costly patent-linkage system and permanently setting long data-exclusivity terms on traditional and biologic drugs. Depending on whether the TPP or the very similar Comprehensive Economic and Trade Agreement (CETA) with the European Union is ratified first, drug costs are expected to rise by between 5 per cent and 12.9 per cent starting around the year 2023.

- An annex of the chapter on transparency and anticorruption (Chapter 26), related to "transparency and procedural fairness for pharmaceutical products and medical devices," could have negative effects on pharmaceutical costs and regulation in the future. Though there is currently no national drug plan in Canada, should one be established, this annex would threaten the ability of the federal government to use certain cost-control measures.

- The dispute-resolution procedures related to investment (Chapter 9) and other parts of the agreement (Chapter 28) create unnecessary and unforeseeable risks to public policy on medicines. Specifically, an investor–state dispute settlement (ISDS) process would allow investors (e.g., brand-name pharmaceutical corporations) in TPP countries to challenge government measures outside the normal court system, in largely unaccountable private tribunals whose decisions are binding. Canada is already facing such a challenge from U.S. drug firm Eli Lilly, which is demanding $500 million in compensation for Canadian court decisions invalidating two of its patents on the grounds they were granted based on claims about the drugs that could not be demonstrated.

Technical barriers to trade (Chapter 8)

The TPP includes several chapters related to government regulation, including those on so-called sanitary and phytosanitary measures (Chapter 7), technical barriers to trade or TBT (Chapter 8) and regulatory coherence (Chapter 25). These chapters, which build on similar rules in the World Trade Organization (WTO) agreements and many Canadian free-trade agreements, are absolute; they do not concern themselves solely with discriminatory treatment between foreign and domestic firms or goods. Rather, government action is restricted for all, based on the belief that regulation should be no more trade-restrictive than necessary. The TPP chapter on TBT includes several articles that pertain to the regulation of medicines and other pharmaceutical products that could be described as WTO-plus. Article 8.7 on transparency in the main body of this chapter sets forth the following requirement:

> *Each Party shall allow persons of another Party to*
> *participate in the development of technical regulations,*
> *standards and conformity assessment procedures by its*
> *central government bodies on terms no less favourable than*
> *those that it accords to its own persons.*[2]

What this means in practice is that the other TPP countries will have the opportunity to provide comments about Canadian regulatory requirements for drug marketing or postmarket monitoring of drug safety and effectiveness. Both Japan and the United States have very powerful pharmaceutical industries that could end up having an indirect effect on Canadian regulations through the participation of the U.S. and/or Japanese governments. The U.S. government in particular has a very close relationship with the pharmaceutical industry. At a recent WTO meeting of the Council for Trade-Related Aspects of International Property Rights (TRIPS), U.S. negotiators pushed back against requests from the least-developed countries (the LDC group) for an indefinite extension to their existing exemption from some TRIPS requirements that would, if enforced, create unsustainable costs for governments. The deputy U.S. Trade Representative was reported to have said the U.S. government could not accede to the demands from the LDCs because certain stakeholders (presumably including the pharmaceutical industry), already upset that the TPP negotiations had not produced the results the industry wanted, would not suffer another U.S. step-down on intellectual property.[3] (The U.S. and the LDC group compromised at the end of November 2015 on a seventeen-year extension.)[4]

In addition to Article 7, Annex 8-C of the TBT chapter applies specifically to pharmaceuticals. The five following articles within this annex could potentially affect Canada.

i) Article 7

> *The Parties shall seek to collaborate through relevant international initiatives, such as those aimed at harmonisation, as well as regional initiatives that support those international initiatives, as appropriate, to improve the alignment of their respective regulations and regulatory activities for pharmaceutical products.*

In the past, regulatory harmonization, primarily through the International Conference on Harmonization (ICH), has had positive and negative effects on drug regulation in Canada.[5] Until late 2015, the ICH was controlled by the U.S., European Union and Japanese drug regulatory agencies and brand-name industry associations in these countries. In October 2015, the ICH changed its name to the International Council for Harmonization and expanded its membership.[6] The effect that the structural changes in the ICH will have on the standards that it recommends is speculative, so it is unknown whether further harmonization will lead to lower or higher regulatory standards in Canada.

ii) Article 11

> Each Party shall make its determination whether to grant
> marketing authorisation for a specific pharmaceutical
> product on the basis of:
>
> (a) information, including, where appropriate, pre-clinical
> and clinical data, on safety and efficacy;
>
> (b) information on manufacturing quality of the product;
>
> (c) labelling information related to the safety, efficacy and
> use of the product; and
>
> (d) other matters that may directly affect the health or
> safety of the user of the product.
>
> To this end, no Party shall require sale or related financial
> data concerning the marketing of the product as part of the
> determination. Further, each Party shall endeavour to not
> require pricing data as part of the determination.

This article sets out the information that regulatory authorities should consider in making a marketing decision. But depending on how it is interpreted, what is not included may be just as important. For example, the article does not say anything positive or negative about regulatory authorities adopting a "medical need" clause as one of the requirements for approving new drugs. Norway had such a clause before it joined the European Medicines Agency. To meet the medical need test, new drugs approved in Norway had to offer an advantage over existing products: they should be better therapeutic alternatives than those already on the market or there should be a clear-cut medical need for any new product.

Between 1981 and 1983, the absence of medical need was cited in 147 of the 233 new drug applications rejected by Norwegian authorities.[7] Medical need does not mean follow-on drugs in the same class will automatically be rejected, since at times a second or third drug in a class is superior to the first. Rather, the fact a drug is superior to a placebo should not necessarily lead to marketing approval as is currently the situation in Canada. If the four criteria for drug approval laid out in this article of the TBT annex are interpreted as a floor (i.e., additional criteria can be used), then Health Canada would be free to adopt a medical need clause in the future. If, however, the criteria are treated like a restrictive list, the option of adopting a Norway-like needs test — with its positive health and cost-savings potential — will vanish forever as an option for Canada.

iii) Article 12

> *Each Party shall administer any marketing authorisation*
> *process that it maintains for pharmaceutical products in*
> *a timely, reasonable, objective, transparent and impartial*
> *manner, and identify and manage any conflicts of interest*
> *in order to mitigate any associated risks.*

The impact of this article may depend on which country's standards are used to judge an authorization's timeliness. Article 8(c) does make allowances for the "available resources and technical capacity" of the parties. In that regard, the TPP may not require that Canada review drugs as quickly as the U.S. Food and Drug Administration, with its superior resources. (The median approval time in the U.S. is 304 days compared to 350 days in Canada.)[8] However, Canada could be compared to a country of similar size, such as Australia, and vice-versa. Currently, Health Canada reviews drugs slightly faster than its Australian equivalent.[9] Faster regulatory approvals by Health Canada have been shown to lead to a greater chance a product will subsequently acquire a serious safety warning or be withdrawn from the market for safety reasons.[10]

iv) Article 12(c)

> *If a Party requires marketing authorisation for a*
> *pharmaceutical product, the Party shall ensure that any*

> *marketing authorisation determination is subject to an*
> *appeal or review process that may be invoked at the*
> *request of the applicant. For greater certainty, the Party*
> *may maintain an appeal or review process that is either*
> *internal to the regulatory body responsible for the marketing*
> *authorisation determination, such as a dispute resolution or*
> *review process, or external to the regulatory body.*

This article says the appeals process for manufacturers whose products have been denied marketing authorization could be either internal to the regulatory body or conducted by an outside body. Health Canada currently has an internal appeals process. Should the department at some point in the future choose to use an external body for appeals, it could conceivably involve industry representatives, since this article says nothing about the composition of such a body.

v) Article 17

> *The Parties shall seek to improve their collaboration on*
> *pharmaceutical inspection, and to this end, each Party shall,*
> *with respect to the inspection of a pharmaceutical product*
> *within the territory of another Party:*
>
> *(c) notify the other Party of its findings as soon as possible*
> *following the inspection and, if the findings will be publicly*
> *released, no later than a reasonable time before release. The*
> *inspecting Party is not required to notify the other Party of*
> *its findings if it considers that those findings are confidential*
> *and should not be disclosed.*

If national governments are to be required to change their pharmaceutical policies to meet new internationalized standards, this article surely represents a missed opportunity for establishing a superior international standard. Instead of necessitating that inspections of manufacturing facilities be made public, the TPP would allow each party to claim this information is confidential and should therefore not be released. Health Canada has a poor track record when it comes to transparency, despite recent minor improvements; this article would specifically allow the department to continue its current policy of secrecy.[11]

Investment and dispute settlement (Chapters 9 and 28)

Like almost all Canadian free-trade agreements, the TPP includes a chapter on investment protection along with a controversial investor–state dispute settlement process (Chapter 9). As described in more detail by Gus Van Harten in his chapter, ISDS provides a venue for foreign investors to sue another party (country) to the treaty in private arbitration for actions taken by federal, provincial or local governments that are alleged to violate the substantial rights contained in the treaty's investment chapter. Those rights include protections against discriminatory treatment (e.g., where foreign and national investors are treated differently by a government action) and expropriation without compensation. But the vast majority of ISDS claims involve other vaguely worded clauses on a foreign investor's "minimum standards of treatment," or their "legitimate expectations," which ISDS tribunals have too frequently interpreted in an expansive way that seriously undermines democratic processes and, occasionally, national legal systems.

Disputes under ISDS clauses in treaties like the TPP are heard outside of the judicial system of the country that is being sued; in general these decisions are not subject to appeal. The tribunals that hear these cases are comprised of three private individuals (usually lawyers) from a rather small pool of arbitrators, many of whom also sometimes serve as lawyers for investors making ISDS charges.[12] As the European Commission has noted, "This situation can give rise to conflicts of interest — real or perceived — and thus concerns that these individuals are not acting with full impartiality when acting as arbitrators."[13] University of Toronto law professor David Schneiderman is among a growing list of experts on ISDS who claim the conflict is very real, conferring "enormous discretion" over what is and is not a legitimate government measure on "an elite corps" of investment layers. "As enforcers, investment tribunals have an immense amount of room to manoeuvre in determining whether governments have run afoul of treaty text," he commented recently.[14]

EU decision-makers are so concerned about the potential for abuse, the European Commission recently proposed replacing all European treaties containing ISDS, including the CETA with Canada, with a more transparent and (they suggest) judicial investment court. The TPP, on the other hand, makes no attempt to reform the flaws of the ISDS system. For example, TPP negotiators relegated a modest code of conduct for ISDS arbitrators to a side agreement to be finalized by participating countries at some point before the pact goes into effect. The vagueness of enforceable investment rules in the TPP combined with this extraordinary discretion vested in arbitrators creates potential problems for regulation in any number of policy areas, including related to pharmaceuticals and efforts to control drug costs.

The U.S. pharmaceutical company Eli Lilly is already using the ISDS provisions in NAFTA to sue Canada for $500 million, claiming the decision of the Canadian courts to overturn patents on two products, on the grounds that the patents made claims about the drugs that could not be substantiated, amounts to expropriation without compensation and violates its minimum standards of treatment as protected in the treaty.[15] For any domestic investor or firm in Canada, the ruling of a superior court would be the final say. The investment chapters in treaties like NAFTA and the TPP give multinational firms the ability to sidestep the law.

The TPP investment text could have, but in the end does little to curb claims such as Eli Lilly's and may, in fact, make matters worse. Procedurally, the TPP would extend ISDS to investors from all TPP countries, including Japan, which is home to a large pharmaceutical industry. Substantively, and unlike NAFTA, the TPP's investment chapter explicitly covers intellectual property rights in its definition of investment and contains no general exception for matters related to public health. Problematically, the TPP investment chapter also cross-references and incorporates (e.g., in Article 9.8.5) rights contained in the WTO TRIPS Agreement. According to a recent assessment of the Eli Lilly case, this cross-referencing is dangerous "given the extensive private and public enforcement rights that right-holders already have and given drug companies' proclivities to bring lawsuits against governments."[16] On the same point, the U.S. government watchdog group Public Citizen argues:

Pharmaceutical firms could use the TPP to demand cash compensation for claimed violations of WTO rules on creation, limitation or revocation of intellectual property rights. Currently, WTO rules are not privately enforceable by investors . . . An Annex in the TPP investment text could empower the three private lawyers of ISDS tribunals, which have a clear track record of interpreting vague terms broadly to favor foreign investors, to impose their binding interpretation of TRIPS' intentionally flexible terms on the very governments that negotiated those terms. This move, which risks making TRIPS obligations enforceable via ISDS, could restrict governments' policy space to ensure access to affordable medicines.[17]

Intellectual property (Chapter 18)

The intellectual property rights chapter of the TPP has probably drawn the most critical attention in Canada, though mainly for its copyright, trademark and other provisions that may affect Canada's tech sector, Internet governance and privacy rights. But the articles in this chapter also cover a variety of areas of importance to pharmaceutical policy such as data-exclusivity (ownership of the safety and efficacy data from clinical trials by the company that paid for the trials), patent term extensions (to make up for any delays in processing patent applications or regulatory delays) and a requirement that countries link the marketing approval of generics to the expiration of patents owned by the originating brand-name company. Previous federal governments have made concessions on all of these issues in the past; in NAFTA, for example, attached to promises (later broken) by the brand-name drug sector to increase research and development in Canada, and as part of CETA.[18] But there are some differences between the IP chapters in CETA and the TPP that might affect how much drug costs will increase in Canada if the treaties are ever implemented.

Canada already allows brand-name companies to block the approval of generic competition by alleging the generic company is violating a patent that is still valid. In the CETA negotiations, Canada agreed to reforms that would give brand-name companies the right to appeal in cases where they lose a court case on this issue — a right not included in the TPP. Moreover, CETA appears to extend data protection to non-innovative drugs whereas the TPP does not. In common, both pending trade deals would lock in additional patent protection beyond the internationally required twenty-year term (patent term extension) for delays in marketing approval for new drugs. In the case of CETA, this period could be up to two years, while the length of the extension is not specified in the TPP. In a previous article, Marc-André Gagnon and I calculated that the CETA provisions described above could increase Canadian drug costs by between 6.2 per cent and 12.9 per cent starting about eight years after ratification.[19] This was assuming the EU treaty would be ratified first, which is not at all clear at this point. Because of the differences between CETA and the TPP, if the TPP came into effect first, Canadian drug costs would initially rise by 5 per cent, since the data-exclusivity provisions in the TPP do not cover as wide a range of products as those in CETA.[20] Regardless of timing, both will lock in a specific pharmaceutical strategy of longer patents and stronger brand-name protections for Canada (and all other signatory countries) that cannot be modified in the future without the agreement of all of the other TPP parties. There is one new provision in the TPP, not present in CETA, which could affect Canadian drug regulation. Article 18.48.4 states the following:

> *With the objective of avoiding unreasonable curtailment of the effective patent term, a Party may adopt or maintain procedures that expedite the processing of marketing approval applications.*

This clause allows for wider use of expedited review processes (i.e., approval mechanisms that are shorter than the standard 300-day process). The likely adverse effect of more rapid approvals on drug safety has already been mentioned.

Transparency and anti-corruption (Chapter 26)

This chapter serves the dual purpose of requiring that TPP countries "promptly" publish any "laws, regulations, procedures and administrative rulings of general application with respect to any matter covered by this Agreement," and that they put in place the means to combat corruption in matters related to international trade and investment. An annex of the chapter (Annex 26-A Transparency and Procedural Fairness for Pharmaceutical Products and Medical Devices) could have negative effects on pharmaceutical costs and regulation in the future.

The second article of the transparency annex lays out a series of principles the parties have to follow, among them the recognition of "the importance of research and development, including innovation. . .related to pharmaceutical products," "the need to promote timely and affordable access to pharmaceutical products," and "the need to recognize the value of pharmaceutical products. . .through the operation of competitive markets." Innovation, in the pharmaceutical industry's terms, typically means any new therapeutic molecule. Combined with the timely access requirement in the TPP, the term is usually interpreted by industry to mean that any new drug should be listed on public drug formularies as soon as possible after it is approved for marketing.

The principles at the start of the transparency annex are not the same as treaty-level obligations. They are only aspirational statements and not legally enforceable; the parties must only "acknowledge" their importance. As such, they should not pose a problem if Canada were to refuse to approve a product, even if it is a new molecule, or if a provincial drug plan refuses to subsidize a new drug. In the same way, it is unlikely these non-enforceable principles could be used to require provincial plans to make a listing decision within a particular period of time. While the principles of the transparency annex cannot be enforced, its remaining three articles can be, though not through the formal state-to-state dispute settlement procedures provided for in Chapter 28.

Article 3 of the annex, on "procedural fairness," deals with how countries set reimbursement prices for pharmaceuticals, requiring them to do so "within a specified period of time," without defining what that might be. If a party cannot complete the review within this time it "shall disclose the reason for the delay to the applicant and shall provide for another specified period of time for completing consideration of the proposal." The same paragraph allows companies to appeal a negative reimbursement decision to either an independent body or to the same expert group that made the original decision (the decision of what appeal mechanism to use is up to the country), provided that the review process includes a substantive reconsideration of the application.

None of the provisions of this paragraph apply to the operations of the Patented Medicine Prices Review Board, as the regulatory body only sets a maximum introductory price for new patented medicines. Nor would the TPP's transparency annex affect the functions of the Pan-Canadian Pharmaceutical Alliance that negotiates prices for brand-name and generic drugs for provincial drug plans. The annex explicitly states, "Canada does not currently operate a national health care programme within the scope of this Annex." However, should Canada, at some point in the future, adopt some form of pharmacare incorporating a system of price regulation, then the provisions in this paragraph could apply. But even then, the original decision about prices would not necessarily be overturned, since any review could be carried out by the same governmental body that did the initial review. Importantly, whichever review process is adopted, it is only available for reviewing decisions not to list a pharmaceutical or medical device for reimbursement (i.e., it would not apply to pricing recommendations or determinations).

Article 4 permits pharmaceutical companies to "disseminate to. . .consumers through the manufacturer's website. . .truthful and not misleading information regarding its pharmaceutical products that are approved for marketing in the Party's territory." Companies are already allowed to do this in Canada, and while there has not been any systematic analysis of the information on websites, other forms of direct-to-consumer advertising have proven to be very deceptive.[21] If a future Canadian government took action to preclude information on websites this provision might be invoked to stop this measure.

Article 5, on consultation, includes this clause:

> To facilitate dialogue and mutual understanding of issues
> relating to this Annex, each Party shall give sympathetic
> consideration to and shall afford adequate opportunity for

*consultation regarding a written request by another Party to
consult on any matter related to this Annex.*

A similar clause in the Australia–United States Free Trade Agreement
(AUSFTA) provoked initial concerns it could have negative consequences
for the way Australia regulates drug approvals and decides whether or not
to fund drugs, but these concerns were not borne out. Consultations per
se should not present any threat to Canada, especially since the text of the
article limits its applicability to issues arising from this particular annex.
The Canadian government could, for example, specify that consultations
must take place in an open forum and be chaired by health officials (not
trade bureaucrats). The government could also exclude industry players
outright at this stage. The only obligation in the annex is to consult, with
no provisions for making decisions or even offering recommendations.
In the AUSFTA, the Australian government ensured that a non-expert
body could not remake the decisions reached by its expert bodies with
respect to approvals or funding. The Medicines Working Group that arose
out of the AUSFTA has only met twice in the last ten years and the discussions have been limited to issues arising from the relevant annex of
that agreement, so it quickly ran out of things to talk about. Should the
Canadian government adopt the same attitude as the Australian government did, consultations pose little threat.

Conclusion

Beyond the text of the TPP, there are additional risks to Canada from
how the agreement might be interpreted by the U.S. government and the
pharmaceutical industry, which was not satisfied with the outcome of the
TPP negotiations, especially with respect to the provisions on intellectual
property rights. For example, where industry had pushed for twelve years
of data-exclusivity protection for biologics, TPP countries would only
agree to a maximum of eight years. As a result, the industry will probably
be very aggressive in pushing for the strictest interpretation of the various
provisions of the TPP that relate to medications.

In summary, the TPP could have profound effects on the criteria that
Canada uses to decide on drug safety and effectiveness, how new drugs

are approved (or not) for marketing, post-market surveillance and inspection, the listing of drugs on public formularies and how individual drugs are priced in the future. Some of these implications are necessarily speculative since they depend on future actions that Canada might take (e.g., with respect to national pharmacare), how the various articles in the TPP are interpreted by dispute panels and how aggressive the pharmaceutical industry is in pursuing its newfound rights in the deal. But they are important enough to warrant careful consideration in any weighing of the costs and benefits of ratifying the TPP

CHAPTER 4
The TPP and the Environment

Jacqueline Wilson

In February 2016, a World Trade Organization (WTO) dispute panel ruled that India's national solar program was illegal under the General Agreement on Tariffs and Trade (GATT 1994) because of its domestic technology quotas. Two years earlier, the local content requirements in Ontario's *Green Energy Act* were similarly found to be illegal at the WTO. In March 2015, a North American Free Trade Agreement (NAFTA) investment arbitration panel held that a company's rights were violated because the Canadian government adopted the decision of an independent environmental assessment panel to reject a planned quarry project.

The limitations that trade agreements put on environmental policy-making are becoming clearer with each new case like these. It's the reason the United States Trade Representative (USTR) assured the public that the Trans-Pacific Partnership (TPP) contains "the most robust enforceable environment commitments of any trade agreement in history."[1] This chapter exposes the USTR position for the significant overstatement that it is.

The language in the TPP's environment chapter is weak and unenforceable while, as examined elsewhere in this book, the investment protections for corporate investors are strong and binding on governments. TPP parties are given discretion to decide whether and how to act on environmental issues, and in any event they are unlikely to file disputes related to the environment. Importantly, for federal states like Canada and Australia, the chapter also covers only central governments, leaving the provinces off the hook altogether — a privilege these levels of government do not have under the rest of the agreement.

Vague and discretionary rules

The primary reason why the TPP environment chapter will not sufficiently protect the environment is that the language is vague, leaving significant room for TPP member countries to exercise discretion about taking action to address environmental issues.

Article 20.3: General Commitments

Environmental protection measures vary widely between TPP member countries. Rather than encourage the adoption of high standards across the region, Article 20.3.2 of the environment chapter allows each party to determine "its own levels of domestic environmental protection and its own environmental priorities."[2] Article 20.3.5 provides states with further discretion to determine whether or how to investigate and prosecute violations of domestic environmental rules. In other words, state sovereignty is treated as inviolable with regard to setting minimum levels of environment protection, while elsewhere in the agreement strong environmental measures that might interfere with trade and investment are exposed to challenge under the TPP's investment chapter (see chapter by Gus Van Harten).

Article 20.4: Multilateral Environmental Agreements

The TPP's reliance on the current state of environmental law in each member country is also reflected in Article 20.4.1, which affirms the state's commitment to implement the multilateral environmental agreements to which it is already a party. There is no requirement for TPP parties to adopt any additional multilateral environmental agreements or to uphold the standards in particular agreements to which it is not a party.

Article 20.5: Protection of the Ozone Layer

Article 20.5.1 leaves significant discretion to TPP member countries about the strength and breadth of any measures to address protection of the ozone layer by only committing parties to "take measures to control the production and consumption of, and trade in, [ozone depleting] substances," rather than setting a particular environmental standard to be met.[3] It is also doubtful that Article 20.5.2, which recognizes the importance of public participation in accordance with the law or policy of the TPP party, will in any way improve public participation in environmental decision making.[4]

Article 20.6: Protection of the Marine Environment from Ship Pollution

The language in Article 20.6 is similarly problematic because each party commits to "take measures to prevent the pollution of the marine environment from ships," but there is no commitment to adopt, maintain or implement laws to meet a particular standard that would truly address the problem. Article 20.6.2 again only recognizes "the importance of public participation and consultation in accordance with [each TPP party's] law or policy," which will not require improved public participation.

Article 20.10: Corporate Social Responsibility

There is a significant equity issue raised by the radical difference between the strong, enforceable rights for investors in the investor–state dispute settlement (ISDS) scheme compared to the weak, unenforceable obligations imposed on investors in Article 20.10. The article on corporate social responsibility is essentially meaningless and imposes absolutely no mandatory requirements on corporations acting in other TPP countries. It asks each party to "*encourage* enterprises. . .to adopt *voluntarily*, into their policies and practices, principles of corporate social responsibility that are related to the environment" (emphasis added).[5]

Article 20.13: Trade and Biodiversity

The weak language of Article 20.13 is similar to Articles 20.5 and 20.6 and is unlikely to require any further action from a TPP party to protect biodiversity. It says each party "shall promote and encourage the conservation and sustainable use of biological diversity, in accordance with its law or policy."[6] Article 20.13.3 recognizes the importance of indigenous and local community knowledge and practice in maintaining biodiversity, and Article 20.13.5 recognizes the importance of public participation, but again only in accordance with the party's existing law and policy.

Article 20.14: Invasive Alien Species

Article 20.14 is vague and unenforceable. The parties recognize that "the movement of terrestrial and aquatic invasive species across borders through trade-related pathways can adversely affect the environment."[7] A TPP environment committee, to be established once the agreement comes into force, is to work with the TPP committee on sanitary and phytosanitary measures to identify co-operative opportunities to share information.[8]

Article 20.15: Transition to a Low Emissions and Resilient Economy

This article includes some of the weakest language in the environment chapter. It does not even promote or encourage action on climate change, let alone require it. The words "climate change" do not appear in the environment chapter and it is not explicit that "low emissions" refers to the greenhouse gas emissions listed in the United Nations Framework Convention on Climate Change. Instead, this article recognizes that "each Party's actions to transition to a low emissions economy should reflect domestic circumstances and capabilities," and states that the TPP countries shall co-operate to address matters of joint or common interest.[9]

The final version of this article is much weaker than the version released by Wikileaks in November 2013.[10] In the leaked version of the text, the article was titled "Trade and Climate Change."[11] The parties were to acknowledge "climate change as a global concern that requires collective action" and recognize the importance of implementing their respective commitments under the United Nations Framework Convention on Climate Change.[12] This earlier version of the chapter also had the parties

- Recognize that trade and climate change policies should be mutually supportive;[13]

- Note efforts in a range of international fora to "increase energy efficiency; develop low-carbon technologies and alternative and renewable energy sources; promote sustainable transport and sustainable urban infrastructure development; address deforestation and forest degradation; reduce emissions in international maritime shipping and air transport; improve monitoring, reporting, and verification of greenhouse gas emissions; and develop adaptation actions for climate change";[14]

- Agree to discuss best practices "in designing, implementing, and operating mechanisms to reduce carbon emissions, including market and non-market measures";[15] and

- Recognize their "respective commitment in APEC to rationalize and phase out, over the medium term, inefficient fossil fuel subsidies that encourage wasteful consumption, while recognizing the importance of providing those in need with essential energy services."[16]

None of these provisions appear in the final text of the TPP.

Article 20.16: Marine Capture Fisheries

Article 20.16 provides more guidance for TPP parties than other articles in the environment chapter. However, other than the mandatory requirement to reduce specific subsidies, the parties are given broad discretion to address these serious environmental issues. The scope of Article 20.16 is similar to Articles 20.5, 20.6 and 20.13, in that TPP member countries agree to recognize "the importance of taking measures aimed at the conservation and the sustainable management of fisheries."[17] Each party "shall seek to operate a fisheries management system" that regulates marine wild- capture fishing.[18] TPP countries also only commit to "promote the long-term conservation of sharks, marine turtles, seabirds, and marine mammals, through implementation and effective enforcement of conservation and management measures." A list of suggested measures for parties to take is included, such as a prohibition on finning, but only "as appropriate."[19]

Article 20.16.5 does provide a mandatory requirement to control, reduce and eventually eliminate all subsidies that contribute to overfishing and overcapacity if the fishing negatively affects fish stocks "that are in an over-fished condition,"[20] or the subsidies are to fishing vessels that are listed by the flag state or a relevant regional fisheries management organization (RFMO) or arrangement for illegal, unreported and unregulated (IUU) fishing.[21]

For all other subsidies that contribute to overfishing or overcapacity, the parties are only required to make "best efforts" to refrain from intro-ducing new, or extending or enhancing existing, subsidies.[22] The parties have three years to eliminate subsidies for overfishing and overcapacity that negatively impact fish stocks already in an overfished condition. Vietnam has negotiated an additional two-year period to eliminate these subsidy programs.[23] There is no time period for eliminating subsidies relating to fishing vessels listed by the flag state or relevant RFMO pursu-ant to paragraph 5(b) of this article.

Each party shall notify the other parties of subsidies covered by Article 1.1 of the WTO Agreement on Subsidies and Countervailing Measures,[24] and they shall, "to the extent possible," inform the parties about other subsidies not covered by this agreement, including fuel subsidies.[25] Each party also commits to several actions to combat IUU fishing, including to "support monitoring, control, surveillance, compliance and enforcement systems," to "implement port State measures," and to strive to act consis-tently with RMFO standards, even if it is not a member.[26]

Article 20.17: Conservation and Trade

Article 20.17.2 provides that each TPP member country shall "adopt, maintain and implement laws, regulations and any other measures to fulfil its obligations under the Convention on International Trade in Endangered Species of Wild Fauna and Flora (CITES)." However, the rest of the article is vague and discretionary. For example, Article 20.17.3 does not set an environmental standard and instead requires the parties "to promote conservation and to combat the illegal take of, and illegal trade in, wild fauna and flora." Parties shall undertake several actions, including "joint activities on conservation issues of mutual interest," but only "as appropriate," and the parties only "endeavour to implement, as appropriate, CITES resolutions."[27]

Article 20.17.5 requires parties to "take measures to combat. . .the trade of wild fauna and flora that. . .were taken or traded in violation of that Party's law or another applicable law."[28] The enforceability of Article 20.17.5 is weakened by the following paragraph, which highlights each party's "right to exercise administrative, investigatory and enforcement discretion" and to "make decisions regarding the allocation of administrative, investigatory and enforcement resources."[29] Footnote twenty-five provides that each party retains the right to determine what constitutes "credible evidence."

Narrow coverage of environmental rules

While the language of many TPP environment chapter articles is vague and discretionary, its reach is also narrowed by the definition of "environmental law" in Article 20.1, which is limited to any statute or regulation of the central government of each TPP party.[30] There appears to have been no effort to expand the scope of protections or include subnational governments in the negotiations of the environment chapter.

Under the General Commitments section, Article 20.3.4 provides that "no Party shall fail to effectively enforce its environmental laws through a sustained or recurring course of action or inaction in a manner affecting trade or investment between the Parties." A TPP party wishing to raise issues regarding another party's subnational laws not included in the definition of environmental law can only "request a dialogue" pursuant to Article 20.12.9.

For Canada, environmental law is defined as "an Act of the Parliament of Canada or regulation made under an Act of the Parliament of Canada that is enforceable by action of the central level of government."[31] This definition is restrictive because the federal government is not solely responsible for the protection of the environment in Canada; environmental protection is not a specifically assigned power and relevant powers are divided in sections 91 and 92 of the *Constitution Act, 1867*.[32]

The scope of this definition has varying importance depending on the division of power in each TPP country. For instance, the inclusion of only central government laws in Australia is significant because, as in Canada, environmental laws are made and enforced by both national and sub-national authorities.[33] In contrast, most environmental regulation in Peru should be covered by a definition that includes central government laws.[34]

Violations must prove trade impacts

A further weakness of the TPP environment chapter is that it does not regulate a TPP party's environmentally detrimental actions in general. Rather, it seeks to prevent such actions only if they can be demonstrated to affect trade between the parties. The commitment in Article 20.3.4 is that a party shall not "fail to effectively enforce its environmental laws through a sustained or recurring course of action or inaction in a manner affecting trade or investment between the Parties." Article 20.12.9 similarly provides for a dialogue regarding a sustained or recurring course of action or inaction by a subnational level of government only if it affects trade or investment between the parties. This threshold for compliance is weaker than the requirement in Article 22.1 of the North American Agreement on Environmental Cooperation (NAAEC), the environmental side-agreement of the NAFTA, which allows a party to challenge actions that show a "persistent pattern of failure by that other Party to effectively enforce its environmental law," but does not require that the complaint show how those actions affect North American trade or investment flows.[35]

The TPP's restriction on enforcement is repeated in several parts of Chapter 20. Article 20.5: *Protection of the Ozone Layer* provides that a party shall be deemed in compliance with this provision if it "maintains the measure or measures listed in Annex 20-A implementing its obligations under the Montreal Protocol." However, footnote 5 provides that a violation of Article 20.5 is not established unless the challenging party can also show that "the other Party has failed to take measures to control the production and consumption of, and trade in, certain substances that can significantly deplete and otherwise modify the ozone layer in a manner that is likely to result in adverse effects on human health and the environment, *in a manner affecting trade or investment between the Parties*" (emphasis added).

Similarly, a footnote to Article 20.6: *Protection of the Marine Environment from Ship Pollution* requires that a challenging party show "the other Party has failed to take measures to prevent the pollution of the marine environment from ships in a manner affecting trade or investment between the Parties." Article 20.9: *Public Submissions* suggests that submissions from a person in a TPP country about that country's implementation of the chapter should "explain how, and to what extent, the issue raised affects trade or investment between the Parties."[36] Footnote twenty-three to Article 20.17: *Conservation and Trade* requires the complaining country to demonstrate how another party to the TPP has failed to "fulfil its obligations under *CITES* in a manner affecting trade or investment between the Parties."

Notably, this language requiring that a violation of the chapter affect trade or investment between the parties is not reproduced in Article 20.16: *Marine Capture Fisheries*. As discussed above, this article imposes more specific requirements on the TPP parties than other articles in the environment chapter. The restriction for enforcement is also not reproduced for Article 20.13: *Trade and Biodiversity* or Article 20.14: *Invasive Alien Species*, but these articles are vague and unenforceable in any event.

Overly complicated state-to-state dispute resolution

Enforcement of the environment chapter will ultimately require political will by TPP party governments. Similar approaches to state-to-state dispute settlement involving environmental protections in other trade agreements have not worked in the past and there is no reason to believe that this chapter will be better enforced. For example, several U.S. environmental groups have documented the reluctance of the U.S. government to use the enforcement mechanism in other free-trade agreements. In the case of Peru, the United States has failed to enforce environmental protections despite very clear evidence of illegal logging contrary to the terms of the U.S.–Peru Free Trade Agreement.[37]

The environment committee established by Chapter 20 of the TPP consists of senior government representatives or their designees from each party and is therefore not at all independent of the parties.[38] The committee's role includes providing reports on implementation of the chapter, discussing co-operative activities under the chapter, and resolving matters referred to it under Article 20.21: *Senior Representative Consultations*.[39]

Consultations

There is a significant focus on consultations to resolve disputes between parties to the TPP. The state-to-state dispute settlement mechanism in the environment chapter provides for three levels of consultation between disputing parties before a matter can be forwarded to an arbitration panel. Article 20.20.2 states that "a Party may request consultations with any other Party. . .regarding any matter arising under this Chapter." If the consultation under Article 20.20 does not resolve the matter, a consulting party may request a further consultation with the TPP party's Environment Committee representative.[40] Finally, a party may request a third consultation between ministers.[41] All consultations are confidential and without prejudice to the rights of any party in future proceedings.[42] There is no requirement for the public to be notified that these consultations are taking place.

Once these three stages of consultation are completed, Article 20.23 allows parties to request more consultation under Article 28.5, or seek the establishment of a panel under Article 28.7 in Chapter 28: *Dispute Settlement*.[43] However, before the matter can be sent to a dispute panel, Articles 20.23.3 and 20.23.4 create an additional barrier to adjudication by requiring a party, for a matter arising under articles 20.3.4 or 20.3.6, to "consider whether it maintains environmental laws that are substantially equivalent in scope to the environmental laws that would be subject to the dispute." If a responding party considers that the requesting party does not maintain equivalent environmental laws, the parties shall discuss the issue during further consultations.[44]

Dispute settlement in Chapter 28

If a TPP member country that has completed the three levels of consultation decides to forward the matter to arbitration, there are significant issues with the rules outlined in the dispute settlement chapter (Chapter 28). Article 28.9.5 provides that in disputes related to the environment chapter (Chapter 20), the two panelists, but not the chair of the panel, must have expertise or experience in environmental law or practice. Public participation in arbitration is not assured because the panel is only required to "consider requests" from non-governmental entities to participate. Public participation is also limited to non-governmental entities in the territory of one of the disputing parties, and must take the form of a written submission only.[45] Public participation is further limited by disclosure requirements that only require a party to the TPP to "make its best efforts" to release its written submissions and oral statements as soon as possible after the documents are filed.[46] The article contemplates some documents not being released to the public until just before the final report of the panel is issued.[47]

When the panel ultimately provides a final report to the disputing parties, it is to be released to the public, subject to the protection of confidential information. However, the panel is not allowed to disclose "which panellists are associated with majority and minority opinions."[48]

Articles 28.19 and 28.20 govern implementation of the final report. Compensation and suspension of equivalent benefits to remedy noncompliance are temporary measures; full implementation of the agreements through elimination of the nonconformity is preferred.[49] Although this remedy appears fairly stringent, its utility is limited by the unwillingness of countries to use these state-to-state dispute resolution mechanisms to address environmental protections in trade agreements. On the other hand, governments have challenged environmental policy in other countries before WTO dispute resolution panels on many occasions, claiming such measures violate trade and investment protections.

Ineffective citizen complaint provisions

The citizen complaint provisions in the environment chapter provide little detail and are unlikely to be an effective way to enforce the requirements of the TPP. For example, Article 20.8 only requires each party to "make use of existing, or establish new, consultative mechanisms, for example national advisory committees, to seek views on matters related to the implementation of this Chapter."[50] A person of a party may only challenge its own government's implementation of the chapter and may only make written submissions.[51] "Person of a Party" is defined in

Article 1.3: *Initial Provisions and General Definitions* as a "national or an enterprise of a Party." The TPP party is required to respond "in a timely manner" to a submission, although that time frame is not defined, and to "make. . .its responses available to the public."[52]

There are few other details about the citizen complaint process in the environment chapter. Article 20.9.2 requires each party to "make its procedures for the receipt and consideration of written submissions readily accessible and publicly available." There are also broad guidelines for considering eligible submissions, including that they "explain how, and to what extent, the issue raised affects trade or investment between the Parties," and that the submission "not raise issues that are the subject of ongoing judicial or administrative proceedings."[53] If the person from a party does make a written submission under Article 20.9.1, there is no opportunity to follow up on or enforce the complaint. Article 20.9.4 only provides that another TPP party[54] may request that the Environment Committee "discuss the submission and written response." Escalation of an environmental issue is limited to state-to-state consultations.

This process is weaker than the citizen suit provisions under the NAAEC, which has been strongly criticized as too difficult to enforce. Despite its failings, the NAAEC process at least produces a factual record in certain circumstances, which is not contemplated in the TPP.[55]

Conclusion

The TPP environment chapter will not protect the environment. The requirements of the parties with respect to protection of the environment are vague and discretionary, frequently only requiring governments to take measures to address environmental problems. The scope of the environment chapter is also restricted by its limited application to the laws of the central government of each TPP country. The mechanisms to enforce the environment chapter are also flawed. Where state-to-state dispute resolution exists in other trade agreements, governments have been reluctant to take other countries to arbitration on matters of environmental protection. If the provisions are used, the complaining TPP party must generally show that the respondent party's environmentally detrimental actions affect trade or investment, which triggers a slow consultation process leading up to potential state-to-state dispute settlement. The citizen-suit provisions are also minimal and unlikely to be effective in enforcing the protections in the environment chapter. Far from including "the most comprehensive environmental commitments. . .ever negotiated in a trade agreement," as expressed by the USTR, the TPP at best represents the status quo for environmental protection, and will not offer any safeguard against environmentally destructive provisions found elsewhere in the agreement.

Food safety and the TPP

Climate change is expected to increase risks related to food safety, plant and animal health due to variances of temperatures, and the spread of animal and plant diseases. Under the TPP, regulations regarding these risks are covered in a section called Sanitary and Phytosanitary Measures (SPS). And once again, the TPP's push toward deregulation increases climate risk...

The TPP takes several steps that would limit countries' ability to regulate to ensure food safety at their border. To expedite food exports, the TPP includes a Rapid Response Mechanism to quickly resolve trade-related restrictions. But it is trade officials, not food-safety experts, who are designated by the SPS chapter to lead the consultative team charged with sorting out food safety disputes. Further, the design and strict time limits set forth for rapid response give food exporters the power to demand justification from inspectors regarding decisions to restrict imports on food safety grounds. Such a mechanism gives companies yet another lever to challenge food safety regulations.

The TPP also sets forth very low standards for using scientific data in assessing risks of new food and agricultural technologies that go beyond World Trade Organization (WTO) standards. Rather than rely on publicly published research within the peer-reviewed literature, the TPP gives particular weight to private industry studies submitted under the protection of Confidential Business Information requirements. This is of particular concern as we enter into the age of complex and powerful new gene-editing technologies through synthetic biology, of which most countries (including the U.S.) do not have a regulatory regime established to protect public health and the environment. The result is another mechanism for companies to tilt the regulatory playing field in their favour as those standards are developed.

While not explicitly stated, it appears that food safety disputes would be eligible for ISDS (investor–state dispute settlement) challenges by corporations, given the very broad definition of "investment" in the investment chapter. The TPP SPS chapter does include a country-to-country dispute settlement mechanism that is expected to be much quicker than at the WTO level, and compensation is expected to be more rapid. All these elements give food company exporters more tools to challenge regulatory efforts to ensure food safety.

Excerpted from the report, "The climate costs of free trade: How the TPP and trade deals undermine the Paris climate agreement," by Ben Lilliston, Institute for Agriculture and Trade Policy (IATP), September 2016.

CHAPTER 5
Does the TPP Work for Workers?

Laura Macdonald and Angella MacEwen

Contemporary trade agreements commonly include a chapter on labour, or a labour side accord, which is supposed to guarantee that the agreement will not contribute to the tendency toward a "race to the bottom" in the global economy.[1] For example, Chapter 19 of the Trans-Pacific Partnership (TPP) includes provisions that are supposed to ensure that "core labour standards," as defined by the International Labour Organization (ILO), are respected by signatory states.[2] In promotional material for the agreement, Global Affairs Canada states the TPP

> *provides the opportunity to raise and improve labour standards and working conditions in TPP member countries through an ambitious level of obligations to ensure that national labour laws and policies in partner countries respect international labour standards. Canada is committed to fundamental labour rights, and supporting high labour standards through a fully enforceable TPP Chapter is a key part of that commitment.*[3]

This is not the view of labour federations from many of the participating TPP countries, as well as a range of human rights–focused non-governmental organizations (NGOs) and academics, who argue the labour chapter fails to provide sufficient tools to address labour rights violations — even where they are most apparent, as in Brunei, Malaysia, Mexico, and Vietnam.[4] The experience of workers under similar free-trade agreements provides ample evidence to back this position.

The text of the TPP labour chapter is modelled on earlier labour accords or chapters starting with the labour side accord to the North American Free Trade Agreement (NAFTA), which came into effect January 1, 1994. Since signing NAFTA, the United States and Canada have continued to promote labour provisions tied to trade agreements, and there has been some progress in making these provisions stronger. Nevertheless, like the NAFTA side accord, these agreements remain largely ineffective for addressing labour rights violations, and they fail to counteract the negative impacts on working people of other, stronger provisions in contemporary trade agreements. As the ILO pointed out recently, "no complaint has given rise to a decision of a dispute settlement body or even led to sanctions."[5]

This chapter will first review the contentious history of labour provisions in recent free-trade agreements to clarify the weaknesses of this approach as a tool to support labour rights. It then breaks down the TPP labour provisions and their likely impact on working conditions and labour law. Based on this history and our reading of the agreement, we can only conclude the TPP will reproduce an ineffective rights regime while further expanding a free-trade model that has perpetuated labour rights violations across the world.

From NAFTA to the TPP: Do labour clauses work?

It is helpful to look at the labour provisions in NAFTA, not just because this is probably the most important trade agreement affecting Canada, but also because it has served as a model for other Canadian and U.S. FTAs, including the TPP. NAFTA was initially negotiated without a labour side accord or labour chapter within the agreement itself. The North American Agreement on Labour Co-operation (NAALC) was a political response to the intense opposition to NAFTA from labour unions and their allies in the United States. Canada, like Mexico, was a reluctant signatory to the NAALC. After his election in 1992, former president Clinton insisted on the inclusion of labour and environment side accords in NAFTA to appease opponents of the agreement and ensure its passage in Congress.

According to the text of the NAALC, Canada, the United States and Mexico committed to "improve working conditions and living standards in each Party's territory," and to promote, "to the maximum extent possible," the eleven labour rights set out in an annex to the agreement.[6] The side-agreement approach had several key weaknesses. First, it meant the labour provisions could not be enforced through the dispute resolution processes in NAFTA itself. Secondly, the NAALC did not create new common labour standards, but merely committed the members to enforce their own existing labour legislation. The agreement does mention some "guiding principles," which mostly reflect standard ILO principles. However, the parties are just encouraged to promote these principles and not necessarily to enforce them.[7] Thirdly, and most importantly, there were no effective sanctions attached to violations of the labour side agreement.

The NAALC established national administrative offices (NAOs) in the labour departments of each signatory state. Individuals, labour union leaders and human rights defenders from each of the three countries can file complaints about the behaviour of one of the other states to their country's NAO.[8] If the NAO decides to accept a case for review, it begins a formal investigation, and may hold public hearings and issue a report. Different types of violation result in different types of punishment — from ministerial consultation, in the case of standards related to industrial organization (e.g., the right to strike), to possible trade sanctions in the case of submissions that involve allegations of child labour, minimum wage disputes or health and safety violations.[9] A flurry of labour cases were submitted in the five years after the NAALC came into force. But their number trickled after that to the point where today the agreement is rarely used. Trade unions and other workers' rights advocates found that the formal complaint mechanism almost never resulted in ministerial consultations or sanctions. The NAFTA countries also created a North American Commission for Labour Co-operation (NACLC), which was initially based in Washington, DC, to oversee the labour side agreement. Initially the NACLC would handle follow-up actions from

NAFTA ministerial consultations, special research projects and other tri-national labour co-operation activities. The member states had so little commitment to the process that, as the number of complaints under the NAALC slowed, the body eventually disappeared.

Not only are the NAALC sanctions for labour violations much weaker than those available in NAFTA to promote the interests of corporations and investors, the process for bringing cases to adjudication is longer and more cumbersome. NAOs report to the labour ministries in each country, and as such cannot guarantee impartiality. In the case of Canada, the effectiveness of the process is further limited by the constitutional mandates of the provinces, many of which (British Columbia, Saskatchewan, Ontario, New Brunswick, Newfoundland and Labrador) did not ratify the NAALC.[10] In Mexico, the country that might have been expected to benefit most from the labour side accord, systematic violations of labour rights abound in a broader context of widespread human rights violations that endangers labour and human rights activists and undermines the country's system of industrial relations. Human rights violations have escalated rapidly in the country over the past ten years, exemplified by the disappearance of forty-three students from the teacher's college in Ayotzinapa, Guerrero, in 2015. These young men are now presumed dead. As Amnesty International reported in its 2015–16 country assessment of Mexico,

> *Impunity persisted for grave human rights violations including torture and other ill-treatment, enforced disappearances and extrajudicial executions. More than 27,000 people remained missing or disappeared. Human rights defenders and journalists continued to be threatened, harassed or killed. The number of detentions, deportations and complaints of abuse of irregular migrants by the authorities increased significantly. Violence against women continued to be widespread. Large-scale development and resource exploitation projects were carried out without a legal framework regarding the free, prior and informed consent of Indigenous communities they affected.*[11]

The most serious problem faced by Mexican trade unions is the failure of the Mexican government to enforce labour and other laws, particularly those around freedom of association and collective bargaining. Many workers are "represented" by employer-dominated unions that sign collective agreements (so-called protection contracts) the workers themselves have never seen or ratified. Workers who attempt to form independent unions are frequently targeted by violence from employers and the employer-dominated unions, often with the collusion of state officials. This situation has been the subject of public reports under the NAALC, but no trinational action has ever been taken.[12] The ILO has also raised serious concerns about the threats to freedom of association in the country that have not yet been addressed through any NAFTA mechanism. As a result, wages are artificially depressed, and more multinational corporations are moving operations to Mexico to take advantage of the systematic exploitation of Mexican workers — exactly the opposite of the higher standards that were promised when NAFTA was signed.

Labour provisions since NAFTA

Following NAFTA, U.S. trade unions and their Democratic allies in Congress continued to push the United States Trade Representative (USTR) to strengthen the labour provisions in new free-trade agreements. For example, the U.S.–Jordan and U.S.–Chile FTAs and the Dominican Republic–Central America Free Trade Agreement (DR–CAFTA) included labour provisions in the main text rather than in side agreements. U.S. concerns with DR-CAFTA were particularly strong because of the serious labour and human rights violations in many of the five countries involved (Dominican Republic, El Salvador, Guatemala, Honduras and Nicaragua). As a result, signatory countries were required to detail their current labour laws, list areas where improvement was needed, and report on progress every six months between 2007 and 2010.[13]

In this generation of U.S. labour agreements only one labour provision is enforceable through the same or similar dispute settlement mechanisms as the rest of the FTA.[14] Each party to these treaties agrees it "shall not fail to effectively enforce its labor laws. . .in a manner affecting trade between the Parties." A petitioner must therefore show that a government did not enforce its labour laws before a case can be sent to dispute resolution. For a case to be successful at the dispute resolution stage, the petitioner would then need to prove the labour violation had an impact on trade between the two nations. (This is the same burden of proof required in the TPP labour chapter.)

Failure to enforce labour laws was the basis for the first labour case pursued to the dispute settlement stage by the U.S. government, in response to a 2008 filing by U.S. and Guatemalan labour unions. It took seven years for the case to be heard.

The most recent U.S. model of labour provisions in FTAs was established in the so-called May 10 Agreement, or Bipartisan Trade Deal.[15] The most important provisions it sets out are that countries must adopt, maintain and enforce the four fundamental rights named in the 1998 ILO Declaration, and that violations of the labour chapter are subject to the same dispute settlement mechanism as other violations of U.S. FTAs. The TPP labour chapter is based on this model, which is also found in the U.S. FTAs with Peru (2009), Panama (2012), Colombia (2012) and South Korea (2012).

Since NAFTA, Canada has signed a series of trade agreements, mostly on a bilateral basis, which also contain labour co-operation agreements. The 1997 agreement with Chile was based closely on the NAFTA model. The 2002 agreement with Costa Rica was similar but with an even more reduced system of enforcement. After this point, Canada began to include somewhat stronger mechanisms on labour protections that were influenced by changes in U.S. trade agreement practices. Newer agreements with Peru (2009), Colombia (2011), Jordan (2012), Panama (2013) and Honduras (2014) contain an agreement to implement ILO standards, and specifically reference the 1998 ILO Declaration and the ILO's Decent Work Agenda. The Canada–South Korea agreement (2015) includes a labour chapter, rather than a side agreement on labour co-operation, but it does not specifically refer to the ILO Declaration, only to "internationally recognized labour rights."

Recent Canadian agreements also contain a clause that prohibits parties from engaging in practices that derogate from domestic laws in order to encourage trade or investment. These agreements contain formal dispute settlement processes for cases involving violations of core labour rights, or where there exists a persistent pattern of failure to comply with domestic laws. In the agreements with Panama, Peru and Colombia, however, fines are limited to US$15 million (about C$19 million), and are to be paid into a fund designed to implement the action plan.[16] This limit on sanctions is in stark contrast with awards under investor–state dispute settlement cases, which have gone into the billions and for which there is no upper limit. Furthermore, the imposition of fines is a weaker tool than trade sanctions, including abrogation of preferential trade status, which can be applied to violations of other provisions in the trade agreement itself.[17] The TPP would be the first trade agreement for Canada under which labour obligations are subject to the main dispute-settlement mechanism of the FTA.

Beyond the formal provisions of these agreements, labour unions and other civil society organizations doubt whether many of the countries involved in the TPP will be able to live up to the minimum labour standards therein. They are concerned, with good reason, that other aspects of the free-trade agreement, such as its market liberalization requirements and investor protections, may adversely affect workers and peasants, exacerbating existing conflicts and thus fuelling the systematic violation of workers' rights. For example, in the case of the Canada–Colombia agreement, civil society organizations (CSOs) question the effectiveness of the labour agreement in the context of widespread violations of labour rights and the large number of murders of labour activists in Colombia.[18] Similarly, Gerda van Roozendaal's careful analysis of the impact of the DR-CAFTA on labour rights in Guatemala argues that the agreement represents a failed case of forced diffusion of labour standards, even though labour disputes may be pursued through the agreement's main dispute-resolution mechanism. Van Roozendaal states that the failure results from weak formulation of the labour provisions and sanction mechanisms, and the lack of follow-up action. In a country that has experienced widespread violence against trade union actors and systematic violation of workers' rights, this is not a surprising conclusion.[19] Similar concerns exist for several of the countries involved in the TPP agreement.

ILO fundamental rights

2. Declares that all members, even if they have not ratified the conventions in question, have an obligation arising from the very fact of membership in the [ILO] to respect, to promote and to realize, in good faith and in accordance with the constitution, the principles concerning the fundamental rights which are the subject of those conventions, namely:

(a) freedom of association and the effective recognition of the right to collective bargaining;
(b) the elimination of all forms of forced or compulsory labour;
(c) the effective abolition of child labour; and
(d) the elimination of discrimination in respect of employment and occupation.

Core conventions
Fundamental conventions

- Freedom of Association and Protection of the Right to Organize Convention, 1948 (No. 87)
- Right to Organize and Collective Bargaining Convention, 1949 (No. 98)
- Forced Labour Convention, 1930 (No. 29)
- Abolition of Forced Labour Convention, 1957 (No. 105)
- Minimum Age Convention, 1973 (No. 138)
- Worst Forms of Child Labour Convention, 1999 (No. 182)
- Equal Remuneration Convention, 1951 (No. 100)
- Discrimination (Employment and Occupation) Convention, 1958 (No. 111)

TPP labour chapter analysis

As mentioned already, the labour provisions in the TPP and other recent U.S. FTAs are a product of policy shifts in response to pressure from labour unions to improve on the NAFTA model. Since the May 10 Agreement of 2007, the USTR has included in its FTAs a fully enforceable obligation to "adopt and maintain" fundamental labour rights as stated in the ILO Declaration. This is sometimes referred to as the second generation of worker rights in U.S. FTAs. Four elements of the May 10 Agreement are incorporated in the TPP labour chapter:

1. Requirement to adopt, maintain and enforce the four fundamental rights named in the 1998 ILO Declaration.

2. Clarification that a country cannot defend its failure to enforce labour law on the basis of resource allocation or resource limitations.

3. A prohibition from lowering labour standards covered by the treaty in a manner affecting trade or investment.

4. Labour obligations must be enforceable through the same dispute settlement mechanisms, and have access to the same penalties, as those available for other obligations under the FTA.

The first requirement is somewhat limited because it refers to the ILO Declaration alone, and not the details of the eight core conventions relating to those fundamental rights or to the procedures found in the "follow-up" to the 1998 ILO Declaration. The requirement to enforce labour laws is limited by the necessity that non-enforcement must have occurred "in a manner affecting trade or investment between the parties," and "through a sustained or recurring course of action or inaction." The following sections provide more detailed examination of these four elements.

Requirement to adopt and maintain fundamental labour rights

Article 19.3.1 of the TPP establishes the requirement of signatories to adopt and maintain the four fundamental rights stated in the ILO Declaration. As in prior U.S. FTAs, this requirement is limited by referring to the declaration alone, not to the details of ILO conventions or the follow-up. Article 19.3.2 establishes the requirement to adopt and maintain laws and regulations on minimum wages, hours of work, and occupational safety and health. This article is limited by a footnote clarifying that it refers to "acceptable conditions of work as determined by that Party."[20] Both articles are further limited by the requirement to demonstrate that the failure to adopt or maintain a specific statute or regulation affects trade or investment between the parties.[21] The Canada–European Union Comprehensive Economic and Trade Agreement (CETA) has stronger language in its labour chapter referring to the ILO's Decent Work Agenda and committing to implement ILO conventions that have already been ratified, as well as committing to "continued and sustained efforts" to ratify those ILO core conventions not yet ratified. The TPP presented a real opportunity to advance the language on labour rights, but failed to do so.

Requirement to enforce fundamental labour rights

Article 19.5 of the TPP deals with the enforcement of labour laws. As in the May 10 Agreement, non-enforcement is limited to cases of a "sustained or recurring course of action or inaction in a manner affecting trade or investment between the parties."[22] This presents an extremely high bar for any potential complaints regarding enforcement under the TPP.

Prohibition from lowering labour standards

Article 19.4, the "non derogation clause," deals with weakening or lowering labour standards to encourage trade or investment. Article 19.4(a) specifies a general prohibition on weakening or offering to weaken labour laws with respect to 19.3.1 (fundamental rights), but contains nothing with respect to 19.3.2 (acceptable conditions of work). Article 19.4(b) applies only to special trade and customs areas such as export processing zones (EPZs), and specifies the obligation around non-derogation with respect to both 19.3.1 and 19.3.2. This seems to imply that parties to the TPP would be permitted to weaken laws around minimum wages, hours of work, and occupational safety and health *outside* of EPZs, even if it were clear that doing so would affect trade or investment between the parties. For example, member states must adopt and maintain a minimum wage according to 19.3.2, but they are within their rights to lower that minimum wage outside export processing zones in order to attract investment. If this is the case, it is difficult to imagine a successful TPP labour complaint related to acceptable conditions outside of EPZs.

Equal access to dispute settlement

While the TPP officially offers equal access to dispute settlement for labour violations, there is a lengthy process of co-operation (Article 19.10), co-operative labour dialogue (Article 19.11) and labour consultations (Article 19.15) before a party may request the establishment of a dispute-settlement panel. Cases may be raised by individual workers, unions or other civil society actors, but are actually brought by governments. For example, unions in Canada and Vietnam might make a submission to Canada's labour department on behalf of workers in Vietnam — an institutionally awkward arrangement for protecting labour rights. Documenting violations will be time consuming and expensive given the requirement to demonstrate an impact on trade or investment between the parties. The lack of reference to the details of the ILO core conventions further limits the extent to which existing ILO jurisprudence will be helpful in resolving disputes. On the other hand, the article on co-operation (19.10) is extensive, and may be a more effective route for raising labour standards in TPP nations because of the possibility of trade sanctions if co-operation fails.

Additional features of the TPP

Two additional articles of the TPP labour chapter are mostly symbolic. Article 19.6 recognizes the goal of eliminating forced labour in TPP member country supply chains, and encourages signatories to discourage the importation of goods produced through forced labour. The second,

Article 19.7, encourages voluntary initiatives on corporate social responsibility. It is unclear how either article will be effective.

Conclusion

Labour chapters in free-trade agreements have not evolved significantly in the eight years since the May 10 Agreement in the U.S. The TPP presented an opportunity to raise the bar for labour rights, specifically by referencing core ILO conventions, the "follow-up" to the ILO Declaration and the ILO Decent Work Agenda. This did not happen. For Canada, although the TPP labour chapter is better than previous Canadian FTAs it could not hope to mediate the negative impacts on workers of modern trade and investment agreements. [23]

The case of Mexico shows that labour chapters are ineffective when these agreements create such asymmetry between business and labour in national and regional processes. The U.S.–Guatemala labour case shows just how lengthy, expensive and mostly ineffective the dispute-resolution process can be. It is hardly surprising, then, that labour unions have been among the strongest opponents of recent trade agreements, including now the TPP. The weak and cumbersome labour rights dispute processes in the agreement provide little comfort to workers in any of the participating countries.

Unions from nine of the twelve signatory states to the TPP have proposed an alternative labour chapter that builds on and improves the labour and dispute-resolution chapters of the U.S.–Peru FTA. Unfortunately, while business groups were regularly consulted throughout the TPP negotiating process, labour unions in Canada were given little opportunity to put their alternative proposals on the table. As such, the TPP simply reproduces an ineffective rights regime while further expanding a free-trade model that has perpetuated labour rights violations in many countries. The race to the bottom continues.

CHAPTER 6
Migrant Workers and the TPP

Hadrian Mertins-Kirkwood

It is increasingly common for international free-trade agreements (FTAs) to contain a chapter on temporary entry for business persons. These provisions, included in the Trans-Pacific Partnership (TPP), allow certain categories of workers to cross borders on a temporary basis without going through the usual immigration process. In theory, this is meant to help executives and investors move capital into, or manage their investments in, other countries. In practice, these provisions allow employers to move an unlimited number of certain types of workers between countries regardless of local labour market conditions. The potential negative impact of this practice on the domestic labour force is worrying, since FTAs give employers an opportunity to import their employees rather than hire and train locally, even where unemployment is high and qualified local workers are available.

Unfortunately, past FTAs such as the North American Free Trade Agreement (NAFTA) have had precisely this negative effect.[1] Employers are finding ways to game the FTA system in order to import workers, with little regulatory oversight. To make matters worse, the migrant workers themselves are at risk of abuse and have limited pathways to permanent residency in the places where they are employed.

This chapter identifies the most important provisions in the TPP's temporary-entry chapter from the Canadian perspective, and discusses how these differ from Canada's existing and potential future commitments in NAFTA and the pending Canada–European Union Comprehensive Economic and Trade Agreement (CETA), respectively. The first section breaks down the general obligations in Chapter 12 that apply to all TPP parties. The second section investigates Canada's specific commitments as expressed in its country-specific annex to Chapter 12, including the range of occupations and sectors that are covered by or excluded from the deal.

While it is possible that the economic impacts of the TPP's temporary-entry chapter will be small — at least in the short term — it is clear the TPP will limit the democratic and legislative capacity of governments to shape immigration and labour policy into the future.

Temporary entry for business persons

At just five pages, the temporary-entry chapter in the TPP is among the shortest of the agreement's thirty chapters. The ten articles in Chapter 12 are generally recycled from NAFTA and are consistent with past Canadian FTAs. In short, the chapter requires governments to create a framework for the free movement of workers between TPP countries where various general and party-specific conditions are met. Crucially, access to the temporary-entry provisions is contingent on employment, so the deal does not create opportunities for unemployed or underemployed workers directly. Instead, the chapter primarily benefits the investors and corporations who can use the temporary-entry provisions to more easily hire and transfer employees across borders.

Compared with the temporary-entry provisions in Canada's existing FTAs, the most consequential new obligations in the TPP relate to transparency and accountability in the application process. These new obligations on governments further restrict policy flexibility and may pose an administrative burden on immigration officials. Although it is notable that Chapter 12 of the TPP omits any mention of labour standards, this is also not unusual for a Canadian FTA.

Article 12.2: Scope

Chapter 12 of the TPP does not include an overarching objective comparable to those found in the temporary-entry chapters of NAFTA

(Chapter 16) or CETA (Chapter 10). For example, CETA highlights the "mutual objective to facilitate trade in services and investment by allowing temporary entry,"[2] while NAFTA recognizes the need for parties "to protect the domestic labor force and permanent employment in their respective territories."[3] Instead, the temporary-entry chapter in the TPP jumps straight into the scope, or limits, of the temporary-entry provisions. Importantly, it clarifies that these do not apply to measures "affecting natural persons seeking access to the employment market of another Party, nor shall it (the chapter) apply to measures regarding citizenship, nationality, residence or employment on a permanent basis." The TPP does not create any new labour-mobility rights for workers; the temporary-entry provisions are explicitly restricted to employers hiring internationally or moving employees across borders.

Article 12.2.3 affirms a state's right to regulate immigration measures, but that protection is negated by the caveat that those measures cannot be "applied in a manner as to nullify or impair the benefits accruing to any Party under this Chapter." Generally speaking, this (lack of) protection for the right to regulate is consistent with past FTAs.

The TPP, like NAFTA, makes no mention of minimum wages or other labour standards in its temporary-entry chapter. CETA, on the other hand, contains some (albeit weak) language with respect to minimum wages and collective bargaining in its Article 10.2.5, which states that

> Notwithstanding the provisions of this Chapter, all
> requirements of the Parties' laws regarding employment and
> social security measures shall continue to apply, including
> regulations concerning minimum wages as well as collective
> wage agreements.[4]

Although the TPP's labour chapter (Chapter 19) references minimum wages and the right to bargain collectively, as Laura Macdonald and Angella McEwan explain elsewhere in this book, it contains no meaningful obligations directly related to migrant workers or temporary entry. At best, it includes a commitment for parties to "co-operate" on the "protection of vulnerable workers, including migrant workers, and low-waged, casual or contingent workers,"[5] but co-operation is voluntary and therefore unenforceable.

Article 12.3: Application procedures

While the scope of the temporary entry-chapter is similar to past Canadian FTAs, the TPP introduces new obligations for transparency and accountability. It requires governments to process applications for temporary entry "as expeditiously as possible" and to respond to applicant inquiries "promptly." Since timelines are not defined, it would be difficult to enforce these provisions, but they may still pose an administrative burden to Immigration, Refugees and Citizenship Canada (IRCC), the federal department responsible for administering the temporary-entry rules (see box).

Temporary entry: Who decides who gets in?

Immigration, Refugees and Citizenship Canada (formerly Citizenship and Immigration Canada) is the federal department responsible for the movement of immigrants and migrant workers into the country. When Canada implements an international treaty with temporary-entry commitments, IRCC becomes bound by those provisions and is obligated to enforce and report on them.

The Canada Border Services Agency (CBSA) is responsible for "[screening] foreign workers at Canadian border crossings and airports to ensure that they meet admissibility requirements before issuing work permits and allowing their entry into Canada."[6] Both IRCC and CBSA can process work permit applications, but only CBSA can issue work permits at the border and make final decisions about temporary entry.

In deciding whether to authorize migrant workers, IRCC and CBSA officials refer to the FW 1 (foreign worker manual).[7] The document describes the eligibility criteria for workers covered by Canada's FTAs who apply for a temporary work permit. It includes significant interpretive detail that does not appear in the legal texts of the treaties themselves. CBSA uses another operational manual, the ENF 4 (port of entry examinations), to determine which workers are let into Canada when they arrive at the border.[8]

An employer who wishes to hire a migrant worker can apply for a work permit in advance through IRCC and early approval streamlines the temporary-entry process. However, for professionals and intra-company transferees covered by an FTA (visas T23 and T24 respectively), an advance work permit is not necessarily required. Provided a worker meets the criteria laid out in the FTA and has the required documentation — identification, evidence of employment, and evidence of credentials — they can simply arrive at a border and be issued a work permit on the spot.[9] In those cases, the decision to approve a work permit is not made by an IRCC immigration officer but by a CBSA officer alone.[10]

The TPP's obligation regarding processing fees is less clear than in past deals. In the TPP, fees must only be "reasonable," whereas under NAFTA fees must be limited to "the approximate cost of services rendered."[11] This looser language may give some TPP governments slightly more flexibility in setting processing fees for applicants, although Canada remains bound by the stricter NAFTA language.

Article 12.4: Grant of temporary entry

The TPP includes a protection for domestic licensing requirements in Article 12.4.3, which reads as follows:

> *The sole fact that a Party grants temporary entry to a business person of another Party pursuant to this Chapter shall not be construed to exempt that business person from meeting any applicable licensing or other requirements, including any mandatory codes of conduct, to practise a profession or otherwise engage in business activities.*

Under this provision domestic licensing and certification bodies retain the right to decide who can practise a profession in their jurisdiction. However, this is not the same as saying a party retains the right to make licensing or certification criteria a requirement for entering the country. In fact, Canada's country-specific commitments prohibit any form of labour certification test at the point of entry (discussed below). Therefore, while the TPP preserves a country's right to regulate professionals once they

111

are inside the country, the burden of regulatory enforcement of entry to Canada simply devolved from IRCC immigration officers to occupational licensing bodies and government employment inspections.

Similar language appears in CETA but not in NAFTA. None of these FTAs require mutual recognition of qualifications, although they do encourage licensing bodies to undertake mutual recognition initiatives. Article 12.4 also obligates parties to notify applicants if they are refused entry, which is similar to NAFTA but not an obligation under CETA.

Article 12.6: Provision of information

Like the other transparency provisions in Chapter 12, Article 12.6 introduces new obligations on governments, which in Canada's case may be an administrative burden on IRCC. The parties commit to "promptly publish online" not only information about the application process (consistent with NAFTA and CETA), but also "the typical timeframe within which an application for an immigration formality is processed." Furthermore, the TPP requires parties to establish a mechanism for receiving and responding to inquiries from business persons.

Article 12.8: Co-operation

The TPP encourages regulatory co-operation on migration issues, which is a provision absent from CETA and significantly expanded from NAFTA. Article 12.8 recommends the parties work together on electronic processing systems for visas, border security and processes for expediting entry of certain categories of workers. This article is not binding and no tangible process for co-operation is created. The parties merely promise to "consider undertaking mutually agreed co-operation activities, subject to available resources."

Article 12.9: Relation to other chapters

The provisions of the TPP's chapter on cross-border trade in services (Chapter 10) apply to workers granted temporary entry under Chapter 12 once they have entered the territory of another party. Chapter 10 does not directly apply to measures affecting the entry of foreign workers into a party, whether or not entry is granted under Chapter 12.[12] In other words, the TPP's trade-in-services rules — most notably the provisions on national treatment, most-favoured-nation treatment, and market access — *do not apply* to temporary-entry decisions but they *do apply* to the treatment of foreign service suppliers once they have crossed the border.

This language is broadly consistent with Canada's other FTAs, including CETA, which states the most-favoured-nation obligations apply "to treatment of natural persons for business purposes present in the territory of the other Party," but "[do not] apply to measures relating to the granting of temporary entry to natural persons of a Party or of a third country."[13] This provision in CETA, as in Canada's other FTAs, means the terms of the TPP temporary-entry chapter are not automatically extended to Canada's existing FTA partners. Likewise, the temporary-entry provisions in any future Canadian FTAs will not automatically extend to TPP parties.

Article 12.10: Dispute settlement

Business persons who believe they have been unfairly denied temporary entry under Chapter 12 cannot directly bring a case against the state under the TPP's dispute settlement rules in Chapter 28. Instead, their government must bring a state-to-state case on their behalf. The matter must involve a "pattern of practice" and all other administrative processes must first be exhausted.

Whether a state would ever initiate such a claim on behalf of its residents is uncertain. CETA's temporary-entry chapter does not contain recourse to dispute settlement and there are no documented cases of states violating their NAFTA temporary-entry obligations, so the comparable provisions in NAFTA have not yet been tested. Nevertheless, the possibility of a Chapter 28 case means trade sanctions are on the table if the provisions of TPP Chapter 12 are violated.

Annex 12-A: Canada's schedule of commitments for temporary entry of business persons

Perhaps more interesting than the main text of Chapter 12 — and more significant for the purposes of this analysis — are the individual party annexes, which total seventy-eight pages and include each country's specific commitments. Canada offers commitments for the same four categories of workers (and their spouses) found in NAFTA: business visitors, intra-corporate transferees (ICTs), investors, and professionals and technicians (see Table 8; see also this chapter's appendices for detailed summaries of Canada's commitments).

Table 8: Main Categories of Covered Business Persons under Canada's TPP Commitments				
	Business Visitors	Intra-Corporate Transferees (ICTs)	Investors	Professionals and Technicians
Work permit required	No	Yes	Yes	Yes
Economic needs tests or quotas permitted	No	No	No	No
Maximum length of stay	Six months*	Three years*	One year*	One year*
Spouses permitted (with open work permit)	No	Yes	Yes	Yes
* Permits can be extended indefinitely				

Each of the four categories has a specific definition and raises specific concerns, but they have several things in common. Firstly, Canada is not allowed to use labour certification tests or quotas to limit the inflow of foreign workers in any category. See, for example, this commitment for ICTs:

> Canada shall grant temporary entry and provide a work permit or work authorisation to Intra-Corporate Transferees, and will not:

> (a) require labour certification tests or other procedures of similar intent as a condition for temporary entry; or

> (b) impose or maintain any numerical restriction relating to temporary entry.[14]

The prohibitions on labour certification tests and numerical limits stop Canada from applying its Labour Market Impact Assessment (LMIA) for workers entering Canada under the temporary-entry provisions of the TPP. The LMIA process, which is administered by Employment and Social Development Canada (ESDC), requires employers to prove "there is a need for a foreign worker to fill the job and that no Canadian worker is available to do the job" before they can hire internationally.[15] Without it, employers could choose to bring in migrant workers even where unemployment is high and/or qualified domestic labour is available.[16] Under CETA, these tests are expressly prohibited.[17] In the TPP, the language is less clear but the effect is the same.[18]

As noted above, Article 12.4 allows Canada to require that business persons meet domestic licensing requirements to work in the country, but Canada did not explicitly reserve the right to make domestic licensing requirements a condition for entering the country and/or receiving a work permit. Secondly, with one exception, all of Canada's commitments for temporary entry are reciprocal: covered workers from TPP countries can only enter Canada under the terms of Chapter 12 if the same types of Canadian workers can enter that other TPP country. The occupations covered for each country are discussed below, although it is worth noting that the United States is the only TPP country to make *no country-specific commitments* under Chapter 12 (see box). Consequently, U.S. workers gain no temporary-entry access to Canada under the TPP that does not already exist under NAFTA.

The United States and Temporary Entry in the TPP

In 2003, the United States Trade Representative (USTR) made temporary-entry commitments in two new treaties — the U.S.–Chile FTA and the U.S.–Singapore FTA — without first seeking congressional approval. Congress eventually ratified both deals, but it sparked a debate over whether unelected trade negotiators should be reforming U.S. immigration law without democratic oversight. Opposition culminated in the *Congressional Responsibility for Immigration Act* of 2003, which had bipartisan support but was never voted on.

Although the act never became law, the USTR has refrained from making new temporary-entry commitments in U.S. FTAs ever since, largely due to continued pressure from Congress.[19] This informal policy was codified through the *Trade Facilitation and Trade Enforcement Act* of 2015 (H.R. 644) that amended the USTR's negotiating objectives as described in the *Bipartisan Congressional Trade Priorities and Accountability Act* of

2015. The USTR must now "ensure that trade agreements do not require changes to the immigration laws of the United States or obligate the United States to grant access or expand access to visas."[20]

The USTR's inability to make temporary-entry commitments put it in a unique position in the TPP negotiations. Although the U.S. remains bound by the general obligations of Chapter 12, the USTR did not make any country-specific commitments and therefore offers no tangible access to its labour market for workers from other countries. In response, most other countries made no temporary-entry commitments to the U.S in the TPP.

Thirdly, with the exception of business visitors, Canada offers temporary entry to the spouses of all workers who enter Canada under the terms of Chapter 12. The commitments for spouses are also provided on a reciprocal basis and are exempt from labour certification tests and quotas. For example, the text reads as follows with respect to ICTs:

> *Canada shall grant temporary entry and provide a work permit or work authorisation to spouses of Intra-Corporate Transferees of another Party where that Party has also made a commitment in its schedule for spouses of Intra-Corporate Transferees, and will not:*
>
> *(a) require labour certification tests or other procedures of similar intent as a condition for temporary entry; or*
>
> *(b) impose or maintain any numerical restriction relating to temporary entry.*[21]

Importantly, a spouse who enters Canada under the TPP can receive an "open" work permit that is not restricted to any one employer, industry or region. Therefore, even though an ICT, investor, or professional or technician can only work for the employer that brought them into Canada, their spouse can work in any field anywhere in the country. Open work permits have an unpredictable labour market impact that is difficult to track and often overlooked.

These three issues with respect to temporary entry — the prohibition on economic needs tests, reciprocity and spousal work permits — are common to Canada's other FTAs, including NAFTA and CETA. There are further implications for Canada that are specific to each category of business person covered by the TPP.

Section A: Business visitors

Unique among the four categories of covered business persons, business visitors do not require a work permit or "an equivalent requirement" to enter Canada.[22] For a worker to qualify, their business must not be based in Canada, their "primary source" of remuneration must be outside Canada, and they must be engaged in a specific list of approved activities, including meetings and consultations, research and design, manufacture and production, marketing, sales, distribution, general service and, for some countries, after-sales or after-lease service. CBSA determines whether a business visitor meets the criteria at the point of entry. This definition of business visitor is slightly more flexible than in CETA, which prohibits business visitors from receiving *any* remuneration from inside Canada. Business visitors can stay in Canada up to six months under the TPP, with the possibility of extension, compared to ninety days under CETA. The spouses of business visitors are not covered by any Canadian FTA.

Section B: Intra-corporate transferees

Intra-corporate transferees (ICTs) are employees of a multinational corporation (MNC) of one TPP country who "seek to render services to that enterprise's parent entity, subsidiary or affiliate" in another TPP country. This category is ostensibly designed to facilitate the small-scale, short-term movement of senior managers and workers with unique skills into a company's foreign branch. In practice, these provisions allow MNCs to move a wide range of regular workers (and their spouses) into a country for years at a time, effectively sidestepping the need to hire and train local workers.

Canada's commitments for ICTs in the TPP include four subcategories: specialists, executives, managers and management trainees on professional development. Workers in each of these categories are eligible for a three-year work permit with the possibility of extension (as are their spouses). To be eligible, a worker must have been continuously employed by the company for "one year within the three-year period immediately preceding the date of the application for admission," while also meeting the definition of one of the ICT subcategories. There are no occupational restrictions on ICTs; every industry and profession is covered, including such sensitive sectors as health, education and culture.

The most important subcategory of ICT in the TPP, as in NAFTA and other deals, is the specialist. In the TPP, Canada defines a specialist as "an employee possessing specialized knowledge of the company's products or services and their application in international markets, or an advanced level of expertise or knowledge of the company's processes and procedures." This definition is, in practice, extremely vague. Neither "specialized knowledge" nor "advanced level of expertise" are further defined, which means workers with even limited experience in the organization may legitimately qualify as specialists. The decision to grant temporary entry on these grounds is ultimately made by IRCC or CBSA.

Canada's definition of specialist in the TPP is pulled directly from NAFTA and differs significantly from CETA, which requires that a specialist have "uncommon" rather than "specialized" knowledge of an organization's products or services. By definition, "uncommon" restricts coverage to a minority of workers. Furthermore, CETA clarifies what counts as an "advanced level of expertise" in the following clause:

> In assessing such expertise or knowledge, the Parties will
> consider abilities that are unusual and different from those
> generally found in a particular industry and that cannot
> be easily transferred to another natural person in the short-
> term. Those abilities would have been obtained through
> specific academic qualifications or extensive experience with
> the enterprise.[23]

The CETA definition of specialist is far more rigorous than the one found in NAFTA or the TPP and therefore less open to interpretation and abuse. Under the TPP, MNCs have significant leeway to move workers across borders with few conditions. Curiously, given the backseat role

U.S. negotiators would have taken in the temporary-entry chapter (see box above), Canada appears to have made no effort to include CETA-like language in the TPP. Specialist ICTs are the only category of business person in the TPP for which Canada's commitments are not reciprocal. Canada has instead specified that specialist coverage is only extended to Australia, Brunei, Chile, Japan, Mexico, New Zealand and Peru. Among those countries, Canada has existing ICT commitments, through FTAs, with Chile, Mexico and Peru.

Section C: Investors

The investors category covers business persons who enter Canada to set up or develop an investment. The definition is short and hinges on the requirement that the business person or their enterprise "has committed, or is in the process of committing, a substantial amount of capital." No definition for "substantial" is provided. In fact, in the context of NAFTA, IRCC's foreign worker manual clarifies "there is no minimum dollar figure established for meeting the requirement of 'substantial' investment."[24] Approval is thus left to the discretion of an immigration official. Investors are eligible for a stay of one year under the TPP with the possibility of extension. Unlike CETA and NAFTA, the spouses of investors are also covered by the TPP's temporary-entry commitments for the same length of stay.

Section D: Professionals and technicians

Professionals and technicians — also known as contractual service suppliers — are business persons of one TPP country who are contracted to supply a service in another TPP country. Whereas an ICT works for the same employer in both countries and is transferred across the border, a professional or technician is brought in by a domestic employer for the duration of a specific contract (up to a maximum of one year with the possibility of extension) either independently as a self-employed contractor or as the employee of a contracted company. Their spouses are also covered for the length of the contract.

The definitions for professionals and technicians are more specific than for other categories of business persons in Chapter 12. Firstly, to be eligible for temporary entry, workers must be engaged in a "specialty occupation," which means any work covered by Canada's National Occupation Classification (NOC) levels 0 (management occupations), A (occupations usually requiring university education) or B (occupations usually requiring college education or apprenticeship training).

The inclusion of skill level B is significant because most of Canada's other FTAs, including CETA, are limited to skill levels 0 and A. Skill level B includes a wide variety of occupations that might not intuitively be considered business persons, such as administrative assistants, photographers, retail sales supervisors and carpenters, to name just a few.[25] That said, in practice most of these occupations are excluded from Canada's country-specific list of commitments (see next section).

Secondly, a professional must meet the following requirements to be eligible for temporary entry under the TPP:

> (a) theoretical and practical application of a body of specialised knowledge, and

> (b) a post-secondary degree of four or more years of study, unless otherwise provided in this schedule, and any additional requirement defined in the National Occupation Classification, and

> (c) two years of paid work experience in the sector of activity of the contract, and

> (d) remuneration at a level commensurate with other similarly-qualified professionals within the industry in the region where the work is performed. Such remuneration shall be deemed to not include non-monetary elements such as, inter alia, housing costs and travel expenses.

The requirements for technicians are slightly different and are described as follows:

(a) theoretical and practical application of a body of specialised knowledge, and

(b) a post-secondary or technical degree requiring two or more years of study as a minimum for entry into the occupation, unless otherwise provided in this Schedule, as well as any other minimum requirements for entry defined in the National Occupation Classification, and

(c) four years of paid work experience in the sector of activity of the contract, and

(d) remuneration at a level commensurate with other similarly-qualified technicians within the industry in the region where the work is performed. Such remuneration shall be deemed to not include non-monetary elements such as, inter alia, housing costs and travel expenses.

These definitions are more exclusive than in NAFTA but more inclusive than in CETA. Under the Canada–EU agreement, professionals must have six years of relevant professional experience compared to two years under the TPP. Technicians under CETA require a university degree compared to a two-year technical degree under the TPP. Additionally, unlike the TPP, technicians under CETA cannot be self-employed (they must be employed by a contracted company). Moreover, as noted above, the CETA commitments only extend to NOC skill levels 0 and A by default. Overall, Canada's general commitments for professionals and technicians under the TPP are broader than in other FTAs, although they are limited by Canada's country-by-country schedule of commitments. That is to say, to be eligible for temporary entry into Canada a professional or technician from another TPP party must not only meet the general criteria outlined above, but they must also be covered by Canada's country-specific lists of occupational categories outlined below.

Canada's country-specific schedules to Section D

To start, Canada has not made any temporary-entry commitments for professionals or technicians from New Zealand, Singapore, the United States or Vietnam. (Canada's commitments are meant to be reciprocal and none of these countries offered comparable new access to Canada in this category.) Brunei is also fully excluded with the sole exception of petroleum engineers. Malaysian technicians are fully excluded and only Malaysian professionals in a limited list of occupations are included.

Coverage for the remaining five countries (Australia, Chile, Japan, Mexico and Peru) varies slightly but follows the same pattern. For professionals, all occupations in NOC levels 0 and A are included *except* for those expressly excluded in Canada's commitments — this is known as a negative list approach. For technicians, all occupations in NOC level B are included *only if* the occupation is listed — this is known as a positive list approach.

The negative list for professionals (i.e., the list of exceptions) excludes the following sensitive occupational sectors:

> *All health, education, and social services occupations and related occupations,*

> *All professional occupations related to Cultural Industries,*

> *Recreation, Sports and Fitness Program and Service Directors,*

> *Managers in Telecommunications Carriers,*

> *Managers in Postal and Courier Services, and*

> *Judges and Notaries.*[26]

Despite these reservations, the list of covered occupations for professionals in the TPP is still more extensive than in CETA or NAFTA, both of which employ a positive list approach. The negative list approach for professionals is consistent with Canada's FTAs with Peru and Colombia, but again the list of exceptions in the TPP is shorter than in both those deals. Under the TPP, for example, Peru gains access for managers in the fields of manufacturing, utilities, construction and transportation, which are occupations that were carved out of Peru's previous treaty with Canada.

The positive lists for technicians from those five countries vary somewhat from party to party. Australia and Peru receive the longest lists, which each include thirty-nine different occupational categories ranging from construction inspectors to pipefitting contractors to plumbers. Japan receives a nearly identical list with the notable exception that contractors in any field are not included.[27] Chile receives a slightly shorter list of thirty-four occupations.[28] Mexico receives a much shorter list of fifteen occupations.

Under the TPP, Peru receives access for five occupational categories that are not covered in the Canada–Peru FTA.[29] Chile and Mexico receive access for a handful of occupational categories not covered in either the Canada–Chile FTA or NAFTA.[30]

Potential consequences of the TPP's temporary-entry provisions

The social and economic impacts of any international trade treaty play out over decades and are difficult to forecast with certainty — in part, because states, investors and arbitrators have leeway to interpret the treaty text. With that limitation in mind, we can begin to predict the potential impacts of the TPP's temporary-entry provisions, based on the preceding analysis and on Canada's experience with NAFTA and other FTAs. Past experience suggests the short-term impact of the TPP on the Canadian labour market may be limited. However, the agreement places real and immediate restrictions on government policy flexibility that may have significant macroeconomic and regulatory consequences in the long term.

The main reason to expect a limited short-term labour market impact from the TPP is the presently limited impact of Canadian FTAs on the Canadian workforce. There were 24,879 people working in

Canada under the terms of an international trade treaty on December 31, 2014 (our best measure, although it likely underestimates the total).[31] Those workers accounted for approximately 0.14 per cent of the Canadian labour force at that time.[32] Insofar as the TPP covers mostly the same types of workers under the same general conditions as past FTAs, we might expect an incremental increase, but not an upsurge, in the total number of migrant workers entering Canada due to the TPP. It will probably take some time for industries and employers to adjust to the labour market flexibility created by the TPP. However, there are several reasons to believe the TPP's temporary-entry provisions will have a more significant long-term impact on the Canadian workforce.

Firstly, the TPP opens up Canada's temporary-entry commitments to some major developed countries that do not already have comparable access. Australia and Japan, in particular, are in a strong position to take advantage of Canada's commitments in the TPP. These populous countries are already top sources of migrant workers to Canada and they share important ties with Canada, including economic integration (i.e., foreign direct investment), linguistic familiarity, cultural connections and common standards for education and training.[33] They are also sources of highly skilled professional workers who are more likely to be covered by the terms of Chapter 12 than similar workers from countries like Chile and Malaysia. Japanese auto makers, for example, could easily move engineers from Japan into their Canadian operations under the TPP's intra-corporate transferee rules.

Other TPP countries are not as well positioned to benefit. Under the TPP, Canada makes no new temporary-entry commitments to the U.S., which accounts for around 90 per cent of the migrant workers currently in Canada under the terms of an FTA.[34] Chile, Mexico and Peru already have extensive access to the Canadian labour market under existing FTAs, which has not created a significant inflow of migrant workers from those countries so far. Brunei, Malaysia, New Zealand, Singapore and Vietnam are excluded from Canada's commitments for key categories in the TPP (and those countries are small-scale investors in Canada anyway). Yet the new access offered to Australia and Japan cannot be overlooked, for the reasons listed above.

Secondly, the TPP offers broader occupational coverage for professionals and technicians than in any existing Canadian FTA. A variety of lower-skill occupations are included in Canada's temporary-entry commitments in the TPP, such as mechanics, carpenters and other construction tradespeople, that do not appear in deals like NAFTA. Whereas most Canadian FTAs require a university degree to be considered an eligible professional, the TPP also covers technicians with apprenticeship training. The quantitative impact on the Canadian labour market from this qualitative change is difficult to predict, but it nonetheless represents a departure from the status quo for Canada's temporary-entry commitments, especially with our developed-country partners.

Thirdly, the TPP comes at an opportune time for Canadian employers trying to bypass the domestic labour market and hire internationally. If the Temporary Foreign Worker Program and the rest of Canada's international mobility programs are included, migrant workers make up as much as 2 per cent of the Canadian workforce today, twice the share from a decade ago.[35] The share of migrant workers specifically covered by FTAs as a proportion of the overall workforce has also doubled in the past decade.[36]

The deleterious effects of this precarious, temporary workforce on wages and unemployment in some sectors and regions are well documented, and cases of migrant workers being abused by employers are widespread.[37] FTAs currently play a minor role in these labour market problems at the macro level, as noted above, but at the sectoral level the effects can be severe. Under NAFTA, some Canadian construction workers have been directly displaced by U.S. intra-corporate transferees.[38] Banks and other white-collar employers have also been caught abusing the temporary-entry rules under Canada's FTAs. In one particularly egregious case, RBC forced its Canadian staff to train the intra-corporate transferees who were brought in to replace them.[39]

The TPP does nothing to address employer abuse of Canada's migrant worker programs. We can expect more of it in certain sectors under the TPP, especially as companies become more familiar with the rules for transferring and hiring foreign workers. Indeed, as the Canadian government cracks down on abuses of the more transparent Temporary

Foreign Worker Program, employers may seek out other, less-regulated pipelines for migrant workers. There are no institutional measures to prevent an employer banned from the TFWP from turning to the terms of an FTA to hire the same migrant worker, provided they meet the FTA's requirements. Moreover, even if the TPP did not significantly *worsen* the situation created by the temporary-entry provisions in past FTAs, that would not mean the present situation is desirable. Canada's entire international mobility regime is a troubled model that does little to address the long-term needs of either workers or employers.[40] If Canada has genuine labour shortages, then greater training and greater permanent immigration are necessary. Opening the door to more migrant labour is a stopgap solution with negative knock-on effects for domestic workers and the broader economy.

Conclusions

Consistent with other aspects of the TPP and other Canadian FTAs, the TPP's temporary-entry provisions perpetuate a model of global economic integration that privileges investors and corporations without empowering workers. Specifically, Chapter 12 cedes public authority over the movement of migrant workers to private employers while failing to address the long-term needs of the Canadian labour market. This outcome reflects a closed negotiation process that allowed unelected bureaucrats, and cabinet members in the government, to make important public policy decisions outside of an open public or parliamentary dialogue.

We may not see large-scale labour market disruptions in the short term as a result of the TPP. However, the risks over time are significant, largely due to the constraints placed by the TPP on the government's ability to regulate the domestic labour market. Because Canada forgoes the right to restrict the total number of foreign workers that can be brought into the country under the terms of the TPP, the potential impact on the labour force is substantial. Multinational and domestic companies have been slow to adopt the use of ICTs and foreign professionals so far, but these temporary-entry provisions may become more attractive in the future as investment continues to globalize and industry continues to consolidate.[41] Canadian employers are increasingly turning to migrant workers through existing programs and pathways, and the TPP will give them another tool for importing migrant workers rather than hiring and training domestic workers.

If a future Canadian government decides that the temporary-entry provisions in the TPP are not serving national interests — due to significant distortions in the Canadian labour market, for example — that government will be prohibited from taking key regulatory measures, such as imposing numerical limits or economic needs tests, to address those problems. The TPP's temporary-entry provisions entrench Canada's past policy decisions without attempting to resolve any of the outstanding issues. Unfortunately, once the TPP is ratified, it cannot be changed outside of a complicated and unprecedented twelve-country renegotiation. As such, if a future Canadian government decided to adopt a different approach to international labour mobility, it would be at risk of incurring punitive trade sanctions from other TPP countries. Democratically enacted Canadian law is superseded by this agreement indefinitely.

Appendices

Appendix A1: Summary of Canada's Chapter 12 Commitments		
Category of Business Person	Sub-category of Business Person	Definition or other criteria
A: Business Visitors	Business Visitors (after-sales or after-lease service)	Business persons for whom: (a) the primary source of remuneration for the proposed business activity is outside Canada; and (b) the principal place of business and the predominant place of accrual of profits remain outside Canada
	Business Visitors (all other)	

B: Intra-Corporate Transferees (ICTs)	Specialist	Business persons employed by an enterprise in the territory of a Party who seek to render services to that enterprise's parent entity, subsidiary or affiliate [in Canada]. Canada may require the business person to have been employed continuously by the enterprise for one year within the three-year period immediately preceding the date of the application for admission.	An employee possessing specialized knowledge of the company's products or services and their application in international markets, or an advanced level of expertise or knowledge of the company's processes and procedures.
	Management Trainee on Professional Development		An employee with a post-secondary degree who is on a temporary work assignment intended to broaden that employee's knowledge of and experience in a company in preparation for a senior leadership position within the company.
	Executive		A business person within an organization who: (a) primarily directs the management of the organization or a major component or function of the organization; (b) establishes the goals and policies of the organization, or of a component or function of the organization; and (c) exercises wide latitude in decision-making and receives only general supervision or direction from higher-level executives, the board of directors or stockholders of the business organization.
	Manager		A business person within an organization who: (a) primarily directs the organization or a department or sub-division of the organization; (b) supervises and controls the work of other supervisory, professional or managerial employees; (c) has the authority to hire and fire or take other personnel actions (such as promotion or leave authorization); and (d) exercises discretionary authority over day-to-day operations.
	Spouses of ICTs	n/a	

C: Investors	Investors	Business persons seeking to establish, develop or administer an investment to which the business person or the business person's enterprise has committed, or is in the process of committing, a substantial amount of capital, in a capacity that is supervisory, executive or involves essential skills.
	Spouses of Investors	n/a

MIGRANT WORKERS AND THE TPP

D: Professionals and Technicians	Professional	Specialty occupation means, for Canada, an occupation that falls within the National Occupation Classification levels 0, A, and B.	Business persons engaged in a specialty occupation requiring: (a) theoretical and practical application of a body of specialized knowledge; and (b) a post-secondary degree of four or more years of study, unless otherwise provided in this schedule, and any additional requirement defined in the National Occupation Classification, and (c) two years of paid work experience in the sector of activity of the contract, and (d) remuneration at a level commensurate with other similarly-qualified professionals within the industry in the region where the work is performed. Such remuneration shall be deemed to not include non-monetary elements such as, inter alia, housing costs and travel expenses.
	Technician		A national engaged in a specialty occupation requiring: (a) theoretical and practical application of a body of specialized knowledge, and (b) a post-secondary or technical degree requiring two or more years of study as a minimum for entry into the occupation, unless otherwise provided in this Schedule, as well as any other minimum requirements for entry defined in the National Occupation Classification, and (c) four years of paid work experience in the sector of activity of the contract, and (d) remuneration at a level commensurate with other similarly-qualified technicians within the industry in the region where the work is performed. Such remuneration shall be deemed to not include non-monetary elements such as, inter alia, housing costs and travel expenses.
	Spouses of Professionals and Technicians	n/a	

Appendix A2: Summary of Canada's Chapter 12 Commitments (cont'd)

Category of Business Person	Sub-category of Business Person	Work permit required	Maximum length of stay	Sector/activity restrictions
A: Business Visitors	Business Visitors (after-sales or after-lease service)	No	Six months	After-Sales or After-Lease Service
	Business Visitors (all other)			Meetings and Consultations, Research and Design, Manufacture and Production, Marketing, Sales, Distribution, General Service

B: Intra-Corporate Transferees (ICTs)	Specialist	Yes	Three years	None
	Management Trainee on Professional Development			
	Executive			
	Manager			
	Spouses of ICTs			
C: Investors	Investors	Yes	One year	None
	Spouses of Investors			
D: Professionals and Technicians	Professional	Yes	One year	Varies by country
	Technician			
	Spouses of Professionals and Technicians			None

Note: In all cases, extensions to the maximum length of stay are possible at Canada's discretion.

Appendix B: Canada's Chapter 12 Commitments to TPP Parties

Category of Business Person	Sub-category of Business Person	Australia	Brunei	Chile	Japan	Malaysia	Mexico	New Zealand	Peru	Singapore	United States	Vietnam
A: Business Visitors	Business Visitors (*after-sales or after-lease service*)	✔	✔	✔		✔	✔	✔	✔			✔
	Business Visitors (*all other*)	✔	✔	✔	✔	✔	✔	✔	✔	✔		✔
B: Intra-Corporate Transferees (ICTs)	Specialist	✔	✔	✔	✔		✔	✔	✔			✔
	Management Trainee on Professional Development			✔								
	Executive	✔	✔	✔	✔	✔	✔	✔	✔			✔
	Manager	✔	✔	✔	✔	✔	✔	✔	✔			✔
	Spouses of ICTs	✔	✔	?	?	?	✔		✔			?
C: Investors	Investors	✔	✔	✔	✔	✔	✔	✔	✔	✔		✔
	Spouses of Investors	✔		?	?		✔		✔			?
D: Professionals and Technicians	Professional	✔	✔	✔	✔	✔	✔		✔			✔
	Technician	✔	--	✔	✔	✔	✔		✔			✔
	Spouses of Professionals and Technicians	✔	✔	?	?		✔					?

Note: "?" indicates uncertainty. It is unclear what Canada's threshold for reciprocity is for spouses. Some countries offer temporary entry but not a work permit to Canadian spouses, which may or may not be enough for Canada to offer full access to spouses from those countries.

CHAPTER 7
Foreign-Investor Protections in the TPP

Gus Van Harten

The Trans-Pacific Partnership (TPP) would give foreign investors special rights to protect their assets by suing countries for compensation when they are affected by laws, regulations and other decisions that the foreign investor thinks are unfair. Nothing like these rights exists for other actors in international law, whether they are other foreign nationals, domestic investors or citizens — even in the most extreme situations of mistreatment. Why should foreign investors have this special status and, in effect, a generous public subsidy for assuming economic risks of democracy and regulation that apply to everyone? Promoters of agreements like the TPP often assert that foreign investors need special protection for one or another reason, but in my experience the assertions do not come, as they should, with compelling evidence of a corresponding benefit *for the public.*

Under other trade or investment agreements that allow for this form of investor–state dispute settlement (ISDS), foreign investors have used their special rights to attack legitimate laws and policies in Canada as well as other countries. Prominent ISDS cases include the Philip Morris challenges to anti-tobacco measures in Australia and Uruguay, the Pac Rim claim against mining restrictions in water-stressed El Salvador and the Vattenfall claim against Germany's nuclear phase-out, for example. In Canada, foreign investors — and the lawyers, sitting as arbitrators, who decide the investors' claims — have used similar provisions in NAFTA in expansive or dubious ways. Examples include the Lone Pine Resources challenge to fracking restrictions in Quebec, the Clayton/Bilcon claim against an environmental assessment process in Nova Scotia, the Mobil Investments/Murphy Oil challenge to the regulatory structure for off-shore oil development in Newfoundland and Labrador, the Eli Lilly claim against federal court decisions on Canadian patent law, the S.D. Myers challenge to a federal ban on PCB waste exports (after the U.S. briefly allowed PCB waste imports) and the Ethyl claim against a federal ban on a gasoline additive.[1]

In what areas have investors sued countries?

Foreign investors have invoked their special rights in many areas of public decision making, but some areas are more prominent than others. In a study of 196 claims by foreign investors under trade or investment agreements, thirty-four cases were found to have involved conflicts over natural resources including oil and gas, gold, lumber, fisheries and water.[2] A total of forty cases arose from government decisions on health or environmental protection. The health theme was evident in cases involving health insurance, drinking water, food safety, pharmaceuticals, pesticides regulation and anti-tobacco measures. The environmental theme involved decisions about water, land and biodiversity conservation, pollution control, mining remediation, hazardous waste disposal and liability for environmental contamination. A smaller number of cases involved planning or approvals decisions by local governments. Other common themes included the administration of justice, taxation, economic policy and financial regulation.

In these NAFTA cases, foreign investors used their special rights to challenge and seek public compensation for good-faith decisions that emerged from democratic or court processes in Canada. With the TPP, many more such claims will become possible, even if the sued country (the "respondent state") has already successfully defended against a very similar ISDS claim in the past. In short, the TPP's rights for foreign investors carry major risks for voters and taxpayers in TPP countries while delivering unjustified benefits, at significant public expense, to foreign

132

investors. As I explain later, the financial benefits of these foreign investor rights have thus far gone overwhelmingly to very large multinationals and very wealthy individuals.

Protection beyond the law

There is a simple reason why ISDS lawyers have encouraged foreign investors to use treaties like the TPP to attack countries' decisions, even at a potentially high cost in legal and arbitration fees for both the foreign investor and the sued country. The reason is that the treaties give advantages for foreign investors that are not available to them, or anyone else, in domestic law and other areas of international law. The following list illustrates some of the special legal benefits that ISDS provides for foreign investors and, in turn, how it privileges foreign investors over everyone else:[3]

- There is no right of a government or any other affected party to bring a claim against a foreign investor in ISDS. Instead, foreign investors have been granted the most powerful rights and protections that exist for any private actor in international law, without any corresponding and actionable duties for foreign investors to respect labour standards, the environment, public health, anti-corruption rules, etc.

- Foreign investors can challenge directly any decision of a country — even by its highest legislature, government body or court — at the international level. Typically, international disputes are resolved among countries and their governments, as at the World Trade Organization (WTO), for example.

- Foreign investors can be awarded uncapped amounts of compensation as the primary remedy for sovereign conduct that is deemed by the arbitrators to have been unlawful. This is an extraordinarily powerful and highly unusual aspect of the treaties. It can create major challenges for legislatures and governments attempting to plan for the cost of their decisions. In effect, corporate lawyers and lobbyists working for foreign investors can use this aspect of ISDS to put an unknown price tag on a proposed law or other decision when a deep-pocketed foreign investor objects to the proposal.

- There is no general doctrine of deference or balancing in the ISDS arbitrators' review of legislatures and courts, in contrast to the domestic law of Canada and other countries such as France, the United Kingdom and the United States. These doctrines of deference or balancing were developed historically to accommodate the role of legislatures as elected bodies and the role of governments in dealing with complex or urgent policy questions.

- The provisions that describe the rights and protections of foreign investors — such as "fair and equitable treatment" or "indirect expropriation" or "de facto discrimination" — are very broadly worded. As a result, they give immense power to the lawyers who sit as arbitrators and decide foreign-investor claims. The core power of the arbitrators is to interpret the ambiguous rights and to award public money to foreign investors, with no monetary cap on the amounts that can be awarded. In past cases, the amounts that countries have been ordered to pay have ranged from tens of thousands to billions of dollars per case.

- The foreign investor directly controls or influences half of the makeup of the arbitration tribunal's membership. Normally, judges would be appointed by a public body and as a part of a publicly accountable process.

- The lawyers appointed as arbitrators in each case, especially the "core" arbitrators who have been appointed over and over, stand to profit from their own decisions. Because they do not have secure tenure and are paid a lucrative daily or hourly rate, the arbitrators have an evident interest to encourage claims, which can be brought only by one side (the foreign investors), and to stretch out the proceedings. Due to the absence of conventional safeguards of judicial independence, a range of conflicts of interest arises in the system, typically favouring deep-pocketed potential claimants, i.e., multinational companies and very wealthy individuals.

- There is no opportunity — or a very limited opportunity, depending on the rules under which a foreign investor chooses to bring the ISDS claim — for review of the arbitrators' decisions in any court, whether domestic or international. Instead, review of the arbitrators' awards is done on limited grounds by another tribunal of for-profit arbitrators or by a domestic court in a place that is typically chosen by the arbitrators themselves. In this way, the power of the arbitrators over public money is de-linked from the courts as well as legislatures and governments.

- The arbitrators' awards are widely enforceable against a country's assets located in other countries. Corporate lawyers have adopted creative strategies to chase assets in this context by attempting to seize warships, public art on loan to foreign galleries, or cultural properties — let alone more conventional commercial assets such as money owed by the customers of a country's state-owned companies.

- No right of "standing" is allowed in ISDS arbitration proceedings for other affected parties, besides the foreign investor and the state's national government. For a legal proceeding to be fair, all parties whose legal interests are affected by the process should be given a right of standing to the extent of their interest.

- There is no requirement for a foreign investor to use a country's domestic courts before resorting to ISDS, no matter how fair and independent the domestic courts are. This anomalous situation arises because the TPP does not apply the usual requirement in international law that a foreign national must go to a country's own courts first, where they are reasonably available and offer justice, before bringing an international claim against the country. Thus, implicitly, agreements like the TPP operate from the position that the courts in all countries cannot be relied on to protect foreign investors. Foreign investors are not required to use the courts, or even to demonstrate that the courts are inadequate in some way, before bringing an ISDS claim. Yet the courts in Canada and many other countries are clearly more independent and more fair than ISDS itself.

To repeat, in these and other ways, the TPP gives special privileges to foreign investors. No other system of international protection, beyond other trade and investment agreements that allow for ISDS, comes close to delivering such a powerful legal position to anyone, even in the most extreme situations of mistreatment. By adding to existing agreements that cover far fewer foreign-owned assets, the TPP would vastly expand this lopsided arrangement in which the largest and wealthiest actors in society are given special access to public compensation for risks that apply to everyone and against which no one else has these special protections.

Who benefits financially from ISDS?

Overwhelmingly, the foreign investors that have benefited financially from the rights in agreements like the TPP have been very large companies and very wealthy individuals. Some of these individuals have used legal manoeuvres to make themselves legally "foreign" in order to sue their own country. To illustrate, in a recent study it was found that over 90 per cent of ordered compensation in foreign-investor claims against countries went to corporations with over US$1 billion in annual revenue — most had over US$10 billion — or to individuals with over US$100 million in net wealth.[4] The distribution of ordered compensation, by size and wealth of claimant, is indicated in the following chart.

By following the money in this way, we find that the clearest financial impact of foreign-investor rights has been to require billions of dollars in public money to be paid to multinationals and the very wealthy. For other foreign investors, the money typically spent on lawyers and arbitrators, whose fees amount to about $8 million per case on average,

Figure 6: Compensation by Size/Wealth of Claimant

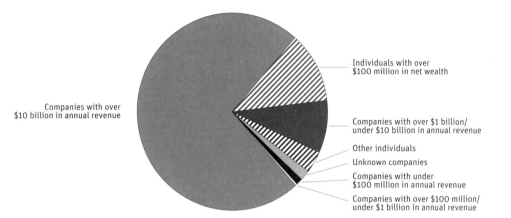

appeared to outpace any financial award to the investor, even in cases where compensation was awarded.[5] Accounting for the factor of legal and arbitration fees, the ISDS system has greatly enriched investment lawyers and arbitrators, who have earned well over $1 billion in fees. The next chart (Figure 7) gives an approximate sense of the financial winners and losers in known ISDS cases, measured by ordered compensation and adjusted for estimated fees paid to lawyers, arbitrators and other professionals in ISDS.

Looking at another measure, the success rates of the largest multinationals (with over $10 billion in annual revenue) has greatly exceeded those of other foreign investors in known ISDS arbitrations. In 71 per cent of the forty-eight cases they initiated, these companies were successful in having their claim heard and in arguing that the respondent country had violated one or more of their investment treaty rights. In contrast, the success rate for other foreign investors across the 166 ISDS cases they brought was 42 per cent.

Perhaps most troubling is the pressure that ISDS allows foreign investors to put on governments behind the scenes. Governments in Canada have responded to the threat of NAFTA ISDS lawsuits from U.S. investors by developing processes to vet regulatory proposals internally. In a study of the impact of ISDS for environmental decision making in Canada

Figure 7: Financial Winners and Losers

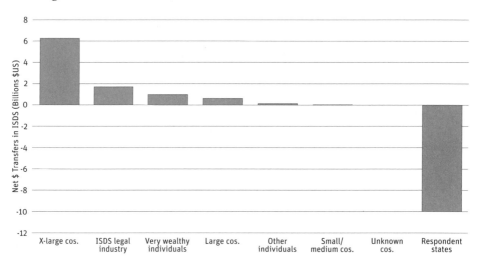

(based on confidential interviews with government officials, especially in Ontario), it was found that government ministries have changed their decision making in order to account for ISDS and other trade litigation risks, that government lawyers play a key role in assessing the risks, and that a ministry's concern for the risks was more acute after the ministry was drawn into a NAFTA case, although institutional learning about ISDS also appeared variable and intermittent.[6] Officials typically declined to discuss specific cases, but referred occasionally to situations in which ISDS or other trade concerns were considered and, in some cases, where they led to changes to a proposal. The findings indicate that governments have changed their decision making in favour of foreign investors in order to avoid financial and political risks of ISDS, apparently at the expense of anyone who has a conflicting interest. Yet, for various reasons, we clearly do not have a full picture of the impacts of ISDS on governments, even with extensive investigative research.

The TPP goes beyond NAFTA

The TPP's rights for foreign investors mimic other trade and investment agreements, but they also go beyond such agreements. First, the TPP would expand vastly the range of foreign investors who enjoy these special rights. Indeed, only two existing agreements — NAFTA and the Energy Charter Treaty — are comparable in scope to the TPP, and only then because those two agreements are the rare cases that currently allow foreign-investor claims among developed economies. As it happens, Canada has the unique position under NAFTA of being the only western developed country that has agreed to these foreign-investor rights with the U.S. The TPP would expand Canada's ISDS exposure (to a reasonable prospect of foreign-investor claims) from, at present, U.S. investors under NAFTA and Chinese investors under the 2014 Foreign Investment Promotion and Protection Agreement (FIPA) to include, most notably under the TPP, companies and wealthy individuals from Australia, Japan and Malaysia.

The TPP is even more important for how it would expand ISDS at a global level. To illustrate, the next chart uses the U.S. economy as a proxy to show how the TPP would expand foreign investor rights worldwide.[7] It compares the amount of foreign-owned assets (i.e., inward foreign direct investment stock) in the U.S. economy that is presently covered by existing ISDS agreements to the amount that would be covered under the TPP. The chart also indicates the expansion that would come from a related trade agreement currently under negotiation: the U.S.–European Union Transatlantic Trade and Investment Partnership (TTIP). As we can see, the TPP and TTIP would together vastly expand the scope of foreign-investor rights from what is presently still an exceptional role in the international economy.

Second, for Canada, the TPP would expand foreign investors' rights, especially the rights of U.S. investors, beyond Canada's current agreements. For example, the TPP would allow foreign investors to claim compensation for violations of "investment agreements" (i.e., contracts) with the federal government.[8] Canada has never before given this added right to foreign investors in a trade or investment agreement. Instead, Canada has held to the sensible position that disputes about a foreign investor's contractual rights should be resolved according to the agreed terms of the contract, including its terms on dispute settlement.

The situation on this point is legally complex, but essentially, by allowing foreign investors to bring international claims for "investment

Figure 8: ISDS Coverage of U.S. Inward FDI Stock

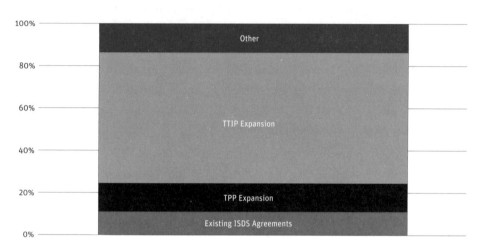

agreements," the TPP would expand the risks for Canadian taxpayers when governments enter into contracts with multinationals to supply goods and services or to deliver or operate privatized services and infrastructure. Federal government contracts would become uniquely enforceable, by foreign companies only, outside Canadian courts if that is what the foreign company prefers, even if the underlying contract refers disputes to Canadian courts. That is risky for taxpayers because, among other things, it allows ISDS arbitrators, who we should recall have a financial interest to encourage foreign investor claims, to award public money to disgruntled foreign companies. The change has potentially wide-ranging implications because procurement contracts or public-private partnerships in Canada would otherwise typically refer disputes to Canadian courts. By this expansion of foreign-investor rights, the TPP would distort the marketplace further in favour of multinationals, by giving them an advantage when they compete for government business. Domestic companies would have to live with the terms of their contracts, while foreign investors, based on the expansive interpretations of ISDS arbitrators on this issue, would have a new TPP right to skirt those terms and resort to their TPP rights instead.

Third, while the TPP mostly reproduces NAFTA's flaws, in situations where the TPP's version of ISDS could provide more regulatory space to countries the reforms are virtually meaningless for Canada because NAFTA is maintained alongside the TPP. Put differently, anything that is new and apparently better in the TPP (such as its exception for some types of anti-smoking measures) is very likely lost because the TPP adds onto, instead of replacing, existing agreements like NAFTA. In this way, the TPP has been designed to create the best of possible legal worlds for foreign investors and the worst for governments, voters and taxpayers in TPP countries.

To explain further, unlike other treaties, in which countries agree explicitly to replace earlier agreements, the TPP "affirms" and thus adds on to existing trade and investment agreements among TPP countries.[9] As a result, for Canada, anything that is apparently better in the TPP compared to NAFTA will very likely be lost in practice because a U.S. investor can bring a claim under NAFTA instead of the TPP. Also, anything worse in the TPP would not be displaced by NAFTA because a foreign investor could choose to bring a claim under the TPP. If a foreign investor was unsure which agreement offered the best chance to win compensation, it could bring a claim under the TPP and NAFTA, making a different argument under each and getting compensation if it won under either. I am not being outlandish here: this sort of manoeuvring is common in ISDS.

For this reason, claims by TPP promoters that the deal is more "progressive" than other agreements are highly misleading. The TPP does not replace other agreements, no matter how comparably "regressive" they might be. It affirms and adds on to them. Considering these factors, if the TPP is adopted it would vastly expand the role of ISDS as a global institution.

Harder to regulate the financial sector

If one compares the TPP to NAFTA, the TPP has more rights for global banks in ISDS. Once again, these added rights come at a potentially huge cost to the public. It appears that TPP negotiators decided that big banks need more, not less, protection from financial regulation. Specifically, the TPP's financial services chapter allows foreign banks to bring claims for compensation that would not be permitted under NAFTA. Unlike NAFTA, the TPP allows such claims based on the TPP's so-called minimum standard of treatment for foreign investors.[10] This supposedly "mini-mum" standard incorporates far-reaching rights for foreign investors to be compensated where they do not receive "fair and equitable treatment" and "full protection and security" from a country. These vaguely worded rights have become notorious after being interpreted expansively by ISDS arbitrators.

By going beyond NAFTA in this way, the TPP would give ISDS arbitrators even more power to award public compensation to banks in a financial crisis, where a government regulates to protect the stability of the financial system. Thus, the TPP would make it harder for financial regulators to predict what arbitrators will decide, years down the road, when a TPP ISDS award is issued. This uncertainty in turn would give banks more leverage behind the scenes to resist regulations when they are devised, at the expense of anyone who may benefit from financial regulation but lacks the power to mount a costly international claim against the country. Overall, this change in the TPP is a win for global banks and a loss for financial regulators, and anyone protected by them, in TPP countries (see box below).

Prudential regulation and NAFTA

"Certain NAFTA investment protections, such as the controversial 'minimum standard of treatment,' do not apply in the financial sector. NAFTA also allows financial regulators to take measures to ensure the integrity and stability of the financial system, even if these regulations violate NAFTA's investment protection rules. This 'prudential carve-out' can be used to block ISDS claims. The TPP, on the other hand, gives ISDS tribunals more power to award public compensation to foreign investors who are allegedly mistreated by financial regulations.

"To illustrate, foreign financial institutions have used ISDS to seek compensation in the context of Europe's financial crisis. In 2008, a Chinese financial services company sued Belgium under a 2005 Belgium–China investment treaty. Ping An, the largest single shareholder in the Belgian-Dutch bank Fortis, alleged that it lost US$2.3 billion when government authorities, who stepped in to rescue the financial giant, later sold off assets over the objections of minority shareholders. While the tribunal ruled against Ping An in May 2015, it did so on jurisdictional grounds and not the merits of the claims of unfair treatment and expropriation. Foreign investors have filed similar ISDS claims against Greece and Cyprus to recover losses incurred under financial restructuring programs."

Canadian Centre for Policy Alternatives

Not fair, not independent

Apart from the details of how the TPP goes beyond NAFTA, there are more fundamental questions at stake in the TPP's expansion of ISDS. The TPP's arbitration process to protect foreign investors contradicts basic principles of judicial independence and fair process. For this reason, it is not compatible with the rule of law.[11] In particular, the TPP gives for-profit lawyers — sitting as arbitrators — the power to decide what sovereign countries can do, and then to award potentially vast amounts of public money to foreign investors. TPP arbitrators are "for profit" because they are paid by the day or by the hour. Unlike judges, they do not have institutional safeguards to remove the evident financial interest to encourage claims by foreign investors. Unlike other kinds of arbitrators, ISDS arbitrators' decisions are subject to little or no scrutiny in any court.

The financial interest of the arbitrators is uniquely present in ISDS arbitration because only one side (the foreign investors) can bring the claims that lead to the arbitrators' appointments and remuneration. Repeat arbitrators in particular have a unique incentive to interpret the law in ways that encourage foreign investors to bring more claims. Missing are the judicial safeguards of a set salary, secure tenure, an objective method of case assignment, a prohibition on working on the side as a lawyer or arbitrator and so on. Worse, the TPP arbitration process is procedurally unfair because, with the exception of the foreign investor and national government of the sued country, it denies full standing to other parties who have a legal interest in the process. That is, anyone else who has a legal interest in the case is not given full rights to access documents, submit evidence and make arguments.

This concern about unfairness is not hypothetical. In various ISDS cases, parties have been affected directly by the arbitration, such as where a provincial government's decision is challenged and its reputation questioned, where an indigenous community's land claim overlaps with a foreign investor's, or where an individual is accused of involvement in corrupt activities.[12] All of these parties have a direct interest in the proceedings, but no right to standing. From the perspective of judicial independence and fair process, these are serious flaws in the ISDS process laid out in the TPP.

Conclusion

The TPP would take us in the wrong direction and be very difficult to reverse. It would expand the transfer of power to ISDS arbitrators from legislatures, governments and courts. The arbitrators would not be accountable like a legislature. They would not be capable of regulating like a government. They would not be independent or fair like a court.

At the core of the TPP's threat to democracy and regulation is the uncertain and potentially huge price tag that its ISDS process would put on any law or regulation that is opposed by a large multinational company or a billionaire investor. The problem is not that foreign investors would be too big to fail; it is that the TPP would make the biggest and richest ones too risky to regulate.

The TPP was an opportunity for countries to step back from and reform the flawed system of foreign-investor rights and ISDS. Instead, the TPP would expand the system massively. That decision is reason enough to reject the TPP in order to protect the established institutions of democracy, sovereignty and the rule of law in TPP countries.

CHAPTER 8
The TPP and Cultural Diversity

Alexandre L. Maltais

Supporters of wholesale globalization believe that cultural policies interfere with market mechanisms and competition. . . We believe this view falls flat when it comes to culture. Furthermore, we are deeply convinced that only when states and governments respect and promote the principle of cultural diversity can all cultures survive and prosper.[1]

—Line Beauchamp, former Quebec culture minister

During the negotiation of the Trans-Pacific Partnership (TPP), Canada supported the idea of including a "cultural exception" in the text in order to preserve federal and provincial cultural policies and give effect to Canada's obligations under UNESCO legal instruments, including the 2005 Convention on the Protection and Promotion of the Diversity of Cultural Expressions (2005 UNESCO Convention). Canadian laws and regulations for the protection of cultural identities and promotion of cultural diversity are often based on, or encouraged by, other international legal instruments.

The rationale behind the cultural exception, which can be found in the North American Free Trade Agreement (NAFTA) and most other Canadian free trade agreements (FTAs), is that market-opening (liberalization) rules in such treaties can seriously threaten or undermine legitimate and essential cultural policy. For example, the Dispute Settlement Body (DSB) of the World Trade Organization (WTO) has, on several occasions, ruled against country protections for domestic cultural rights and heritage on the basis of free-trade principles. In 1997, a WTO panel agreed with the U.S. that Canadian subsidies for cultural goods such as periodicals, and non-tariff barriers applied to U.S. periodicals, violated several provisions of the General Agreement on Tariffs and Trade (GATT 1994).[2] In another WTO dispute initiated by the U.S., the DSB decided, in 2009, that China's limitations on the importation, distribution and sale of U.S. publications and audiovisual products violated parts of the GATT 1994 and the General Agreement on Trade in Services (GATS) — even while panelists recognized there is a link between cultural products and public morals that is subject to an exception under the GATT.[3]

On top of these disputes launched by states, international investment treaties allow foreign corporations and investors to directly challenge domestic cultural regulations — especially as they relate to historical and natural heritage and other immovable cultural property — as a form of indirect expropriation of capital or as a breach of the investor's so-called minimum standards of treatment. In certain cases, ad hoc investment tribunals have rejected government assertions that expropriations may be necessary to protect cultural sites. For instance, in 2000, an investment tribunal decided that Costa Rica should be required to pay a U.S. investor US$16 million as compensation for the expropriation of a hotel near a UNESCO world heritage site protected by international law.[4] In rich and poor countries alike, even the threat of such costly lawsuits, which take place outside the domestic court system and independently of national laws and customs, could be enough to discourage governments from pursuing cultural or heritage protection measures.

Fifteen years ago, Pauline Marois, then Quebec's deputy premier, advocated for the adoption of a new international legal instrument for protecting cultural diversity, recognizing that: "The right of States to freely determine their cultural policies is jeopardized by unfettered and unbridled economic and financial globalization. [This right] is being threatened by the dehumanizing 'free-trade-only' philosophy" (author's translation).[5] Her views were not unique in Canada or Quebec; they reflected a general and long-standing consensus among political leaders in much of the world on the importance of national cultural policies and the need to preserve them when negotiating international trade and investment agreements.

It was this global concern over the impact of "wholesale globaliza- tion," in the words of former Quebec culture minister Line Beauchamp, that fostered the adoption of the 2005 UNESCO Convention. The legally binding treaty recognizes the "distinctive nature of cultural activities, goods and services as vehicles of identity, values and meaning," and reaffirms "sovereign rights of States to maintain, adopt and implement policies and measures that they deem appropriate for the protection and promotion of the diversity of cultural expressions on their territory."[6] Although many other legal instruments on cultural property have been adopted in the context of UNESCO, the 2005 UNESCO Convention is recognized as the leading treaty. It is the source of the idea, undermined in two recently concluded Canadian FTAs, that there should be a "cultural exception" in trade agreements — that, in other words, culture should no longer be considered as merely another commercial product.

Cultural exceptions in the TPP and CETA

During negotiations on the Canada–EU Comprehensive Economic and Trade Agreement (CETA), the former Conservative government committed to a broadly worded carve-out (exclusion) for cultural policy. The govern- ment's strategy was threefold: to secure expressly cultural considerations in the CETA preamble; to achieve an exception for "cultural industries" applicable to certain chapters of the agreement; and to include a number of reservations on specific cultural sectors, regulations, laws and institutions in the CETA annexes.[7] The result is not as strong as advocates for cultural diversity had been hoping, but it does not stray too far from Canada's past practice. Though Canada's strategy was the same in the TPP negotiations, the outcome was quite different — even though Canadian negotiators had many allies at the table.

Leaked official documentation shows that Australia, New Zealand, Chile, Canada, Brunei, Malaysia and Vietnam (the pro-exception group) were all in favour of including a cultural exception in the Pacific agreement, while the United States and the four other negotiating countries were definitely against the idea (the anti-exception group).[8] According to Gilbert Gagné and Antonios Vlassis, the division has nothing to do with traditional geographical (North vs. South) or ideological divides; the opposing positions of these two coalitions are based solely on national interest, which I would qualify as "perceived interest."[9] Interestingly, the TPP member states that are also parties to the 2005 UNESCO Convention were not necessarily those in favour of including a cultural exception in the agreement. Likewise, not all non-parties to the 2005 UNESCO Convention were against the idea of a more "culture-friendly" TPP (see Table 9 below).

Table 9: TPP Country Support for "Cultural Exception" and Participation in 2005 UNESCO Convention.		
TPP negotiating parties (as of January 2016)	In favour of the "cultural exception"	Parties to the 2005 UNESCO Convention[10]
Australia	X	X
Brunei	X	
Canada	X	X
Chile	X	X
Japan		
Malaysia	X	
Mexico		X
New Zealand	X	X
Peru		X
Singapore		
United States		
Viet Nam	X	X

Neoliberal cultural considerations in the TPP preamble

It is tempting to skip the preamble in free-trade agreements such as the TPP, since the language tends to be aspirational and is not enforceable via dispute settlement. The preamble can, however, have a mitigating effect on pressures in the agreement to liberalize in sensitive areas of legitimate public policy. This is because international law provides that a treaty shall be interpreted "in the light of its object and purpose." Thus, one could argue that provisions of the TPP — like the CETA, which also includes cultural considerations in its preamble — should be interpreted as more "culture-friendly."

In practical terms, the "international judges" of free trade (i.e., arbitrators on investor–state tribunals, members of the WTO Dispute Settlement Body, etc.) may be more inclined to adopt a harmonious interpretation of seemingly contradictory international trade and investment rules on one side, and UNESCO cultural obligations on the other, if the intentions of the parties are clearly spelled out in advance. For instance, the objective of sustainable development that was included in the preamble of the Marrakesh Agreement (establishing the WTO) was a decisive factor in the DSB's interpretation of state obligations under the GATT in the *U.S. – Shrimp* case.[11]

In addition to non-economic considerations, including the importance of environmental protection, labour rights, good governance and respect for the rule of law, TPP negotiating parties agreed to mention cultural considerations in the preamble of the agreement. The relevant paragraph reads as follows:

The Parties to this Agreement, resolving to: . . .

RECOGNIZE the importance of cultural identity and diversity among and within the Parties, and that trade and investment can expand opportunities to enrich cultural identity and diversity at home and abroad.[12]

This language is insufficient to give effect to Canada's obligations under UNESCO treaties, or to mitigate the negative impact of the TPP on cultural policies at the national and provincial levels, for three main reasons. First, it completely ignores all international legal instruments on the protection of culture, including the 2005 UNESCO Convention. We can contrast this with the CETA, which explicitly refers to and reaffirms state obligations under the cultural treaty in a fashion that could positively (i.e., in a culture-friendly manner) affect Canada–EU disputes related to

149

cultural policy. Second, while the TPP preamble foresees opportunities for the promotion of culture and diversity through trade and investment, it fails to acknowledge the threats and challenges in the agreement. The suggestion is that more trade inevitably enriches culture — a typically neoliberal concept frequently contradicted by pragmatic approaches to cultural protection and diversity.

Third, the TPP preamble misses another opportunity to enshrine cultural considerations in a paragraph on states' "right to regulate," in which parties "resolve to preserve the flexibility. . .to set legislative and regulatory priorities, safeguard public welfare, and protect legitimate public welfare objectives, such as public health, safety, the environment, the conservation of living or non-living exhaustible natural resources, the integrity and stability of the financial system and public morals."[13] Here, again, the TPP approach differs from what Canada and the European Union agreed to in CETA, which explicitly recognizes the "promotion and protection of cultural diversity" as legitimate policy objectives. A trade or investment dispute panel established under the TPP may arrive at different results in a conflict over cultural policy depending on whether the list of legitimate objectives is treated as exhaustive or descriptive.

Canada has signed other free trade agreements that provide a much stronger commitment to cultural diversity and protection than even CETA or NAFTA (where the cultural exception was first expressed).[14] For instance, the following language was included in the preambles of Canada's FTAs with Peru (2009), Jordan (2012), Panama (2013) and Honduras (2014):

> *Recognizing that states **must maintain the ability to preserve,** **develop and implement their cultural policies** for the purpose of strengthening cultural diversity, given the **essential role that** **cultural goods and services play in the identity and diversity** **of societies and the lives of individuals** (emphasis added).*[15]

Other FTAs with Costa Rica (2002), the European Free Trade Association (2009) and South Korea (2015) include a similar paragraph in their respective preambles.[16] It is a clear sign of Canada's historical concern with preserving the right to regulate for cultural protection and promotion. The TPP preamble, on the other hand, makes no reference to international instruments for the protection of culture, does not explicitly recognize the preservation of cultural diversity as a legitimate policy objective, and takes a neoliberal view of cultural promotion (i.e., that more trade and investment can have only positive impacts on culture). The final text reflects the absence of consensus within negotiating parties split on the cultural exception.

A conditional and limited general cultural exception

In general, FTAs like the TPP require states to treat national and foreign goods, services and investors the same way, but they may also prohibit governments from intervening in the economy in ways that might encourage local development and protect local jobs or industries, or from passing public safety regulations. As the late Stephen Clarkson and others have noted, FTAs like the TPP are constitution-type documents designed to restrict the policy space of signatory states (their federal, subnational and even municipal governments) in the interests of "freeing" or liberalizing trade and investment flows.[17] As such, governments will try to exclude sensitive policy areas, including culture, where they want to maintain some space to govern and regulate in the public interest.

In the past, as noted above, Canadian governments of all political stripes have sought a broad general exception for culture and cultural industries in Canada's trade and investment treaties. Proximity to the U.S. and its dominant entertainment industry has stoked recurring Canadian concerns about cultural assimilation and the survival of local industries and public institutions capable of nurturing distinctive artistic and cultural expression. Constrained by higher unit costs — the result of a small population in a large country — Canadian cultural industries, from broadcasting to publishing, have consistently advocated for protection.[18] These efforts have been strongly opposed by successive U.S. administrations. In a climate of increasing globalization, U.S. negotiators have enthusiastically exploited trade and investment agreements to advance one of their most commercially successful export industries.

Article 29.8 of the TPP chapter on Exceptions and General Provisions, regarding "Traditional Knowledge and Traditional Cultural Expressions," reads as follows:

> *Subject to each Party's international obligations, each Party may establish appropriate measures to respect, preserve and promote **traditional knowledge** and **traditional cultural expressions** (emphasis added).*

It is interesting that this shows up under Section B: General Provisions, alongside a paragraph on disclosure of information, and not the exceptions section proper. There does not appear to be a good reason why the exception for traditional knowledge and culture should not appear in the same section as the standard exceptions for security policy, temporary safeguard measures (taken to maintain economic order), and the GATT Articles XX (b) and (g), which provide protection (as weak as it has proven to be) for measures "necessary to protect human, animal or plant life or health," and "relating to the conservation of living and non-living exhaustible natural resources."[19]

Beyond its placement in the text, the TPP general exception for culture has two other particularities related to its conditionality and limited scope. In the first case, note the exception is subject to "each Party's international obligations." This raises the question of whether it is a true exception at all, since the parties' international obligations presumably include the TPP itself, as well as any cultural treaties they have signed. In other words, the exception may be circular, since cultural policy would only be protected to the extent that it complies with the liberalizing pressures in the TPP. In practical terms, the exception is also phrased such that only TPP member states that are party to other international instruments on the protection of traditional knowledge and traditional cultural expressions would be allowed to invoke the exception for the purpose of maintaining cultural policy space.

For example, in the context of a TPP-related trade dispute, Canada could argue its policies for the protection of traditional cultural expressions fulfil obligations in the 2005 UNESCO Convention to which it is a party. Similarly, Malaysia could invoke the TPP general cultural exception to justify maintaining its regulations protecting the traditional knowledge of indigenous people and local communities, as the country is a party to the 2003 UNESCO Convention for the Safeguarding of the Intangible Cultural Heritage.[20] On the contrary, the United States could hardly use the TPP exception to justify a national measure aimed at preserving archaeological sites or structures located in the ocean, as it has not signed the 2001 Convention on the Protection of the Underwater Cultural Heritage.

The scope of the TPP cultural exception is also strangely limited. The concepts of *traditional knowledge* and *traditional cultural expressions* are both included in UNESCO instruments, but are more often used in the framework of the World Intellectual Property Organization (WIPO). Although there is no universally accepted definition of "traditional knowledge," the WIPO suggests the term includes "the intellectual and intangible cultural heritage, practices and knowledge systems of traditional communities, including indigenous and local communities."[21] With regard to "traditional cultural expressions," the WIPO says it relates to "tangible and intangible forms in which traditional knowledge and cultures are expressed, communicated or manifested."[22] Regardless of their exact definitions, these two concepts are much narrower than the idea of *cultural diversity* in the 2005 UNESCO Convention, where it is defined as:

> *the manifold ways in which the cultures of groups and*
> *societies find expression. These expressions are passed on*
> *within and among groups and societies. Cultural diversity is*
> *made manifest not only through the varied ways in which*
> *the cultural heritage of humanity is expressed, augmented*
> *and transmitted through the variety of cultural expressions,*
> *but also through diverse modes of artistic creation,*
> *production, dissemination, distribution and enjoyment,*
> *whatever the means and technologies used.*[23]

In light of the objective of the 2005 UNESCO Convention to "protect and promote the diversity of cultural expressions," the limited scope of the TPP's cultural exception may not suffice to preserve the integrity of Canada's cultural policies and ensure Canada's compliance with its international obligations under UNESCO legal instruments.

Canada's insufficient cultural reservations

To make up for weaknesses in the TPP's general exceptions related to culture, Canada sought and has secured reservations (carve-outs) to specific TPP chapters in separate annexes to the core agreement. This technique allows Canada and other TPP parties to list (or grandfather) measures, regulations or laws that appear, on the face of it, to be inconsistent with the agreement on its entry into force, as well as those sectors of activity in which the government would want to maintain policy flexibility (i.e., to take future measures that would otherwise violate the agreement). The drawback, of course, is that a country may forget to include certain cultural protection policies in its list of so-called nonconforming measures, or fail to anticipate new sectors of economic activity a government may one day want to shield from trade and investment disciplines, making future policy measures vulnerable to government-to-government dispute settlement or investor–state arbitration.

Canada's key cultural reservations in the TPP concern particularly the investment chapter, which grants foreign investors or corporations from TPP countries rights to national treatment and most-favoured-nation treatment, as well as more vaguely defined and interpreted "minimum standards of treatment," while also prohibiting "performance requirements" on incoming investment, such as the use of domestic goods or services, export quotas, technology transfer, etc. Many of these investor protections conflict with Canadian cultural policy and the *Investment Canada Act* generally. Canada's investment reservations in the TPP therefore stipulate the following:

> *An investment subject to review under the* Investment Canada Act *may not be implemented unless the Minister responsible for the* Investment Canada Act *advises the applicant that the investment is likely to be of net benefit to Canada. This determination is made in accordance with six factors described in the Act, summarized as follows:* . . .

*(e) the **compatibility of the investment with** national industrial, economic and **cultural policies**, taking into consideration industrial, economic and **cultural policy objectives** enunciated by the government or legislature of any province likely to be significantly affected by the investment. . .(emphasis added).*

Foreign investments in cultural businesses are also subject to specific rules under the TPP. Another Canadian reservation specifies that, "the specific acquisition or establishment of a new business in designated types of business activities relating to Canada's cultural heritage or national identity may be subject to review. . .in the public interest." It should be noted that two identical reservations were made by Canada in the CETA context. Other Canadian cultural reservations in the TPP concern trade in services, state-owned enterprises (to protect the CBC) and government procurement (to exclude public contracts on services related to culture or cultural industries). For example, with certain exceptions, Canada "reserves the right to adopt or maintain any measure that affects cultural industries and that has the objective of supporting, directly or indirectly, the creation, development or accessibility of Canadian artistic expression or content."

This cultural reservations approach — also used in the CETA negotiation context — is not as effective as a broad general exception for cultural policy, which has its own limitations. That is because the more cultural policy is boxed in by agreements like the TPP — the more its definition is legalized in this way — the more culture becomes vulnerable to the "ratchet" effect in FTAs: future governments are free to change their cultural policy as long as the new policy is less, and never more, restrictive to trade and investment. Even where future policy flexibility is preserved, its exercise must fall within the scope and terms of each party's reservations, which only apply against certain, not all, TPP services and investment obligations. For example, it is not possible to shield cultural laws, policies, regulations and other measures from "minimum standards of treatment" and "expropriation" clauses that are most often cited by foreign investors in investor–state disputes. This feature of FTAs and investment treaties makes it harder for governments to reform policy so that it more effectively shields culture from free-trade disciplines.

Another Canadian cultural reservation (carve-out) from the TPP's chapters on Cross-Border Trade in Services (Chapter 10) and Investment (Chapter 9), included under Annex II covering protection for future policy measures, appears to be a significant concession to the U.S. and a step back from Canada's already insufficient cultural exception policy. The "exception to the exception," as Michael Geist describes it, reads as follows:

> *Canada reserves the right to adopt or maintain any measure that affects cultural industries and that has the objective of supporting, directly or indirectly, the creation, development or accessibility of Canadian artistic expression or content, **except**:*
>
> *a) **discriminatory requirements** on services suppliers or investors to make financial contributions for Canadian content development; and*
>
> *b) measures **restricting the access to on-line foreign audiovisual content*** (emphasis added).

The origin of this reservation lies in the U.S.-led opposition to an "unreasonably broad" cultural exception in the TPP.[24] In a blog post, Geist writes that while he is supportive generally of a loosening of Canadian content rules and fewer restrictions on streaming audiovisual services (e.g., Netflix, YouTube, iTunes), "it is shocking to find the Canadian government locking itself into rules that restrict its ability to consider expanding Cancon contributions to entities currently exempt from payment or adopting rules that limit regulatory jurisdiction over foreign online video providers that target Canadian consumers."[25]

However, the situation is even worse than Geist suggests because this is not the first or only "major departure from longstanding Canadian trade policy," as he puts it. In fact, the traditional Canadian negotiating approach would need to have a much larger scope to have any hope of achieving a full exception covering all aspects of cultural heritage, and ensuring compliance with all Canada's obligations under international legal instruments including the UNESCO treaties. Canada has already made major negotiation concessions in the CETA by agreeing on an asymmetric and limited cultural exception based on cultural reservations at the provincial and federal levels.[26]

Conclusion

There was a fundamental difference in the CETA and TPP negotiating dynamics that ultimately determined the limits of the cultural exception in both agreements. European member states had no opposition in principle to the idea of protecting culture, and both the EU and Canada are parties to the 2005 UNESCO Convention. Divisions between Canadian and EU negotiators in the CETA process related to the means of giving effect to UNESCO obligations and how to express this as a cultural exception in the agreement, as well as the scope of the exception. In the TPP negotiations, the U.S. and several other countries were radically opposed to the idea of acknowledging a distinction between cultural products and other commercial products, as well as to recognizing the legitimacy of state intervention for protecting or promoting national cultural expressions.

Though Canadian negotiators took a similar approach on culture in the TPP as they did in the CETA, and even had allies at the TPP table, Canada fell far short of attaining the moderately effective cultural exception that has been sought by previous Canadian governments in all free-trade agreements. Instead, the outcomes far more closely reflect the views and interests of the U.S. government and entertainment industry. This is a setback for Canadian advocates of cultural diversity and their international allies. It is far from clear whether the partial and fragmented cultural exclusions the Canadian government ultimately settled for in the TPP can be relied on to adequately safeguard Canadian cultural identity and industries in the future.

CHAPTER 9
The Trouble with
the TPP's Copyright Rules

Michael Geist

As the Trans-Pacific Partnership (TPP) negotiations neared a conclusion in 2015, the intellectual property chapter generated enormous concern from copyright experts who feared it would dramatically alter the balance between the interests of creators and users. Those concerns were borne out by the final text, which significantly exceeds international norms, pays short shrift to user interests, and requires legislative changes in many countries including Canada. How did we get here?

Remember that Canada was not an initial participant in the TPP negotiations. The Harper government began working on entry into the TPP in 2009, leading to a formal request, in 2011, for participation in the negotiations.[1] When, a year later, the U.S. held a consultation on the possibility of Canada joining the talks, the International Intellectual Property Alliance (IIPA), the lead lobby group for the movie, music and software industry, urged against it until a Canadian copyright bill could be passed that satisfied U.S. expectations. The Canadian government promised it would oblige this request, and noted it had signed the Anti-Counterfeiting Trade Agreement (ACTA).[2]

The U.S. demands had an enormous impact on the contents of the 2012 Canadian copyright bill, particularly its restrictive digital-lock rules, which were at the very top of the U.S. priority list.[3] The Canadian government was not shy about acknowledging how much pressure the U.S. was bringing to bear. For example, Canada enacted anticounterfeiting legislation in 2014 that James Moore, then industry minister, admitted to be one of the U.S. conditions for TPP participation.[4] Moore said,

> *This legislation contributes to a more effective relationship between Canada and the United States on raising Canada to the international standard and meeting the standard that the American government frankly asked the government of Canada to meet in order for us to move forward with our participation in the Trans-Pacific Partnership negotiations so we think we've checked all the necessary boxes.*

Even with those changes, the U.S. used the TPP negotiations to pressure Canada into making even more copyright reforms. This chapter examines the policy implications of three of the biggest: term extension, digital locks and the role of Internet intermediaries.

Copyright term extension

The term of copyright in Canada is presently set at the life of the author plus an additional fifty years, which is consistent with the international standard in the Berne Convention. This is also the standard in half of TPP countries: Japan, Malaysia, New Zealand, Brunei and Vietnam also provide protection for life-plus-fifty years. The TPP will add twenty years to the term of copyright protection in Canada and these countries.

From a Canadian perspective, the issue of extending the term of copyright was raised on several prior occasions and consistently rejected by governments and trade negotiators. For example, term extension was discussed during the 2009 national copyright consultation, but the Canadian government decided against it. Furthermore, the European Union initially demanded that Canada extend the term of copyright in the proposed Canada–EU Comprehensive Economic and Trade Agreement (CETA), but that too was effectively rebuffed.[5]

From a policy perspective, the decision to maintain the international standard of life plus fifty years is consistent with the evidence that term extension creates harms by leaving Canadians with an additional twenty years during which no new works will enter the public domain, with virtually no gains in terms of new creativity. In other words, in a policy world in which copyright strives to balance creativity and access, term extension restricts access but does not enhance creativity. This has been confirmed by many economists, including in a study commissioned by Industry Canada (now the Department of Innovation, Science and Economic Development).[6] Moreover, studies in other countries that have extended copyright terms conclude it ultimately costs consumers as additional royalties are sent out of the country.[7] In the case of the TPP, the term extension is a major windfall for the United States and a net loss for Canada (and most other TPP countries). In fact, New Zealand, which faces a similar requirement, has estimated the extension alone will cost its economy NZ$55 million (about C$51 million) per year.[8] The Canadian cost is undoubtedly far higher.[9]

The damage caused by the term extension involves more than just higher costs to consumers and educational institutions. It also creates a massive blow to access to Canadian heritage.[10] In the fall of 2015, Broadview Press, an independent academic publisher that has been a vocal proponent of copyright, warned about the dangers of the term extension to its business and the academic community.[11] Broadview CEO Don LePan described how "unlimited, or excessively long, copyright terms have often kept scholars from publishing (or even obtaining access to) material of real historical or cultural significance." He held up Broadview's editions of *Mrs. Dalloway* and *The Great Gatsby* as examples of top-notch texts available in Canada but not the U.S. where terms are longer. The publisher is

> *looking at publishing similar editions of works by other*
> *authors who have been dead for more than fifty but fewer*
> *than seventy years — works such as Orwell's* Animal
> Farm *and* 1984, *for example; a Broadview edition of such*
> *works, with the appendices of contextual materials that*
> *are a feature of almost every Broadview edition, would*
> *provide highly valuable context for students at all levels.*

We are also looking forward to January 1, 2016, when we will finally be able to make the superb Broadview edition of [T.S. Eliot's] The Waste Land and other Poems *— with its excellent explanatory notes and extensive range of background material on modernism — available in Canada.*

If the TPP is approved in Canada, wrote LePan, "say goodbye to those Orwell and Eliot editions." The TPP-mandated copyright term extension would likewise directly affect twenty-two Governor General's Award–winning fiction and nonfiction authors whose work would take decades longer to enter the public domain.[12] These include Margaret Laurence, Gabrielle Roy, Marian Engel, Marshall McLuhan and Donald Creighton (see box). In addition to Canadian authors there are many well-known international figures that will be kept out of the public domain in Canada, such as John Steinbeck, Martin Luther King, Andy Warhol, Woody Guthrie and Elvis Presley.

Not quite public domain

Governor General's Award–winning books scheduled to enter the public domain over the next twenty years that will have to wait until after 2037 if the TPP is ratified:

Fiction
- Igor Sergeyevich Gouzenko (*The Fall of a Titan*)
- Winifred Estella Bambrick (*Continental Revue*)
- Colin Malcolm McDougall DSO (*Execution*)
- Germaine Guèvremont (*The Outlander*)
- Philip Albert Child (*Mr. Ames Against Time*)
- Gabrielle Roy (*The Tin Flute*)
- Jean Margaret Laurence (*The Stone Angel, A Jest of God*)
- Marian Engel (*Bear*)
- Hugh Garner (*Hugh Garner's Best Stories*)

Non-fiction

- James Frederick Church Wright (*Slava Bohu*)
- Laura Goodman Salverson (*Confessions of an Immigrant's Daughter*)
- Edgar Wardell McInnis (*The Unguarded Frontier*)
- Evelyn M. Richardson (*We Keep a Light*)
- William Sclater (*Haida*)
- Marjorie Elliott Wilkins Campbell (*The Saskatchewan*)
- William Lewis Morton (*The Progressive Party in Canada*)
- Josephine Phelan (*The Ardent Exile*)
- Donald Grant Creighton (*John A. Macdonald, The Young Politician*)
- Frank Hawkins Underhill (*In Search of Canadian Liberalism*)
- Herbert Marshall McLuhan (*The Gutenberg Galaxy*)
- Noah Story (*The Oxford Companion to Canadian History and Literature*)
- Francis Reginald Scott (*Essays On the Constitution*)

While the damage to the public domain in Canada stands as one of the worst aspects of the TPP's intellectual property chapter, there is the potential for an implementation approach that would mitigate some of the harm. As Australian law professor Kim Weatherall points out in her excellent review of the TPP copyright provisions, earlier versions of the agreement would have prohibited the implementation of any formalities, such as registration, for copyright.[13] The no-formalities rule was dropped from the final TPP text.[14]

The Berne Convention prohibits the use of formalities for works covered by the treaty, but Canada could conceivably treat the term beyond Berne (i.e., the twenty years after life-plus-fifty-years) as a supplementary regime that falls outside of the Berne standard.[15] If Canada (and potentially other countries) treated the additional protection as supplemental, it could require copyright registration and notification of the extended term in order to qualify for further protection. Copyright registration would not eliminate all the harm to the public domain, but it would mean that only those who desire the extension would take the positive steps to get it, thereby reducing the costs of the TPP's unnecessary copyright term extension.

Digital locks

One of the most controversial aspects of the 2012 Canadian copyright reform process involved the anti-circumvention provisions, often referred to as "digital lock" rules. The U.S. pressured Canada to include anti-circumvention rules, which were required for ratification of the WIPO Internet treaties, within the copyright reform package. They feature legal protections for technological protection measures (TPMs, a broader umbrella that captures digital rights management, or DRM) and rights management information (RMI). TPMs can be used to control access to, and use of, digital content. The proliferation of TPMs alongside legislation designed to protect digital locks represents a perfect storm of danger to consumers, who may find themselves locked out of content they have already purchased, while sacrificing their privacy and free speech rights in the process.

There was an enormous amount of scholarly analysis on these issues throughout Canada's reform process.[16] Moreover, McGill University professor David Lametti, now a Liberal MP and the parliamentary secretary for international trade, wrote about the incoherence of digital-lock rules.[17] The academic analysis was decidedly negative about the legal reforms, as was that of the broader public, which made the issue a top priority as part of the 2009 Canadian copyright consultation.[18]

This background is necessary, since it is important to understand that the digital-lock rules currently found in Canadian copyright law already represent a government decision to cave to U.S. pressure to go far beyond what is required of governments under the WIPO Internet treaties. It should also be noted that the digital-lock rules introduced by the Liberals in a 2005 bill were far more flexible and balanced than the ones passed by the Conservative government in its 2012 legislation. Yet, despite the 2012 reforms, the TPP will require Canada to make further changes to its digital-lock rules and lock Canada into a "WIPO+" model that removes the ability to restore the flexibility found in the WIPO Internet treaties. In other words, once the TPP takes effect, the restrictive digital-lock rules will be locked into Canadian law.

The TPP affects both the rights management information rules and technological protection measures provisions. For RMI, Article 18.69 of the TPP requires Canada to add criminal liability to the list of potential remedies. This marks a significant change from the 2012 copyright reform package, reflecting a U.S. desire for increased criminalization of copyright law. Canada opposed the change during the TPP negotiations, at least up to the Hawaii round in August 2015, but ultimately caved in the final draft.[19] There are no similar criminal requirements in the pending Canada–EU trade agreement.

Article 18.68 of the TPP contains extensive requirements for technological protection measures that go beyond what is required by the WIPO Internet treaties. In fact, the TPP digital-lock rules also exceed those found in CETA and the Canada–South Korea Free Trade Agreement, with more restrictive rules on the creation of circumvention exceptions as well as criminal liability requirements.[20] While these other agreements — whether the WIPO Internet treaties or other trade agreements — permit more flexible approaches, if the TPP takes effect it will trump them for Canadian law purposes by requiring a different standard for digital-lock protection.

The restrictive approach in the TPP may also apply to the creation of new digital-lock exceptions. As part of the contentious debate over the implementation of anti-circumvention rules in Canadian copyright law in 2012, the government tried to assure concerned stakeholders it had established specific mechanisms within the law to create additional exceptions to the general rule against circumvention. The law includes a handful of exceptions for issues such as security or privacy protection, but there is also a process for adding new limitations to the general rule.

There are two possible avenues for new limitations and exceptions. First, Section 41.21(1) of the *Copyright Act* allows the Governor in Council to make regulations for an exception where the law would otherwise "unduly restrict competition."[21] Second, Section 41.21(2)(a) identifies other circumstances to consider for exceptions, including whether the circumvention rules could adversely affect the fair-dealing criteria in the act.[22] In addition to those two potential regulation-making models for new exceptions and limitations, Canadian law also establishes the possibility of creating a positive requirement on rights holders to unlock their locked content. It states that the Governor in Council may make regulations

requiring the owner of the copyright in a work, a performer's
performance fixed in a sound recording or a sound recording
that is protected by a technological protection measure to
provide access to the work, performer's performance fixed
in a sound recording or sound recording to persons who
are entitled to the benefit of any of the limitations on the
application of paragraph 41.1(1)(a) prescribed under
paragraph (a). The regulations may prescribe the manner in
which, and the time within which, access is to be provided,
as well as any conditions that the owner of the copyright is
to comply with. [23]

This is not like other limitations or exceptions in the legislation, as it does not envision the possibility of permitting a user to circumvent a digital lock. Instead, it lays the groundwork to create a requirement to unlock content. However, the TPP may still not permit even this flexibility. Article 18.68.4(i) of the intellectual property chapter is limited to creating exceptions or limitations on the prohibition against circumvention, and does not include language to permit mandated unlocking.[24] It says,

a Party may provide certain limitations and exceptions to
the measures implementing paragraph 1(a) or paragraph
1(b) in order to enable non-infringing uses if there is an
actual or likely adverse impact of those measures on those
non-infringing uses, as determined through a legislative,
regulatory, or administrative process in accordance with
the Party's law, giving due consideration to evidence when
presented in that process, including with respect to whether
appropriate and effective measures have been taken by rights
holders to enable the beneficiaries to enjoy the limitations
and exceptions to copyright and related rights under that
Party's law.[25]

The absence of a positive obligation to unlock is not surprising since it is not found in U.S. law. The Canadian government may try to argue that a positive obligation to provide unlocked content is a form of exception, yet the TPP adds another weapon to the arsenal of rights holders steadfastly opposing this type of requirement.

Copyright takedowns

The TPP's effort to regulate how Internet service providers (ISPs) and hosts address allegations of copyright infringement on their networks and sites was another major issue addressed by negotiators. The goals of the U.S. and Canadian governments in the talks were clear from the outset: the U.S. wanted to export the notice-and-takedown system in its *Digital Millennium Copyright Act* (DMCA) to the rest of the TPP, while Canada wanted to preserve its newly created notice-and-notice approach. In fact, Canada rushed through the notice-and-notice system without regulations (causing major problems of misleading notices) in order to argue that it should not be required to adopt the U.S. approach.[26] The hallmark of the U.S. system is that it requires content takedowns without court oversight. By contrast, the Canadian approach, which has operated informally for over a decade but took effect as a law in 2015, seeks to balance the interests of copyright holders, the privacy rights of Internet users and the legal obligations of Internet providers.

Under the Canadian notice-and-notice system, copyright owners are entitled to send infringement notices to Internet providers, who are legally required to forward the notifications to their subscribers. The notices must include details on the sender, the copyright works and the alleged infringement. If the Internet provider fails to forward the notification, it must explain why or face the prospect of damages that run as high as $10,000. Internet providers must also retain information on the subscriber for six months (or 12 months if court proceedings are launched). For ISPs, the system creates significant costs for processing and forwarding notices. However, assuming they meet their obligations of forwarding the notice, the law grants them a legal "safe harbour" that removes potential liability for the actions of their subscribers.

The TPP compromise allows Canada to maintain the notice-and-notice system, but no other TPP member country can adopt it in order to comply with the ISP liability and notice rules in the intellectual property chapter. The Canadian rules can be found in Annex 18-E of the intellectual property chapter, which states that the standard ISP rules in the agreement do not apply to a country that meets the conditions of the annex "as from the date of agreement in principle of this Agreement." Since that date is now long passed (October 4, 2015), no other TPP country can implement the notice-and-notice system to meet its TPP obligations. It should be noted that Chile, which objected to the special treatment for Canada, obtained a similar exception for its system based on Annex 18-F of the U.S.–Chile Free Trade Agreement.

The compromise highlights one of the major sources of trouble with the TPP. More than a mere trade agreement, the TPP is a clear effort by the U.S. to export its regulatory framework to other countries, creating a competitive advantage for U.S. companies. Canada and Chile were able to push back to retain their systems, but no other TPP country (present or future) will be permitted to adopt those systems to meet their treaty obligations. This compromise presumably comes at the behest of the major U.S. movie, music and software industries, which have used their lead lobby group to criticize both Canada and Chile over their systems.[27]

For those countries stuck with the TPP's implementation of U.S. law, University of Idaho professor Annemarie Bridy points out that the agreement is "less speech-protective and more prone to over-enforcement and abuse."[28] For example, the TPP does not contain a mandatory counter-notice system that would allow users to effectively challenge claims of infringement by requiring providers to repost their content. Moreover, the TPP has fewer requirements for the contents of takedown notices as compared to the DMCA, with no requirement for rights holders to state their good-faith belief that the content in the notice infringes copyright. The absence of a good-faith-belief requirement is a major omission given that it has played a role in litigation in the U.S. where rights holders misuse the takedown system.

The decision to lock in the DMCA notice-and-takedown system within the TPP comes just as the U.S. Copyright Office undertakes a public study of its costs and burdens on rights holders, service providers and the general public.[29] As with the discussion above on digital locks, the risk that the

TPP may mandate a particular approach that limits domestic reforms is an enormous problem for all stakeholders, regardless of their perspective.

Perhaps the most telling provision in the Internet provider section comes at the very end, in Article 18.82.9, which states, "The Parties recognize the importance, in implementing their obligations under this Article, of taking into account the impacts on right holders and Internet Service Providers." [30] There is no reference to users or the general public, as if those impacts simply do not matter. This reflects the TPP negotiating approach in which the broader public is not even an afterthought. It is missing altogether.

Conclusion

Canadian policy-makers have long recognized that domestic copyright policy interests are best served by multilateral negotiations, which enable the development of consensus positions that meet international minimum standards but allow for flexible implementation. The copyright provisions in the TPP reflect the risk of bilateral and plurilateral talks, which can often lead to U.S.-dominated policies being foisted on other participants. The copyright provisions in the TPP's intellectual property chapter crystallize those concerns, leading to the potential for millions of dollars in royalty payments being transferred out of Canada, the increased criminalization of copyright law and a loss of policy flexibility for future Canadian copyright reforms.

CHAPTER 10
Signed, Sealed and Delivered? The TPP and Canada's Public Postal Service

Daniel Sheppard and Louis Century

In 1867, months after Confederation, the Parliament of Canada enacted legislation creating a single, public postal system. It was a significant endeavour, and an essential one for a new country that needed to connect and unite disparate communities over large distances. On the eve of Canada's hundred-and-fiftieth birthday, our public postal service continues to play this role, in particular for remote communities with low levels of infrastructure. In many places, the post office is the only face of the federal government, and a primary point of access to the rest of the country.

The right to a universal postal service is recognized in international law. Article 3.1 of the Universal Postal Convention, to which Canada is a party, affirms "the right to a universal postal service involving the permanent provision of quality basic postal services at all points in [member countries'] territory, at affordable prices." This right is reflected in the *Canada Post Corporation Act*, which defines the objectives of our public postal service to include providing a standard of service that "will meet the needs of the people of Canada," and that, despite Canada's vast geography, "is similar with respect to communities of the same size."[1]

The act also requires that Canada Post provide the above services on a "self-sustaining financial basis," i.e., that the postal service should pay for itself. While its postage rates must be "fair and reasonable," they must also be "consistent so far as possible with providing a revenue, together with any revenue from other sources, sufficient to defray the costs incurred" by Canada Post in fulfilling its universal service mandate.

This challenge — to provide affordable postal services to all Canadians in a cost-effective manner — has become more difficult in recent years, as developments in communications technology have contributed to a decline in physical mail volumes. In order to remain financially sustainable while still achieving its public interest mandate, Canada Post has expanded to provide services that complement the delivery of letter mail, notably parcel and express delivery services.

The Canadian public cares deeply about the future of public postal services and Canada Post. Just observe the widespread public backlash following the reduction of door-to-door mail delivery under the Conservative government of Stephen Harper. The Liberal government of Justin Trudeau campaigned on a platform to "save" home mail delivery, and, in May 2016, it announced an independent review of Canada Post, "to ensure Canadians receive quality postal services at a reasonable price."[2] This review included public consultations and an examination of potential new revenue-generating lines of business for the corporation. For instance, some argue that Canada Post should follow the model of other industrialized countries by expanding into the provision of basic financial services, also known as postal banking. In announcing the review, the minister of public services and procurement, Judy Foote, said the government was "not ruling out anything" when it came to potential new lines of business.[3]

Unfortunately, any consultative project for reinventing Canada's public postal service must contend with a medley of international trade rules, including those contained in the recently finalized Trans-Pacific Partnership trade agreement (TPP). If ratified, the TPP would create binding obligations on Canada that are enforceable through arbitration proceedings initiated by any of the eleven other signatory states, and in some cases by corporations from those states. Many general rules in the TPP may have an impact on how Canada Post functions today and in the future. The agreement also contains a surprising number of rules targeting postal services that were inserted at the request of U.S. industry groups, notably express delivery services and insurance companies. In contrast to the Canada Post review currently underway, these rules in the TPP were negotiated in secret by trade negotiators and lobbyists, on a fast-tracked basis, without parliamentary oversight or public consultation.

In this chapter we will determine the extent to which the rules contained in the TPP may constrain the current and future activities of Canada Post. This is not an easy task. Much of the TPP language is broad, vague or novel. The application of the rules therein to Canada Post will turn on complex factual considerations and the interpretations of governments and international arbitrators. We focus primarily on how the TPP may impact Canada Post's *current* integrated service model involving the monopoly provision of letter mail supported by revenues from courier and express delivery services.

We conclude that the TPP would not necessarily render Canada Post's current activities unlawful or firmly close the door to innovation in the future. However, the TPP's convoluted, overlapping and ambiguous rules, many of which directly respond to industry lobbying, create real risks of future trade and investment disputes triggered by corporations or member states unhappy with Canada's policy choices in the area of postal services. The risk of costly trade litigation, even when it is largely hypothetical, can influence policy decisions at the front end. On the back end there would always be a possibility that international arbitrators would rule against Canada. These risks could have been avoided had Canada included better reservations to the TPP rules affecting postal services, as some other countries did.

Funding universal letter mail through express delivery services

The TPP does not require the privatization of Canada Post, or insist that its monopoly over letter mail services should be broken up. In fact, by defining limits on the scope of postal monopolies, the TPP presupposes that states can and will maintain public postal systems.[4] But the trade deal does create serious economic challenges for Canada Post by threatening its ability to perform more profitable, non-core services that help make letter mail delivery economically feasible. It is these economic challenges that should concern anyone who wishes to see Canada maintain a viable, universal public postal service across the country.

Providing letter mail service to many of Canada's remote and rural communities is not economically viable on its own. In the past, fees charged on high-volume, lower-cost postal routes in major urban centres provided the revenue to offset unprofitable routes. However, dramatic changes in communications infrastructure have disrupted this model by reducing reliance on letter mail for many Canadians. In 2015, Canada Post delivered 1.6 billion fewer letters than it did in 2006.[5] The rapid and sustained decline in Canada Post's main line of business has required the corporation to find other ways to subsidize service to rural Canada. To date, its most profitable innovation has been entry into the express delivery services industry.

Express delivery services involve the expedited collection, transport and delivery of papers, parcels or other goods while tracking and maintaining control of the items throughout the process. The industry is a key component of the modern e-commerce economy. Long dominated by global logistics companies like FedEx and UPS, the express delivery sector has proven to be highly profitable. While global letter mail volumes have been in steady decline for some twenty years, express delivery services generate in excess of US$130 billion (about C$167 billion) globally, with an annual growth rate of 6 per cent since 1998.[6] It is not at all surprising that postal systems the world over, including Canada Post, have chosen to enter this lucrative field.

Involvement in the express delivery industry has been a highly profitable endeavour for Canada Post. Between 2014 and 2015, while Canada Post saw a 6.1 per cent decline in letters sent, parcel delivery grew by an astonishing 9.7 per cent.[7] Parcels generated over $1.6 billion for Canada Post that year, making up over a quarter of the corporation's 2015 revenue.[8] Without the operation of Xpresspost, Canada Post's brand for its express delivery service, the corporation would have operated at a loss.

Canada Post is also involved in the express delivery market through its 91 per cent stake in Purolator, the Mississauga-based global delivery company. Founded in 1960, Purolator was acquired by Canada Post in 1993 for $55 million. In 2014, Purolator generated pre-tax earnings of over $73 million, offering an additional source of revenue for Canada Post in the express delivery industry. Both of these express delivery services have been foundational in maintaining Canada Post's profitability, and its ability to meet the universal service mandate.

Industry efforts to dismantle Canada Post's integrated service model

Canada Post's involvement in express delivery services, including its relationship with Purolator, has been a source of controversy and risk. Competitor companies, most notably UPS, have long argued that Canada Post's relationship with Purolator is not only anticompetitive but also unlawful under international trade rules. In 2000, UPS launched a lawsuit against the government of Canada under the North American Free Trade Agreement (NAFTA), raising numerous allegations related to issues as diverse as pension regulation and customs processing rules. Among the various complaints UPS raised were allegations that Canada Post violated rules related to equal treatment for foreign investments and competition policy by granting Purolator access to its infrastructure and facilities (thousands of post offices and delivery networks across the country) while denying equal access to UPS, and that Canada Post's own courier services unfairly took advantage of monopoly infrastructure. UPS launched a similar case under European Union competition rules after the European Commission signed off on Deutsche Post's acquisition of a significant interest in DHL.[9]

UPS lost both lawsuits, but the company never abandoned its campaign against these kinds of arrangements by national postal entities. In parallel to their legal battles in North America and Europe under existing trade rules, UPS and other private companies aggressively lobbied the U.S. government for new trade rules that would, from their perspective, level the playing field. These efforts saw expression in a number of bilateral trade agreements between the U.S. and other countries that included special provisions related to express delivery services.

For example, the 2003 Chile–U.S. Free Trade Agreement (FTA) required that Chile, but not the U.S., refrain from imposing new restrictions on express delivery services in its territory.[10] The 2004 Australia–U.S. FTA included language designed to restrict the ability of state postal monopolies to compete with private companies in the express delivery market.[11]

The U.S. also enacted domestic reforms in 2006 that prohibited "subsidization [by the U.S. Postal Service] of competitive products by market-dominant products."[12]

The TPP replicates and expands upon these targeted provisions, and can rightly be seen as representing the high-water mark for efforts by the express delivery industry to establish international trade rules that serve its objectives. Their crowning achievement is Annex 10-B – *Express Delivery Services* of the TPP's services chapter (Chapter 10), which directly targets how postal systems are permitted to operate in the express delivery market. As acknowledged by the U.S. Trade Representative (USTR), the annex was included "to address the unique challenges private suppliers face when competing with national postal entities in express delivery," and includes "new commitments that address longstanding issues for U.S. service suppliers."[13]

The express delivery services annex: a coup for courier companies

The TPP annex on express delivery services imposes a wide range of restrictions and rules that challenge arrangements such as those between Canada Post and Purolator, and even how postal services can engage in express delivery directly, such as through Xpresspost. In doing so, the annex raises the real risk that Canada Post's use of express delivery revenues to maintain universal domestic postal services could be subject to more trade challenges.

The express delivery annex contains two key rules that could challenge Canada Post's continued operations in the express delivery sector. The first prohibits a postal service using money generated from monopoly activities (i.e., the delivery of letter mail) to "cross-subsidize" its own or anyone else's express delivery services.[14] The second rule requires that postal monopolies not "abuse [their] monopoly position" in a way that treats foreign companies (like UPS) less favourably than domestic ones (like Purolator) or undermines cross-border trade in services between signatory states.[15] These provisions go well beyond comparable rules in existing trade agreements such as NAFTA or the World Trade Organization's General Agreement on Trade in Services (GATS).

It is hard to predict what these rules will mean for Canada Post's continued work in the express delivery market. For one thing, the prohibition against cross-subsidization is remarkably difficult to apply in practice. The allegation, broadly speaking, is that Canada Post uses revenues from its exclusive privilege letter operations to subsidize express courier services (both Xpresspost and Purolator). Numerous investigations and reviews, including by Canada Post's auditors, consistently found no evidence of direct financial cross-subsidization.[16] However, this does not preclude arguments by unsatisfied companies that cross-subsidization is occurring indirectly.

The TPP may offer a new venue to assert such claims since the express delivery services annex speaks of "subsidies" in general. International trade law also recognizes the concept of an *indirect* subsidy, which might include the use of mail delivery infrastructure developed over decades to facilitate the processing, tracking and shipment of packages.[17] But evaluating the existence of an indirect subsidy, particularly within a fully integrated corporation like Canada Post, would be extremely difficult conceptually and empirically. Claims that a dominant position is being abused — the second significant rule in the annex — can also be factually complex.[18] Regardless of how difficult it is to work though such arguments, the existence of rules in the TPP directly targeting postal operators constitutes a significant risk that Canada Post's current operations will be scrutinized, criticized and potentially challenged.

State-owned enterprises, designated monopolies, and noncommercial assistance

While the TPP's express delivery services annex poses the most specific and obvious risk to Canada Post's ability to maintain profitability through parcel delivery, several of the agreement's more general provisions present challenges to the corporation's links to Xpresspost and Purolator. Chapter 17 of the TPP contains extensive, complex rules related to state-owned enterprises (SOEs) and "designated monopolies," which would apply to Canada Post and Purolator. Among other things, these rules would prohibit Canada Post from using its monopoly in the letter delivery market to engage — even indirectly through a subsidiary — in anticompetitive practices, in a nonmonopoly market, that negatively impact trade or investment between TPP members.[19] This rule is broader than NAFTA's comparable competition and SOE rules.[20]

Chapter 17 of the TPP also contains expansive rules, unparalleled in prior trade agreements, regulating the provision of "non-commercial assistance" (NCA) to SOEs.[21] The novelty and complexity of the NCA rules makes any prediction of their impact speculative. But the argument has been made, despite any evidence supporting this assertion, that by granting Purolator access to Canada Post infrastructure the latter provides the courier a form of noncommercial assistance.[22]

The TPP requires parties to ensure that their SOEs, like Canada Post, do not provide noncommercial assistance to other SOEs, like Purolator, in a manner that has "adverse effects on the interests of another Party" with respect to the SOE's supply of services into the territory of other TPP parties.[23] To the extent that Purolator's access to Canada Post infrastructure assists it when it comes to its global delivery operations in other TPP member states, this rule provides a further way for the corporation's opponents to argue its activities are unlawful under trade agreements.

The risk of investor–state claims

Neither the express delivery annex nor the SOE and NCA rules of Chapter 17 are subject to the TPP's investor–state dispute settlement (ISDS) system in which foreign investors are permitted to sue a country before international arbitrators for allegedly breaching the agreement's generous investment protections.[24] In other words, while a TPP country could bring a claim regarding postal services against Canada based on these rules, a corporation like UPS could not, or at least not directly. However, a corporation could bring a claim against Canada under some other provision of the TPP that is subject to ISDS, and argue that the rules discussed above should be used as "interpretive aids" to help ground a claim under that other provision.

Like NAFTA, the TPP's investment chapter contains rules safeguarding a foreign investor's right to national treatment and most-favoured-nation treatment, as well as a more vague "minimum standard of treatment." Investors are also protected from direct and indirect expropriation without compensation.[25] All of these protections *are* subject to ISDS and could be used to creatively bring a case that incorporates the postal services rules discussed above.

It is tempting to take some comfort from the decision in *UPS v. Canada* under NAFTA's ISDS process, where a majority of arbitrators rejected the company's claims against Canada Post, many of which were similar to the issues discussed above. However, we cannot lose sight of the fact the TPP is a different agreement than NAFTA; there is no guarantee international arbitrators would interpret its rules in the same way. Given that past ISDS awards are persuasive, not binding, on future arbitrators, and the NAFTA award was not unanimous (a dissenting arbitrator would have found for UPS on at least some of its claims), it is not so difficult to imagine a similar challenge under the TPP resulting in a different outcome.

One thing is certain: the TPP is unique in multilateral trade agreements in its dedicated focus on postal services and their interaction with express delivery. This alone represents a new kind of risk to Canada Post's current activities. It would be very serious if these rules do ultimately get interpreted as prohibiting the kind of integrated letter mail and express delivery service model that characterizes Canada Post today. The current "solution" to the problem of providing universal service in an era of declining letter mail would be seriously challenged, and could force Canada Post to look elsewhere for new revenue streams.

Conclusion

For those who are concerned about the future of Canada Post it is perhaps most frustrating that all of the challenges described here were entirely avoidable. The TPP, like most trade agreements, permits states to exclude existing and future measures, or entire sectors, from its services and investment obligations through the use of reservations. For example, Canada took advantage of the agreement's Annex I and II reservations to protect cultural industries, which has the effect of protecting Canada Post from trade challenges regarding assistance it provides in the delivery of Canadian periodicals.[26]

Other countries, however, went much further in protecting their public postal services from the impact of international trade rules. Japan reserved "the right to adopt or maintain any measure relating to investments in or the supply of. . .postal services in Japan."[27] Singapore reserved "the right to adopt or maintain any measure relating to a Public Postal Licensee."[28] Canada could have included its own reservation granting Canada Post general protections. Yet, behind the closed doors of the TPP's secret negotiations, Canadian negotiators decided, for unknown reasons, not to do so. As a result, we are left with a trade agreement that combines broad, generally applicable rules with specific sections and annexes that directly and explicitly target Canada Post.

It is unfortunate that Canada agreed to these ill-defined new rules, which cast doubt on the federal government's policy-making authority in respect of postal services at the very moment when the public is participating in a consultative project to reimagine the role of our public postal service. Legal interpretations aside, the TPP is a powerful tool that can and will be used by companies to lobby against, and potentially challenge, Canada Post initiatives that cut into their bottom line. The TPP is not fatal to Canada Post's current integrated business model, nor should it impede expansion into new lines of business, but it introduces a number of risky factors into the calculus. It is more than fair to ask whether these new risks are worth it.

CONTRIBUTORS

LOUIS CENTURY is a lawyer at Goldblatt Partners LLP and former law clerk to Justice Richard Wagner of the Supreme Court of Canada. Louis has a diverse civil litigation practice that includes professional regulation, class actions, employment law, police misconduct and constitutional law. He is also a fellow of the Philippe Kirsch Institute.

MICHAEL GEIST is a law professor at the University of Ottawa where he holds the Canada Research Chair in Internet and E-commerce Law. He has a bachelor of laws from Osgoode Hall Law School in Toronto, masters of laws from Cambridge University in the UK and Columbia Law School in New York, and a doctorate in law from Columbia Law School. He has written extensively about the TPP and its implications for digital policy in Canada.

JOHN JACOBS is an international economic policy analyst. His work examines the impact of Canadian trade and investment agreements on mining and economic development within Canada and internationally. He has a PhD from the School of Public Policy and Administration and the Institute of Political Economy at Carleton University and an MA from the International Institute of Social Studies in The Hague, Netherlands. He is the author of numerous public policy publications, a former columnist with the *Chronicle Herald* and a research associate with the Canadian Centre for Policy Alternatives.

ALEXANDRE LAROUCHE-MALTAIS holds a BA in international relations and international law from the University of Quebec in Montreal, as well as a master's degree in international law from the Graduate Institute in Geneva. As former International Trade and Legal Affairs Consultant within the United Nations Conference on Trade and Development (UNCTAD), Alexandre was involved in a trade-related technical assistance program for implementing the World Trade Organization's (WTO) Trade Facilitation Agreement in developing and least-developed countries since 2015. Prior to joining UNCTAD, he worked within the Africa office and the trade facilitation and policy for business section of the International Trade Centre (ITC) in Geneva. From 2010 to 2015, Alexandre worked as a research project manager for l'*Institut de recherche en économie contemporaine* (IREC) on international trade issues.

JOEL LEXCHIN received his MD from the University of Toronto in 1977. He is an emeritus professor in the School of Health Policy and Management at York University in Toronto where he taught health policy. He has worked for twenty-eight years in the emergency department of Toronto's University Health Network and is the author or co-author of over 150 peer-reviewed articles on a wide variety of topics concerned with Canadian and international pharmaceutical policy. His book *Private Profit versus Public Policy: The Pharmaceutical Industry and the Canadian State* was published by University of Toronto Press at the end of October 2016.

ANGELLA MacEWEN is an economist with the Canadian Labour Congress, a research associate with the Canadian Centre for Policy Alternatives and a policy fellow with the Broadbent Institute. She has an undergraduate degree in international development studies from Saint Mary's University in Halifax and a master's degree in economics from Dalhousie University. Her areas of expertise include international trade and economic development, labour market issues and social policy analysis.

LAURA MACDONALD is a professor in the department of political science and the Institute of Political Economy at Carleton University. She has edited collections and published numerous articles in journals on such issues as the role of non-governmental organizations in development, global civil society, citizenship struggles in Latin America, Canadian development assistance and the political impact of the North American Free Trade Agreement (NAFTA) on human rights and democracy across the continent.

HADRIAN MERTINS-KIRKWOOD is a researcher at the Canadian Centre for Policy Alternatives where he focuses on federal and provincial climate-change policy in Canada. He is an ongoing contributor to the CCPA's Trade and Investment Research Project and Alternative Federal Budget.

DANIEL SHEPPARD is a lawyer at Goldblatt Partners LLP where he maintains a broad public law practice with a focus on constitutional litigation and public international law. He is also an adjunct professor at Osgoode Hall Law School where he serves as clinical director of the school's Test Case Litigation Program.

SCOTT SINCLAIR is a senior research fellow with the Canadian Centre for Policy Alternatives where he directs the Trade and Investment Research Project. He has written widely on the impacts of trade treaties and public interest regulation and was a former trade policy advisor with the government of British Columbia.

STUART TREW is the editor of the *CCPA Monitor*, a bimonthly publication of the Canadian Centre for Policy Alternatives. He was previously a trade researcher and campaigner with the Council of Canadians (2006–2014) and before that edited a weekly newspaper in Ottawa. He has a bachelor of journalism and political science from Carleton University.

GUS VAN HARTEN is a professor at Osgoode Hall Law School at York University. Previously he was a faculty member in the law department of the London School of Economics. He specializes in international investment law and administrative law. His books include *Sold Down the Yangtze: Canada's Lopsided Investment Deal with China* (Lorimer, 2015), *Sovereign Choices and Sovereign Constraints: Judicial Restraint in Investment Treaty Arbitration* (Oxford

University Press, 2013) and *Investment Treaty Arbitration and Public Law* (Oxford University Press, 2007).

JACQUELINE WILSON is a lawyer at the Canadian Environmental Law Association and works on law reform and litigation relating to trade, climate change, energy policy and water policy. Prior to joining CELA, Jacqueline was litigation counsel with Canada's Department of Justice. She received her JD degree from the University of Toronto in 2010.

ACKNOWLEDGEMENTS

The editors wish, first and foremost, to express their deep gratitude to all the authors who generously contributed to this project. We also wish to acknowledge Peter Bleyer, Bruce Campbell, Kerri-Anne Finn, Tim Scarth, Gary Schneider, Emily Turk and the staff at the Canadian Centre for Policy Alternatives. Special thanks are due to Hadrian Mertins-Kirkwood, who, in addition to contributing a chapter, assisted and provided input in various ways. We are grateful to Linda McQuaig for her generous comments and support. Thanks are also due to Jim Lorimer, Emma Renda and Laura Cook at James Lorimer & Company. Finally, we are grateful to the members of the Trade and Investment Research Project for their ongoing support.

ENDNOTES

INTRODUCING THE TPP

1. Canadian Press, "'This deal is, without any doubt whatsoever, in the best interests of the Canadian economy': Harper lauds TPP," *National Post*, October 5, 2015, http://news.nationalpost.com/news/canada/canadian-politics/this-deal-is-without-any-doubt-whatsoever-in-the-best-interests-of-the-canadian-economy-harper-lauds-tpp.

2. See, for example, Les Whittington, "Election 2015: A decade of change under Harper," *Toronto Star*, August 8, 2015, https://www.thestar.com/news/canada/2015/08/08/election-2015-a-decade-of-change-under-harper.html.

3. Angus Reid Strategies, "'Three Amigos' Summit: Just one-in-four Canadians say NAFTA has been good for their country," June 27, 2016, http://angusreid.org/three-amigos-summit-nafta.

4. One recent survey indicates that 87 per cent of Canadian business executives support Canada's ratification and implementation of the TPP. See Richard Blackwell, "Canadian executives back TPP, stronger ties with China," *The Globe and Mail*, June 19, 2016.

5. For example, David H. Autor, David Dorn and Gordon H. Hanson, "The China syndrome: Local labor market effects of import competition in the United States," *American Economic Review* 103, no. 6 (2013): 2121–68, http://economics.mit.edu/files/6613; Josh Bivens, "The Trans-Pacific Partnership is unlikely to be a good deal for American workers," Economic Policy Institute, Washington, April 16, 2015, http://www.epi.org/publication/tpp-unlikely-to-be-good-deal-for-american-workers/.

6. President Obama himself, addressing Parliament, observed: "If the benefits of globalization accrue only to those at the very top. . .then people will push back."

7. Stephen Clarkson, "NAFTA and the WTO as supraconstitution," in *Uncle Sam and Us: Globalization, Neoconservatism, and the Canadian State* (Toronto: University of Toronto Press, 2002), 49–72.

8. This point can be illustrated in Canada's case by the far more rapid phase-out period for import tariffs on Japanese vehicles (five years) in Canada versus the term of twenty-five to thirty years for the U.S., an imbalance that will encourage locating new auto assembly investment and reinvestment in the U.S. rather than Canada. See John Holmes and Jeffrey Carey, "The devil is in the details: The TPP's impact on the Canadian automotive industry," Canadian Centre for Policy Alternatives, July 7, 2016.

9. "USTR lawyer says TPP designed to accommodate U.S. certification requirement," *Inside U.S. Trade*, February 26, 2016. "The entry-into-force mechanism of the Trans-Pacific Partnership (TPP) was specifically designed to protect the ability of the United States to carry out its domestic requirement that the president not allow a trade agreement to enter into force until he has certified that each trading partner has complied with its obligations that take effect immediately, according to the lead U.S. lawyer on TPP."

10. Paul Koring, "China will have to play by TPP rules to join world's biggest free-trade league," *The Globe and Mail*, July 29, 2015.

11. In March 2016, the Philippines announced it was giving the U.S. access to four air bases and one army camp as outlined in a 2014 defence pact. That same month, the U.S. deployed three B-2 bombers to a naval support facility in the Indian Ocean in response to increased tensions between China and several countries bordering the South China Sea. The U.S. is also in talks with Japan and South Korea about installing missile defence systems in response to increased ballistic missile tests in North Korea — a move China also opposes. See Trefor Moss, "U.S. set to deploy troops to Philippines in rebalancing act," *Wall Street Journal*, March 20, 2016, http://www.wsj.com/articles/u-s-set-to-deploy-troops-to-philippines-in-rebalancing-act-1458466797); Oriana Pawlyk, "Air Force deploys B-2 bombers to Diego Garcia," *Air Force Times*, March 9, 2016, http://www.airforcetimes.com/story/military/2016/03/09/b-2s-deploy-diego-garcia-asia-pacific/81530974/; Bloomberg/Reuters, "Deployment of U.S. missile defence system could reshape security in East Asia," February 8, 2016, http://www.japantimes.co.jp/news/2016/02/08/asia-pacific/deployment-of-u-s-missile-defense-system-could-reshape-security-in-east-asia/#.V4aWRJMrIUE.

12. Dylan Chambers, "Far from a slam dunk: Eyeing the risks of the TPP for Vietnam," *The Diplomat*, Global Public Policy Institute, Berlin, July 8, 2016, http://thediplomat.com/2016/07/far-from-a-slam-dunk-eyeing-the-risks-of-the-tpp-for-vietnam/.

13. Jeronim Capaldo, Alex Izurieta and Jomo Kwame Sundaram, "Trading Down: Unemployment, Inequality and Other Risks of the Trans-Pacific Partnership Agreement," (working paper for the Global Development and Environment Institute at Tufts University, January 2016), http://www.ase.tufts.edu/gdae/policy_research/TPP_simulations.html.

14. Ali Dadkhah, Dan Ciuriak and Jingliang Xiao, "Better In than Out? Canada and the Trans-Pacific Partnership," C.D. Howe Institute, April 2016, https://www.cdhowe.org/public-policy-research/better-out-canada-and-trans-pacific-partnership.

15. Joseph E. Stiglitz, "The great divide: On the wrong side of globalization," *New York Times*, March 15, 2014, http://opinionator.blogs.nytimes.com/2014/03/15/on-the-wrong-side-of-globalization/?_r=0.

16. OECD, "Pharmaceutical Expenditure," in *Health at a Glance 2015.* (Paris: OECD Publishing, 2015), 178.

17. Recent data from the PMPRB clearly shows that extending monopoly protection and boosting brand-name drug company profits with the hope of generating higher levels of research and development (R&D), and more innovative medicines, has been a failure. For further discussion see the chapter by Scott Sinclair.

18. White House, "The Trans-Pacific partnership: What you need to know about President Obama's trade agreement," https://www.whitehouse.gov/issues/economy/trade.

19. In January 2016, the Citizens Trade Campaign sent a letter to all U.S. senators and congresspersons, signed by more than 1,500 labour and environmental organizations (including 350.org and Greenpeace), urging them to oppose the TPP, http://www.citizenstrade.org/ctc/wp-content/uploads/2016/01/TPPOppositionLetter_010716.pdf.

20. Josh Bivens, "Trade, jobs and wages," Economic Policy Institute Blog, May 6, 2008, http://www.epi.org/publication/ib244/.

21. "A record high of 70 investor-state dispute settlement (ISDS) cases were filed in 2015," according to UNCTAD, "Investor-state dispute settlement: Review of developments in 2015," June 2016, http://investmentpolicyhub.unctad.org/Publications/Details/144.

22. Van Harten's research indicates that 90 per cent of ordered compensation in foreign investor claims against countries went to corporations with over US$1 billion in annual revenue — most had over US$10 billion — or to individuals with over US$100 million in net wealth.

23. Daniel Tencer, "TransCanada's $15-billion lawsuit against Obama fires up anti-free trade movement," *Huffington Post Canada*, July 9, 2016, http://www.huffingtonpost.ca/2016/01/09/transcanada-nafta-keystone-isds_n_8945334.html; and "Greenpeace calls on Italy to reconsider position on EU-Canada trade deal," Greenpeace press release, June 10, 2016, http://www.greenpeace.org/eu-unit/en/News/2016/Greenpeace-calls-on-Italy-to-reconsider-position-on-EU-Canada-trade-deal/.

24. Evidence of Victoria Owen and Susan Haigh, Canadian Association of Research Librarians, to the Standing Committee on International Trade, June 16, 2016, http://www.parl.gc.ca/HousePublications/Publication.aspx?Language=e&Mode=1&Parl=42&Ses=1&DocId=8376768.

25. Steve Chase, "Harper's chief of staff takes lead on Trans-Pacific talks, irking cabinet members," *The Globe and Mail*, June 16, 2012, http://www.theglobeandmail.com/news/politics/harpers-chief-of-staff-takes-lead-on-trans-pacific-talks-irking-cabinet-members/article4296863/.

26. Testimony of Perrin Beatty, president of the Canadian Chamber of Commerce, to the Standing Committee on International Trade, February 23, 2016, http://www.parl.gc.ca/HousePublications/Publication.aspx?Language=e&Mode=1&Parl=42&Ses=1&DocId=8117182.

27. Standing Committee on International Trade, "House of Commons Standing Committee on International Trade to hold hearings in Vancouver, Calgary,

Saskatoon and Winnipeg," press release, March 21, 2016, http://www.parl. gc.ca/HousePublications/Publication.aspx?Language=e&Mode=1&Parl=42&S es=1&DocId=8161270.

28. Edward Mejia Davis, "GOP seizes on recently surfaced video to hit Hillary Clinton on trade," CNN, June 28, 2016, http://www.cnn.com/2016/06/28/ politics/donald-trump-hillary-clinton-tpp/.

29. Hillary Clinton, "America's Pacific century," *Foreign Policy*, October 11, 2011, http://foreignpolicy.com/2011/10/11/americas-pacific-century/; Christine Ahn, "Open fire and open markets: The Asia-Pacific pivot and Trans-Pacific partnership," *Foreign Policy in Focus*, January 14, 2014. http://fpif.org/open-fire-open-markets-asia-pacific-pivot-trans-pacific-partnership/.

30. Audrey Young, "Groser: TPP means 'ugly compromises'," *New Zealand Herald*, October 3, 2015, http://m.nzherald.co.nz/business/news/article. cfm?c_id=3&objectid=11522953.

31. Naomi Klein, *This Changes Everything: Capitalism vs. the Climate* (Toronto: Knopf Canada, 2014).

CHAPTER 1

1. Quote taken from "The Trans-Pacific Partnership: Leveling the Playing Field for American Workers and American Business," *United States Trade Representative*, March 9, 2016, https://ustr.gov/tpp.

2. The governments of Canada and Japan released a "Joint Study" on trade liberalization in 2007 that was based on 2001 data and relied on the contentious computable general equilibrium (CGE) methodology. No recent studies have been made available by the Canadian government. For a critique of the CGE model see Jim Stanford, "Out of equilibrium: The impact of EU-Canada free trade on the real economy," Canadian Centre for Policy Alternatives, October 2010, 22–25, http://www.policyalternatives. ca/sites/default/files/uploads/publications/National%20Office/2010/10/ Out_of_Equilibrium.pdf.

The author's enquiries as to the availability of data and documents to support claimed TPP benefits received the following response:

"As with any international trade initiative, Canada assessed the economic value of being in the TPP negotiations prior to entering and our analysis is ongoing as the negotiations progress. We consider, among other factors, the opportunity to deepen and modernize our trading relationships with countries with which we currently have FTAs (US, Mexico, Chile, Peru), as well as the chance to gain new market access in Asia, including Japan. All 11 of our TPP partners are listed as Priority Markets under the Global Markets Action Plan… In other words, the TPP is fully in line with Canada's economic plan and our trade policy agenda."

But no supporting documents have been provided.

3. Robert Fife, "Trudeau markets Canada as tech hub in bid for global investment at Davos," *The Globe and Mail*, January 20, 2016, http://www.

theglobeandmail.com/news/world/justin-trudeau-to-talk-up-canada-when-he-takes-the-stage-at-davos/article28278339/.

4. Guillaum Dubreuill, "Canadian business is united: It's time for TPP," Canadian Chamber of Commerce, March 15, 2016, http://www.chamber.ca/media/news-releases/Canadian-business-is-united-time-for-TPP/.

5. UNCTADstat, "Economic trends: National accounts: Gross domestic product," http://unctadstat.unctad.org/wds/ReportFolders/reportFolders.aspx.

6. 99.2 per cent of agricultural and 100 per cent of nonagricultural product categories are tariffs-free. See "Trade Profiles — Singapore," World Trade Organization (WTO), January 25, 2016, http://stat.wto.org/CountryProfile/WSDBCountryPFView.aspx?Language=E&Country=SG.

7. "Report — Trade Data Online," Industry Canada, https://www.ic.gc.ca/app/scr/tdst/tdo/crtr.html?naArea=9999&searchType=All&productType=NAICS&reportType=TB&timePeriod=10|Complete+Years&currency=CDN&toFromCountry=CDN&countryList=specific&areaCodes=9&grouped=GROUPED&runReport=true.

8. "Report — Trade Data Online — Import, Export and Investment," Industry Canada, 2015 annual data; and Greg Quinn, "Canada Trade Deficit Unexpectedly Narrows on Surge in Exports," *Bloomberg*, February 22, 2016, http://www.bloomberg.com/news/articles/2016-02-05/canada-trade-deficit-unexpectedly-narrows-on-surge-in-exports.

9. Stanford, "Out of equilibrium," 30. See also the predictions of increased trade deficits upon tariff removal in the Canada-EU study of the Comprehensive Economic and Trade Agreement (CETA), European Commission and the Government of Canada, "Assessing the costs and benefits of a closer EU-Canada economic partnership," Department of Foreign Affairs and International Trade, 2008, 57.

10. Industry Canada Trade Data Online, top 25 total Exports by product, HS 4 codes, 2015.

11. "World development indicators — Canada, exports to GDP," *World DataBank*, December 4, 2015, http://databank.worldbank.org/data/reports.aspx?ReportId=30436&Type=Chart.

12. "World development indicators," *World DataBank*, http://databank.worldbank.org/data/reports.aspx?source=world-development-indicators&preview=on.

13. "World development indicators," *World DataBank*, November 3, 2015, http://databank.worldbank.org/data/reports.aspx?source=2&country=&series=TX.QTY.MRCH.XD.WD&period=&l=en.

14. Simple and weighted average definitions taken from https://www.wto.org/english/res_e/statis_e/popup_indicator_help_e.htm.

15. Alana Semuels, "How the Trans-Pacific Partnership Threatens America's Recent Manufacturing Resurgence," *The Atlantic*, October 8, 2015, http://www.theatlantic.com/business/archive/2015/10/trans-pacific-partnership-

tpp-manufacturing/409591/; also Josh Bivens, "The Trans-Pacific Partnership is unlikely to be a good deal for American workers," *Economic Policy Institute*, April 16, 2015, http://www.epi.org/publication/tpp-unlikely-to-be-good-deal-for-american-workers/.

16. Mary E. Burfisher, et al., "Agriculture in the Trans-Pacific Partnership," United States Department of Agriculture, October 2014, 22–24, http://www.ers.usda.gov/media/1692509/err176.pdf; also WTO, "Trade Profiles — Canada, Japan," January 25, 2016, http://stat.wto.org/TariffProfile/WSDBTariffPFView.aspx?Language=E&Country=CA,JP.

17. Global Affairs Canada, *Report of the Canada-Japan Joint Study on Benefits and Costs of Further Promotion of Bilateral Trade and Investment*, Foreign Affairs, Trade and Development Canada, October 2007, 64, http://www.international.gc.ca/trade-agreements-accords-commerciaux/agr-acc/japan-japon/canjap-report-rapport.aspx?lang=eng#chap1; Burfisher et al., "Agriculture in the Trans-Pacific Partnership," 22, 23.

18. "Trade Profiles — Canada, Japan," World Trade Organization (WTO).

19. These findings are confirmed by a 2007 study (using 2001 data) on the liberalization of Canada-Japan trade which concluded that "In Japan, production in the manufacturing and services sectors would increase, but that of grains and meat products would decrease. In Canada, production in the agricultural and food sectors would increase, but that of most manufacturing sectors would decrease, although to a lesser extent." *Report of the Canada-Japan Joint Study on Benefits and Costs of Further Promotion of Bilateral Trade and Investment*, 64.

20. Source: UNCTADstat, GDP at current prices $US and Merchandise Trade Matrix by product groups, $US, author's calculations.

21. OECD, "STI country profiles: Canada," in *OECD Science, Technology and Industry Outlook 2014* (Paris: OECD Publishing, 2014), 285, http://www.oecd-ilibrary.org/content/chapter/sti_outlook-2014-40-en; also OECD, "Moving up the value chain: staying competitive in the global economy: Main findings," 2007, 20.

22. Suzy H. Nikièma, "Performance requirements in investment treaties," IISD Best Practices Series, December 2014, 2, http://www.iisd.org/sites/default/files/publications/best-practices-performance-requirements-investment-treaties-en.pdf.

23. Ha-Joon Chang, *The East Asian Development Experience: The Miracle, the Crisis and the Future* (Penang, Malaysia; London; New York; New York: Third World Network, Zed, 2006).

24. Daniel Poon, "A pivot to Asia? Canada's 'real' globalization," *Policy Options*, September 2012; also Keith Crane, et al., "The effectiveness of China's industrial policies in commercial aviation manufacturing," *Product Page*, 2014, http://www.rand.org/pubs/research_reports/RR245.html.

25. "The global revival of industrial policy: Picking winners, saving losers," *The Economist*, August 5, 2010, http://www.economist.com/node/16741043;

also Edward Luce, "America reassembles industrial policy," *Financial Times*, April 8, 2012, https://www.ft.com/content/6cbeb150-7da4-11e1-bfa5-00144feab49a (subscription required); also Joseph E. Stiglitz, Joan Esteban and Justin Lin Yifu, *The Industrial Policy Revolution I: The Role of Government Beyond Ideology* (Basingstoke, UK: Palgrave Macmillan, 2013).

26. Philip Cross, "The role of natural resources in Canada's economy," *Canadian Economic Observer* 21, no. 11 (November 2008): 3.3, 3.7, 3.9.

27. Ibid., 3.7.

28. Centre for Study of Living Standards (CSLS), "Productivity trends in natural resources industries in Canada," October 2004.

29. In 2014 the extractives sector paid on average $41.08/hr. whereas manufacturing paid $23.46/hr. Statistics Canada, Table 281-0030.

30. Statistics Canada, Government of Canada, "Contribution of Exports to Jobs, 2011," July 30, 2015, http://www.statcan.gc.ca/daily-quotidien/150730/t002b-eng.htm. This is the most recent data available for this Statistics Canada survey Table 381-0032. "The database measures the contribution of exports to gross value added or GDP by removing the value of the imported intermediate inputs (non-capital purchases from other industries) embodied in exported products. This method provides a measure of the contribution of exports to the GDP of each industry and of the total economy." http://www.statcan.gc.ca/daily-quotidien/150730/dq150730b-eng.htm.

31. Statistics Canada, Table 381-0032.

32. See Table 3, "Canadian-TPP (non-FTA countries)" by Product.

33. Canadian Press, "TPP could harm Canada's dairy more than expected, expert says," CBC, November 14, 2015, http://www.cbc.ca/news/canada/montreal/tpp-dairy-imports-effects-1.3308877.

34. Statistics Canada, Table 281-0024.

35. "Economic mood darkens as rout spreads beyond oil patch," *The Globe and Mail*, February 24, 2016, http://www.theglobeandmail.com/report-on-business/economy/businesses-outside-oil-patch-now-feeling-sting-of-commodity-price-rout-boc/article28105709/; also "UPDATE 3 — Canada government warns of big budget deficits, growth forecast cut," *Reuters*, February 22, 2016, http://www.reuters.com/article/canada-budget-idUSL2N1610YX.

CHAPTER 2

1. Prime Minister of Canada, "Minister of Health mandate letter," November 2015, http://pm.gc.ca/eng/minister-health-mandate-letter.

2. The overall figures put Canada in fourth place behind Greece, but a senior economist with the OECD health division in Paris "pointed out that because the figures provided by Greece include other costs, it may be more accurate to put Canada in the third-highest spot for drug spending." Elizabeth Church, "Canada among top pharmaceutical spenders on OECD list," *The Globe and Mail*, November 4, 2015.

3. OECD, "Pharmaceutical expenditure," in *Health at a Glance 2015*, November 2015, 178.

4. Government of Canada, "TPP Article 18.48 (2)," *Consolidated TPP text*, http:// www.international.gc.ca/trade-agreements-accords-commerciaux/agr-acc/tpp-ptp/text-texte/ toc-tdm.aspx?lang=eng.

5. This estimate is based on calculations of the cost impacts of CETA, adjusted to reflect the specific requirements of the TPP. See Joel Lexchin, "Involuntary medication: The possible effects of the Trans-Pacific Partnership on the cost and regulation of medicine in Canada," Canadian Centre for Policy Alternatives, January 2016.

6. Joel Lexchin and Marc-André Gagnon, "CETA and pharmaceuticals: impact of the trade agreement between Europe and Canada on the costs of prescription drugs," *Globalization and Health*, May 6, 2014, http://www.globalizationandhealth.com/content/10/1/30.

7. "CETA Technical Summary," October 2013, http://international.gc.ca/trade-agreements-accords-commerciaux/agr-acc/ceta-aecg/understanding-comprendre/technical-technique.aspx?lang=eng.

8. Patented Medicine Prices Review Board, "Table 16: Total R&D Expenditures and R&D-to-Sales Ratios of Reporting Companies, 1988–2014" in *Annual Report 2014*, December 10, 2015, http://www.pmprb-cepmb.gc.ca/en/reporting/annual-reports.

9. Patented Medicine Prices Review Board, *Annual Report 2014*, 47.

10. Patented Medicine Prices Review Board, *Annual Report 2014*, 1.

11. Barney Jopson, "Hillary Clinton plans 'exit tax' to tackle inversions: Move could deter deals such as Pfizer's planned $160bn takeover of Allergan," *Financial Times of London*, December 7, 2015, https://next.ft.com/content/50dd21ca-9d39-11e5-8ce1-f6219b685d74 (subscription required).

12. Doctors Without Borders/Médecins Sans Frontières, "The negative impact on public health will be enormous: Statement by MSF on the conclusion of Trans-Pacific Partnership negotiations in Atlanta," October 5, 2015, http://www.msf.ca/en/article/the-negative-impact-on-public-health-will-be-enormous-statement-by-msf-on-the-conclusion-of.

13. Ibid.

14. Nathalie Bernasconi-Osterwalder, "How the Investment chapter of the Trans-Pacific Partnership falls short," International Institute for Sustainable Development, November 6, 2015, http://www.iisd.org/commentary/how-investment-chapter-trans-pacific-partnership-falls-short.

15. Government of Canada, "TPP Chapter 11, Financial Services, Article 11.2(2): Scope," *Consolidated TPP text*, http://www.international.gc.ca/trade-agreements-accords-commerciaux/agr-acc/tpp-ptp/text-texte/11.aspx?lang=eng.

16. Gus van Harten, *Sovereign Choices and Sovereign Constraints: Judicial Restraint in Investment Treaty Arbitration*. (Oxford: Oxford University Press, 2013), 102.

17. For example, foreign investors invoked the minimum standards of treatment provision (NAFTA Article 1105) in 69 out of 77 investor-state claims filed by January 1, 2015. See Scott Sinclair (with Hadrian Mertins-Kirkwood), "NAFTA Chapter 11 Investor-State Disputes to January 1, 2015," Canadian Centre for Policy Alternatives, January 14, 2015, https://www.policyalternatives.ca/publications/reports/nafta-chapter-11-investor-state-disputes-january-1-2015.

18. Those efforts to reregulate the health insurance market were themselves reversed by a subsequent government. The debate about whether to create a single-payer system is ongoing.

19. Luke Eric Peterson, "German court sees no clash between Achmea v. Slovakia arbitral award and EU law, and is unmoved by persistent arguments of European Commission," *Investment Arbitration Reporter*, January 8, 2015. (Subscription required.)

20. Joel Dahlquist and Luke Eric Peterson, "Arbitrators nixed DCF valuation of temporary harms In Achmea v. Slovakia I case, and declined to order state to refrain from future BIT breach," *Investment Arbitration Reporter*, June 18, 2014.

21. During the twenty-year history of NAFTA, consensus on binding interpretive notes has only been reached once, in 2001 regarding interpretive notes on transparency and minimum standards of treatment.

22. As of 2015, UNCTAD identifies 667 investor–state cases worldwide. United Nations Conference on Trade and Development, "Investment Agreements Navigator," http://investmentpolicyhub.unctad.org/IIA.

23. In December 2015, Philip Morris's legal challenge against Australia under a Hong Kong Bilateral Investment Treaty was terminated. Because the claim was dismissed on jurisdictional grounds, the substantive issue of whether or not plain-packaging rules run afoul of international investment treaties remains unresolved. "Philip Morris suit against Australia dismissed on jurisdictional grounds," *Inside U.S. Trade*, December 23, 2015.

24. The TPP contains an exception from certain of the chapter's performance-requirements prohibitions, for measures "*necessary* to protect human, animal, or plant life or health." The inclusion of this exemption from aspects of one TPP obligation will likely be read as inferring that the drafters intended to make public health measures subject to other TPP provisions, unless explicitly exempted. "Article 9.9 (3) (d): Performance Requirements," http://www.international.gc.ca/trade-agreements-accords-commerciaux/agr-acc/tpp-ptp/text-texte/toc-tdm.aspx?lang=eng.

25. "(T)he treaty partners assured the public that language 'underscores that countries retain the right to regulate in the public interest, including on health, safety, the financial sector and the environment.' That provision, however, is subject to compliance with all of the other investor protections in the chapter, fully negating the preservation of policy space." Lisa Sachs and Lise Johnson, "TPP would let foreign investors bypass the Canadian public interest," *The Globe and Mail*, November 25, 2015.

26. According to the text: "A tobacco control measure means a measure of a Party related to the production or consumption of manufactured tobacco products (including products made or derived from tobacco), their distribution, labelling, packaging, advertising, marketing, promotion, sale, purchase, or use, as well as enforcement measures, such as inspection, recordkeeping, and reporting requirements. For greater certainty, a measure with respect to tobacco leaf that is not in the possession of a manufacturer of tobacco products or that is not part of a manufactured tobacco product is not a tobacco control measure." "TPP Article 29.5: Tobacco Control Measures, note 12," http://www.international.gc.ca/trade-agreements-accords-commerciaux/agr-acc/tpp-ptp/text-texte/toc-tdm.aspx?lang=eng.

27. The mandate letter directs the health minister to "Introduce plain packaging requirements for tobacco products, similar to those in Australia and the United Kingdom." Prime Minister of Canada, "Minister of Health Mandate Letter," November 2015, http://pm.gc.ca/eng/minister-health-mandate-letter.

28. These are all regulatory priorities of the new federal government as set out in the ministerial mandate letter. Prime Minister of Canada, "Minister of Health Mandate Letter," November 2015, http://pm.gc.ca/eng/minister-health-mandate-letter.

29. Center for Policy Analysis on Trade and Health (CPATH), "Protect public health in TPP talks," http://www.cpath.org/id59.html.

30. Jim Grieshaber-Otto and Scott Sinclair, "Bad Medicine: Trade treaties, privatization and health care reform in Canada," Canadian Centre for Policy Alternatives, 2004, https://www.policyalternatives.ca/publications/reports/bad-medicine.

31. For transparency purposes, Canada has included an illustrative, nonbinding list of nonconforming measures maintained at the subnational level of government. But all existing nonconforming measures, whether they appear on the list or not, are protected. "TPP Annex I: Non-Conforming Measures — Canada," http://www.international.gc.ca/trade-agreements-accords-commerciaux/agr-acc/tpp-ptp/text-texte/31-1-a3.aspx?lang=eng.

32. United States Trade Representative, "TPP chapter summary: Cross Border Trade in Services," https://ustr.gov/sites/default/files/TPP-Chapter-Summary-Cross-Border-Trade-in-Services.pdf .

33. The full reservation reads, "Canada reserves the right to adopt or maintain a measure for providing public law enforcement and correctional services, as well as the following services to the extent that they are social services established or maintained for a public purpose: income security or insurance, social security or insurance, social welfare, public education, public training, health and child care." "TPP Annex I: Non-Conforming Measures — Canada," http://www.international.gc.ca/trade-agreements-accords-commerciaux/agr-acc/tpp-ptp/text-texte/31-2-a3.aspx?lang=eng.

34. For a discussion of the differing views of Canadian and U.S. governments during the NAFTA subnational reservations exercise, see Matthew Sanger and Scott Sinclair, "Putting Health First: Canadian Health Care Reform in a

Globalizing World," Canadian Centre for Policy Alternatives, 2004, 13–15; also *Inside NAFTA*, November 29, 1995.

35. NAFTA Annex II-C-9 applies against the national treatment (1102, 1202), the services chapter's most-favoured nation treatment (1203), local presence (1205) and senior management and board of directors (1107) articles.

36. Nevertheless, through NAFTA's most-favoured nation treatment clause, U.S. and Mexican investors would be entitled to the most favourable treatment given to European investors under CETA in the Canadian health care sector. Furthermore, this amounts to a unilateral, nonreciprocal commitment by Canada. Nonconforming U.S. subnational measures would still enjoy the protection of the NAFTA Annex I general reservation, as carried over into the TPP. Meanwhile, only those Canadian sub-national measures that are expressly reserved under CETA's negative listing approach would be protected from challenge by U.S. or Mexican investors.

37. The RFP for the testing services could arguably be excluded from the TPP trade-in-services chapter by virtue of being government procurement. But since the provincial nursing bodies are independent entities, the success of such an argument is questionable.

38. Michael Geist, "How the TPP may put your health care data at risk," *Toronto Star*, October 13, 2015, http://www.thestar.com/business/2015/10/13/how-the-tpp-may-put-your-health-care-data-at-risk-geist.html.

39. "TPP Article 10.7.3. Non-Conforming Measures," http://www.international.gc.ca/trade-agreements-accords-commerciaux/agr-acc/tpp-ptp/text-texte/toc-tdm.aspx?lang=eng.

40. "Paragraphs 1 through 7 shall not apply to the non-conforming aspects of measures that are not subject to the obligations under Article 10.3 (National Treatment) or Article 10.5 (Market Access) by reason of an entry in a Party's Schedule to Annex I, or to measures that are not subject to the obligations under Article 10.3 (National Treatment) or Article 10.5 (Market Access) by reason of an entry in a Party's Schedule to Annex II." "TPP Article 10.8.8. Domestic Regulation," http://www.international.gc.ca/trade-agreements-accords-commerciaux/agr-acc/tpp-ptp/text-texte/toc-tdm.aspx?lang=eng.

41. This section was written by Hadrian Mertins-Kirkwood, who authored Chapter 6 of this book on the TPP's temporary-entry chapter.

42. Chantal Blouin, "NAFTA and the mobility of highly skilled workers: The case of Canadian nurses," *The Estey Centre Journal of International Law and Trade Policy* 6, no. 1 (2005).

43. See Appendix 1603.D.1 in "Chapter Sixteen: Temporary Entry for Business Persons," *Text of the North American Free Trade Agreement (NAFTA)*, http://www.international.gc.ca/trade-agreements-accords-commerciaux/agr-acc/nafta-alena/text-texte/16.aspx?lang=eng.

44. "Chapter 9: Investment. Article 9.19: Submission of a Claim to Arbitration," *Trans-Pacific Partnership*, https://ustr.gov/trade-agreements/free-trade-agreements/trans-pacific-partnership/tpp-full-text.

45. Gus van Harten, *Sovereign Choices and Sovereign Constraints: Judicial Restraint in Investment Treaty Arbitration* (Oxford, UK: Oxford University Press, 2013).

46. A footnote to the TPP definition of investment agreement explains that: "For the avoidance of doubt, this subparagraph does not cover correctional services, healthcare services, education services, childcare services, welfare services or other similar social services." "Chapter 9: Investment. Article 9.1. Definitions," *Trans-Pacific Partnership*, 9-4, https://ustr.gov/trade-agreements/free-trade-agreements/trans-pacific-partnership/tpp-full-text.

47. "Chapter 9: Investment. Article 9.1. Definitions," *Trans-Pacific Partnership*, 9-4.

48. Deborah Gleeson, "Preliminary analysis of the final TPP Healthcare Transparency Annex: Annex 26-A: Transparency and Procedural Fairness for Pharmaceutical Products and Medical Devices," School of Psychology and Public Health, La Trobe University, December 12, 2015, 1.

49. "Transparency Chapter — Annex on Transparency and Procedural Fairness for Healthcare Technologies," *Trans-Pacific Partnership*, June 22, 2011, http://www.citizenstrade.org/ctc/wp-content/uploads/2011/10/TransPacificTransparency.pdf.

50. "Annex 26-A. Transparency and Procedural Fairness for Pharmaceutical Products and Medical Devices. Schedule to Annex 26-A," *Trans-Pacific Partnership*, http://www.international.gc.ca/trade-agreements-accords-commerciaux/agr-acc/tpp-ptp/text-texte/26.aspx?lang=eng#26a.

51. Jon Johnson, "How will international trade agreements affect Canadian health care?" in *Putting Heath First: Canadian Health Care Reform in a Globalizing World*, ed. Matthew Sanger and Scott Sinclair (Ottawa: Canadian Centre for Policy Alternatives, 2004).

CHAPTER 3

1. For recent estimates of the macroeconomic impact of the TPP on member countries, see World Bank Group, "Global Economic Prospects: Spillovers and Weak Growth," January 2016, 227: "The impact on NAFTA members (all also members of TPP) would be small, on the order of 0.6 percent of GDP, because trade represents a modest share of GDP and because existing barriers to their trade (which is already mostly among them) are already low for the most traded commodities." See also Jeronim Capaldo and Alex Izurieta, "Trading Down: Unemployment, Inequality and Other Risks of the Trans-Pacific Partnership Agreement," January 2016, 18: "While projected employment losses [from the TPP] are small compared to the labour force, they clearly signal an adverse effect of liberalization not taken into account in full-employment models. In TPP countries, the largest effect will occur in the U.S., with approximately 450,000 jobs lost by 2025. Japan and Canada follow, with approximately 75,000 and 58,000 jobs lost respectively."

2. In this and all instances, citations from the TPP text are taken from the Global Affairs Canada website and adjusted for Canadian spelling. http://www.international.gc.ca/trade-agreements-accords-commerciaux/agr-acc/tpp-ptp/text-texte/toc-tdm.aspx?lang=eng.

3. Knowledge Ecology International, "US, AU and CA try to block WTO LDC drug patent waiver because PhRMA's not happy enough with the TPP," 2015, http://keionline.org/node/2337.

4. "WTO members approve TRIPS non-violation extension, debate e-commerce language," *Bridges*, November 26, 2015, http://www.ictsd.org/bridges-news/bridges/news/wto-members-approve-trips-non-violation-extension-debate-e-commerce.

5. Joel Lexchin, "Harmony in drug regulation, but who's calling the tune? An examination of regulatory harmonization in Health Canada," *International Journal of Health Services* 42, 2012, 119–36.

6. "ICH announces organizational changes as it marks 25 years of successful harmonization," International Council for Harmonization press statement, http://www.ich.org/about/organisational-changes.html.

7. Bjørn Jøldal, "Regulation for need — the Norwegian experience," *Journal of Social and Administrative Pharmacy* 2, 1984, 81–4.

8. Centre for innovation in Regulatory Science (CIRS), "The impact of the changing regulatory environment on the approval of new medicines across six major authorities 2004–2013," 2014, http://cirsci.org/publications/R&D Briefing 55 16122014.pdf.

9. Ibid.

10. Joel Lexchin, "New drugs and safety: what happened to new active substances approved in Canada between 1995 and 2010?" *Archive of Internal Medicine* 172, 2012, 1680–1; also Joel Lexchin, "Postmarket safety warnings for drugs approved in Canada under the Notice of Compliance with conditions policy," *British Journal of Clinical Pharmacology*, 2014.

11. David Bruser and Jesse McLean, "Canadians kept in dark about defective drugs," *Toronto Star*, September 11, 2014.

12. Pia Eberhardt and Cecilia Olivet, "Profiting from Injustice: How law firms, arbitrators and financiers are fuelling an investment arbitration boom," Transnational Institute and Corporate Europe Observatory, 2012, https://www.tni.org/files/download/profitingfrominjustice.pdf

13. European Commission, "Investment in TTIP and beyond — the path for reform," http://trade.ec.europa.eu/doclib/docs/2015/may/tradoc_153408.PDF.

14. David Schneiderman, "A CETA investment court is not the solution," *The Globe and Mail*, March 5, 2016, B7.

15. Kazi Stastna, "Eli Lilly files $500M NAFTA suit against Canada over drug patents," CBC News, September 13, 2013, http://www.cbc.ca/news/business/eli-lilly-files-500m-nafta-suit-against-canada-over-drug-patents-1.1829854.

16. Brook K. Baker and Katrina Geddes, "Corporate power unbound: investor-state arbitration of IP monopolies on medicines — Eli Lilly v. Canada and the Trans-Pacific Partnership Agreement," September 28, 2015, Northeastern University School of Law Research Paper no. 242, http://ssrn.com/abstract=2667062 or http://dx.doi.org/10.2139/ssrn.2667062

17. Public Citizen, 2015.

18. Joel Lexchin and Marc-Andre Gagnon, "CETA and pharmaceuticals: impact of the trade agreement between Europe and Canada on the costs of prescription drug," *Globalization and Health* 10, 2014, 30.

19. Ibid.

20. Marc-Andre Gagnon, personal communication, December 2, 2015.

21. Joel Lexchin and Barbara Mintzes, "A compromise too far: a review of Canadian cases of direct-to-consumer advertising regulation," *International Journal of Risk and Safety in Medicine* 26, 2014, 213–25.

CHAPTER 4

1. See USTR website for the TPP, under "Preserving the Environment," https://ustr.gov/tpp/#preserving-the-environment.

2. "Article 20.3.2: General Commitments." All references to the text of the TPP use the version of the text published on the website of the New Zealand Ministry of Foreign Affairs and Trade, https://www.mfat.govt.nz/en/about-us/who-we-are/treaty-making-process/trans-pacific-partnership-tpp/text-of-the-trans-pacific-partnership/.

3. "Article 20.51.: Protection of the Ozone Layer."

4. "Article 20.52.: Protection of the Ozone Layer."

5. "Article 20.10: Corporate Social Responsibility."

6. "Article 20.13.2: Trade and Biodiversity."

7. "Article 20.14.1: Invasive Alien Species."

8. "Article 20.14.2: Invasive Alien Species."

9. "Article 20.15.2: Transition to a Low Emissions and Resilient Economy."

10. "Secret TPP Treaty: Environment chapter for all 12 nations," *WikiLeaks*, January 15, 2014. Citing: Trans-Pacific Partnership Environment Working Group chairs. "Environment Chapter Consolidated Text." Trans-Pacific Partnership Agreement negotiations, November 24, 2013, https://wikileaks.org/tpp2/static/pdf/tpp-treaty-environment-chapter.pdf.

11. "Article SS.15: Secret TPP Treaty: Environment Chapter for all 12 Nations," 15.

12. "Article SS.15 (1): Secret TPP Treaty: Environment Chapter for all 12 Nations," 15.

13. "Article SS.15 (2): Secret TPP Treaty: Environment Chapter for all 12 Nations," 15.

14. "Article SS.15 (3): Secret TPP Treaty: Environment Chapter for all 12 Nations," 16.

15. "Article SS.15 (4): Secret TPP Treaty: Environment Chapter for all 12 Nations," 16.

16. "Article SS.15 (6): Secret TPP Treaty: Environment Chapter for all 12 Nations," 16.

17. "Article 20.16.1: Marine Capture Fisheries."

18. "Article 20.16.3: Marine Capture Fisheries."

19. "Article 20.16.4: Marine Capture Fisheries."

20. "Article 20.16.5(a): Marine Capture Fisheries."

21. "Article 20.16.5(b): Marine Capture Fisheries."

22. "Article 20.16.7: Marine Capture Fisheries."

23. "Article 20.16.6: Marine Capture Fisheries," and footnote 18.

24. *Agreement on Subsidies and Countervailing Measures*, World Trade Organization, https://www.wto.org/english/docs_e/legal_e/24-scm.pdf.

25. "Article 20.16.11: Marine Capture Fisheries."

26. "Article 20.16.14: Marine Capture Fisheries."

27. "Article 20.17.3: Conservation and Trade."

28. Another applicable law is defined in footnote 26 as the law of the jurisdiction where the take or trade occurred and is only relevant to whether the take or trade was illegal.

29. "Article 20.17.6: Conservation and Trade."

30. "Article 20.1: Definitions."

31. Ibid.

32. *The Constitution Act, 1867* (UK), 30 & 31 Vict, c 3, reprinted in RSC 1985, App II, No 5, ss 91, 92.

33. "Article 20.1: Definitions."; also Jon Carson and Robyn Glindemann, "Environmental law and practice in Australia: Overview," *Global Guide 2015/2016: Environment*, Thomson Reuters, http://global.practicallaw.com/1-502-8908.

34. Alberto Delgado, Alberto Ventura and Sandra Lock, "Environmental law and practice in Peru: Overview," *Global Guide 2015/2016: Environment*, Thomson Reuters, http://global.practicallaw.com/8-602-1506.

35. "Article 22(1). Commission for Environmental Cooperation," *North American Agreement on Economic Co-operation*, http://www.cec.org/about-us/NAAEC.

36. "Article 20.9(2)(d): Public Submissions."

37. "The Trans-Pacific Partnership and the environment: An assessment of commitments and trade agreement enforcement," Center for International Environmental Law, November 2015, 4–5, http://www.ciel.org/wp-content/uploads/2015/11/TPP-Enforcement-Analysis-Nov2015.pdf.

38. "Article 20.19.2: Environment Committee and Contact Points."

39. "Article 20.19.3: Environment Committee and Contact Points."

40. "Article 20.21.1, .2: Senior Representative Consultations."

41. "Article 20.22: Ministerial Consultations."

42. "Article 20.22.3: Ministerial Consultations."

43. "Article 20.23.1: Dispute Resolution."

44. "Article 20.23.4: Dispute Resolution."

45. "Article 28.13(e): Rules of Procedure for Panels."

46. "Article 28.13(d)(i): Rules of Procedure for Panels."

47. "Article 28.13(d)(ii): Rules of Procedure for Panels."

48. "Article 28.18: Final Report."

49. "Article 28.19: Non-Implementation — Compensation and Suspension of Benefits and Article 28.20: Compliance Review."

50. "Article 20.8.2: Opportunities for Public Participation."

51. "Article 20.9.1: Public Submissions."

52. "Article 20.9.1: Public Submissions."

53. "Article 20.9.2(d) and (e): Public Submissions."

54. A Party is defined as any State or separate customs territory for which this Agreement is in force in Chapter 1, Article 1.3 of the TPP.

55. "Article 15: Commission for Environmental Cooperation," *North American Agreement on Economic Cooperation*, http://www.cec.org/about-us/NAAEC.

CHAPTER 5

1. Kimberly A. Nolan García, "Transnational advocates and labor rights enforcement in the North American Free Trade Agreement," *Latin American Politics and Society* 53, no. 2, 30.

2. "Chapter 19: Labour Chapter," *Trans-Pacific Partnership*, https://www.mfat. govt.nz/assets/_securedfiles/Trans-Pacific-Partnership/Text/19.-Labour-Chapter.pdf.

3. Global Affairs Canada, "The Labour Chapter," 2015, http://www. international.gc.ca/trade-agreements-accords-commerciaux/agr-acc/tpp-ptp/ understanding-comprendre/18-labour.aspx?lang=eng.

4. AFL-CIO, "The Trans-Pacific Partnership: Four countries that don't comply with U.S. trade law," http://www.aflcio.org/content/ download/150491/3811471/file/TPPreport-NO+BUG.pdf.

5. International Labour Organization, "Can trade liberalization and social progress go hand-in-hand?" 2013, http://www.ilo.org/newyork/voices-at-work/WCMS_229471/lang--en/index.htm. The United States is currently engaged in a labour enforcement case against Guatemala, under the DR–CAFTA. A decision has not yet been issued. Further details on the U.S.–Guatemala labour enforcement case can be found online: https://ustr. gov/issue-areas/labor/bilateral-and-regional-trade-agreements/guatemala-submission-under-cafta-dr.

6. The North American Agreement on Labour Cooperation, http://www.labour. gc.ca/eng/relations/international/agreements/naalc.shtml.

7. Angel Torres, "A wishful thought: Enforceability and avoidance of labor provisions in foreign trade agreements," *Law and Business Review of the Americas* 20, 2014, 627. The "guiding principles" referred to in the NAFTA agreement are: 1) The freedom of association and protection of right to organize; 2) The right to bargain collectively; 3) The right to strike; 4) The prohibition of forced labor; 5) Labor protections for children and young people; 6) Minimum employment standards, including minimum wage; 7) The elimination of employment discrimination; 8) Equal pay for women and men; 9) The prevention of occupational injuries and illnesses; 10) Compensation for occupational injuries and illnesses; and 11) Protection of migrant workers. North American Agreement on Labor Cooperation (NAALC), September 13, 1993, Annex 1.

8. Stephen Clarkson, *Does North America Exist?* (Toronto: University of Toronto Press, 2008), 104.

9. Nolan, 2011, 40.

10. Government of Canada, "Labour Program," http://www.labour.gc.ca/eng/relations/international/agreements/naalc.shtml.

11. Amnesty report, https://www.amnesty.org/en/countries/americas/mexico/report-mexico/.

12. AFL-CIO, "Mexico: Labor Rights Concerns," 2015, http://www.aflcio.org/Issues/Trade/Trans-Pacific-Partnership-Free-Trade-Agreement-TPP/Labor-Rights/Mexico-Labor-Rights-Concerns; Arturo Alcalde Justiniani; ¿Dónde quedó el acuerdo laboral paralelo al TLCAN? http://www.rmalc.org/historico/tratados/tlcan/documentos/2007/acuerdo%20laboral%20paralelo%20al%20TLCAN.pdf. See also "Observation (CEACR) – adopted 2010, published 100th ILC session (2011), Freedom of Association and Protection of the Right to Organise Convention, 1948 (No. 87) – Mexico (Ratification: 1950)," http://www.ilo.org/dyn/normlex/en/f?p=1000:13100:0::NO:13100:P13100_COMMENT_ID:2326537:NO; Observation (CEACR) - adopted 2012, published 102nd ILC session (2013), Discrimination (Employment and Occupation) Convention, 1958 (No. 111) — Mexico (Ratification: 1961), http://www.ilo.org/dyn/normlex/en/f?p=1000:13100:0::NO:13100:P13100_COMMENT_ID:3079532:NO; "Observation (CEACR) - adopted 2012, published 102nd ILC session (2013), Worst Forms of Child Labour Convention," 1999 (No. 182) - Mexico (Ratification: 2000), http://www.ilo.org/dyn/normlex/en/f?p=1000:13100:0::NO:13100:P13100_COMMENT_ID:3085618:NO.

13. Torres, "A wishful thought," 630–31.

14. Mary Jane Bolle, *Overview of Labor Enforcement Issues in Free Trade Agreements,* Congressional Research Service, 2016.

15. Ibid.

16. Lorand Bartels, "Social issues: Labour, environment, and human rights," in ed. Simon Lester, Bryan Mercurio and Lorand Bartels *Bilateral and Regional Trade Agreements: Commentary and Analysis* (Cambridge, UK: Cambridge University Press, 2015), 379.

17. Pierre-Alexandre Cardinal, "Labour rights and the Canada/Colombia Free Trade Agreement: A fundamentally flawed culture," *Revue québécoise de droit international* 26, no. 1 (2013),11.

18. Mark Rowlinson and Sheila Katz, "Labour rights in Colombia and the Canada-Colombia labour side agreements," in Canadian Council for International Cooperation, *Making a Bad Situation Worse: An Analysis of the Text of the Canada-Colombia Free Trade Agreement*, 2009, 10.

19. Gerda van Roozendaal, "The diffusion of labour standards: The case of the U.S. and Guatemala," *Politics and Governance* 3, no. 2 (2015), 27.

20. "Chapter 19: Labour Chapter," *Trans-Pacific Partnership*, footnote 5.

21. "Chapter 19: Labour Chapter," *Trans-Pacific Partnership*, footnote 4.

22. "Chapter 19: Labour Chapter," *Trans-Pacific Partnership*, Article 19.5(1).

23. ILO, *Social Dimensions of Free Trade Agreements*, 2015, http://www.ilo.org/wcmsp5/groups/public/---dgreports/---inst/documents/publication/wcms_228965.pdf.

CHAPTER 6

1. In the context of NAFTA, for example, former U.S. Assistant Secretary of Labor Joaquin Otero has noted the "countless cases where abuses of non-immigrant visas resulted in massive layoffs of American workers." See Joaquin F. Otero, "Comment" on George J. Borjas, "Economic research and the debate over immigration policy," in *Social Dimensions of U.S. Trade Policies*, eds. Alan V. Deardorff and Robert M. Stern (Ann Arbor: The University of Michigan Press, 2000), 85.

2. "Article 10.2(1)," *Canada-European Union Comprehensive Economic and Trade Agreement (CETA)*. Note that all references to CETA use the legally-scrubbed version of the text released in February 2016, not the preliminary text released in September 2014. The final version is accessible from the European Commission at http://trade.ec.europa.eu/doclib/docs/2016/february/tradoc_154329.pdf.

3. "Article 1601," *North American Free Trade Agreement (NAFTA)*.

4. CETA 10.2(5).

5. "Article 19.10.6(n)(iii)," *Trans-Pacific Partnership*.

6. Immigration, Refugees and Citizenship Canada, "How to hire a temporary foreign worker (TFW): A guidebook for employers," August 27, 2015, http://www.cic.gc.ca/english/resources/publications/tfw-guide.asp.

7. Citizenship and Immigration Canada, *FW 1: Foreign Worker Manual*, January 29, 2013, http://publications.gc.ca/collections/collection_2013/cic/Ci63-27-2013-eng.pdf.

8. Immigration, Refugees and Citizenship Canada, *ENF 4: Port of Entry Examinations*, February 10, 2016, http://www.cic.gc.ca/english/resources/manuals/enf/enf04-eng.pdf.

9. Workers covered by an FTA fall under exemption R204(a) in the *Immigration and Refugee Protection Regulations (SOR/2002-227)*, http://laws-lois.justice.gc.ca/eng/regulations/SOR-2002-227/section-204.html.

10. CBSA officers receive fifty hours of online instruction, eighteen weeks of classroom instruction, and twelve to eighteen months of on-the-job training before they can make immigration decisions. Canada Border Services Agency, "From recruit to officer trainee — training and development programs," July 9, 2014. http://www.cbsa-asfc.gc.ca/job-emploi/hso-asf/training-formation-eng html.

11. NAFTA 1603.4.

12. The trade in services chapter covers measures affecting "the presence in the Party's territory of a service supplier of another Party" (TPP 10.2.1(d)), which would include any foreign worker granted temporary entry under Chapter 12. At the same time, Article 12.9 makes it clear that Chapter 10 does not "impose any obligation on a Party regarding its immigration measures." Moreover, Article 10.2.4 reiterates that Chapter 10 does not impose "any obligation on a Party with respect to a national of another Party who seeks access to its employment market or who is employed on a permanent basis in its territory, and does not confer any right on that national with respect to that access or employment."

13. CETA 10.6.2(b) and CETA 10.6.3.

14. TPP 12-A(Canada)(B)(4).

15. Citizenship and Immigration Canada, "What is a Labour Market Impact Assessment?" February 2, 2016, http://www.cic.gc.ca/english/helpcentre/answer.asp?q=163&t=17.

16. For a deeper discussion of the LMIA process and its relationship to Canada's FTAs, see Hadrian Mertins-Kirkwood, *Labour mobility in Canada: Issues and policy recommendations*, Canadian Labour Congress, December 8, 2014, http://canadianlabour.ca/issues-research/labour-mobility-canada-issues-and-policy-recommendations.

17. See, for example, CETA 10.8.3.

18. Canada's Annex 12-A does not explicitly prohibit Canada from imposing "economic needs tests" for some categories of workers, but the prohibition on labour certification tests and numerical limits ultimately serves the same purpose. The World Trade Organization has previously concluded that economic needs tests should be interpreted broadly to include all forms of quantitative restrictions or any tests that "condition market access." See paragraph 24 in Council for Trade in Services, "Economic needs tests: Note by the Secretariat," *World Trade Organization S/CSS/W/118*, November 30, 2001.

19. See, for example, this letter dated April 22, 2015 from U.S. Trade Representative Michael Froman to Republican Congressman Chuck Grassley: http://www.grassley.senate.gov/sites/default/files/judiciary/upload/Immigration%2C%2004-22-15%2C%20letter%20from%20USTR%2C%20immigration%20in%20trade%20agreements.pdf.

20. Sec. 914(a), *H.R.644 — Trade Facilitation and Trade Enforcement Act of 2015*, 114th Congress (2015-2016), introduced on February 2, 2015, became public law on February 24, 2016, https://www.congress.gov/bill/114th-congress/house-bill/644 .

21. TPP 12-A(Canada)(B)(5).

22. TPP 12-A(Canada)(A)(3).

23. CETA 10.1.

24. Citizenship and Immigration Canada, *FW 1: Foreign Worker Manual*, 173.

25. For the full list, see "National Occupational Classification Matrix 2011," Employment and Social Development Canada, March 2, 2015, http://www5. hrsdc.gc.ca/NOC/English/NOC/2011/html/Matrix.html.

26. For Japan, "Researchers, except for those working in an academic entity" are also excluded.

27. Whereas the other countries receive access for "contractors and supervisors" in a number of different fields, Japan only receives access for supervisors in those same fields. Japan also does not receive access for electricians or plumbers.

28. Unlike Australia, Japan and Peru, Chile's list does not include architectural technologists and technicians; industrial designers; drafting technologists and technicians; land survey technologists and technicians; and technical occupations in geomatics and meteorology.

29. The new coverage is for architectural technologists and technicians; industrial designers; drafting technologists and technicians; land survey technologists and technicians; and technical occupations in geomatics and meteorology. Curiously, the Canada–Peru FTA includes chefs and underground production and development miners, which the TPP does not.

30. Neither the Canada–Chile FTA or NAFTA distinguish between professionals and technicians, so a direct comparison of occupational coverage is difficult. New coverage in the TPP appears to be mainly in the construction and engineering sectors (e.g., construction inspectors, carpentry contractors, electricians).

31. We use a "spot check" measure of valid work permits, rather than a count of total entries in any given year, because migrant workers may enter Canada multiple times in one year or stay in Canada for longer than one year at a time. Nevertheless, the spot check approach likely underestimates the total number of migrant workers because it assumes workers leave the country when their permits expire, which is not always the case.

    Unless otherwise noted, figures provided in this section are based on data produced for the Canadian Centre for Policy Alternatives by Citizenship and Immigration Canada (dated May 2015).

32. FTA workers in Canada on December 31, 2014, as a share of total employed persons in Canada in 2014 (approximately 17.8 million). Statistics Canada, "Table 282-0012: Labour force survey estimates (LFS), employment by class of worker, North American Industry Classification System (NAICS) and sex," CANSIM, January 8, 2016, http://www5.statcan.gc.ca/cansim/a26?lang=eng&id=2820012.

33. On December 31, 2013, Australia was the fifth-biggest source of work permit holders under the International Mobility Programs (after the United States,

France, India and the United Kingdom). Japan was seventh overall, behind Ireland. See "3.4. International Mobility Program work permit holders by top 50 countries of citizenship and sign year, 2004 to 2013," Citizenship and Immigration Canada, December 31, 2014, http://www.cic.gc.ca/english/resources/statistics/facts2013/temporary/3-4.asp.

34. Author's estimate. NAFTA accounted for 97 per cent of all FTA work permits on December 31, 2014, and the ratio of American to Mexican entries under all branches of the International Mobility Programs is approximately 14:1 (see CIC, "3.4" above), so the U.S. share of total entries is roughly 90 per cent.

35. Hadrian Mertins-Kirkwood, "The hidden growth of Canada's migrant workforce," in *The Harper Record 2008–2015*, eds. Teresa Healy and Stuart Trew (Ottawa: Canadian Centre for Policy Alternatives, 2015).

36. Temporary business persons accounted for 0.07 per cent of the labour market in Canada in 2004 (same methodology as above). Even without the TPP, this figure will likely continue to rise as the Canadian economy continues to integrate with Canada's existing FTA partners.

37. Mertins-Kirkwood, *Labour Mobility in Canada*.

38. Canadian Press, "Foreign worker permits for Conifex Power plant raise questions in B.C.," *CBC News*, June 23, 2014, http://www.cbc.ca/news/canada/british-columbia/foreign-worker-permits-for-conifex-power-plant-raise-questions-in-b-c-1.2685242.

39. Kathy Tomlinson, "RBC replaces Canadian staff with foreign workers," *CBC News*, April 6, 2013, http://www.cbc.ca/news/canada/british-columbia/rbc-replaces-canadian-staff-with-foreign-workers-1.1315008.

40. Armine Yalnizyan, "Immigration policy should foster new Canadians, not temporary workers," *The Globe and Mail*, July 6, 2015, http://www.theglobeandmail.com/report-on-business/rob-commentary/immigration-policy-should-foster-new-canadians-not-temporary-workers/article25328607 .

41. For a deeper discussion of Canadian corporate concentration in the era of trade and investment liberalization, see Jordan Brennan, *Ascent of Giants: NAFTA, Corporate Power and the Growing Income Gap* (Ottawa: Canadian Centre for Policy Alternatives, 2015).

CHAPTER 7

1. For a list of recent cases: Scott Sinclair, "NAFTA Chapter 11 Investor–State Disputes to January 1, 2015," Canadian Centre for Policy Alternatives, January 14, 2015.

2. Gus Van Harten, *Sovereign Choices and Sovereign Constraints* (Oxford University Press, 2013).

3. For a further discussion: Gus Van Harten, *Investment Treaty Arbitration and Public Law* (Oxford University Press, 2007).

4. Gus Van Harten and Pavel Malysheuski, "Who has benefited financially from investment treaty arbitration? An evaluation of the size and wealth of

claimants," Osgoode Legal Studies Research Paper no. 14, January 11, 2016, http://papers.ssrn.com/sol3/papers.cfm?abstract_id=2713876.

5. David Gaukrodger and Kathryn Gordon, "Investor-state dispute settlement: A scoping paper for the investment policy community," *OECD Working Papers on International Investment 2012/03*, OECD Publishing, 2012, http://www.oecd.org/investment/investment-policy/WP-2012_3.pdf.

6. Gus Van Harten and Dayna Nadine Scott, "Investment treaties and the internal vetting of regulatory proposals: A case study from Canada," *Journal of International Dispute Settlement* 7, no. 1, 2016.

7. Data compiled by author by comparing U.S. treaties currently in force that allow for ISDS claims to the most recent annual OECD data (for 2012) on U.S. FDI positions: OECD.stat. *FDI positions by partner country*, 2012, https://stats.oecd.org/Index.aspx?DataSetCode=FDI_FLOW_PARTNER.

8. "Article 9.18.1(a)(i)(C)," *Trans-Pacific Partnership*, https://ustr.gov/sites/default/files/TPP-Final-Text-Investment.pdf.

9. "Article 1.2.1(b)," *Trans-Pacific Partnership*, https://ustr.gov/sites/default/files/TPP-Final-Text-Investment.pdf.

10. "Article 11.2.2," *Trans-Pacific Partnership*, https://ustr.gov/sites/default/files/TPP-Final-Text-Investment.pdf. Compare: "Article 1401(2)," *North American Free Trade Agreement (NAFTA)*, http://www.international.gc.ca/trade-agreements-accords-commerciaux/agr-acc/nafta-alena/text-texte/toc-tdm.aspx?lang=eng.

11. For further discussion: Gus Van Harten, "Investment treaty arbitration, procedural fairness, and the rule of law," in ed. Stephan Schill, *International Investment Law and Comparative Public Law* (Oxford University Press, 2010).

12. Gus Van Harten, "The EC and UNCTAD reform agendas: Do they ensure independence, openness, and fairness in investor-state arbitration?" in eds. Steffen Hindelang and Markus Krajewski, *Shifting Paradigms in International Investment Law* (Oxford University Press, 2016).

CHAPTER 8

1. Speech by the Quebec Minister of Culture and Communications for the Informal Meeting of European Union Ministers of Culture, June 2005, Luxembourg, http://www.eu2005.lu/en/actualites/discours/2005/06/27quebec/index.html

2. René Lemieux and Joseph Jackson, "Cultural exemptions in Canada's major international trade agreements," Library of Parliament, 1999, http://www.lop.parl.gc.ca/content/lop/researchpublications/prb9925-e.htm.

3. World Trade Organization, "Dispute DS363 – China: Measures affecting trading rights and distribution services for certain publications and audiovisual entertainment products," 2012, https://www.wto.org/english/tratop_e/dispu_e/cases_e/ds363_e.htm.

4. Compañia del Desarrollo de Santa Elena S.A. v. Republic of Costa Rica (ICSID Case No. ARB/96/1).

THE TRANS-PACIFIC PARTNERSHIP AND CANADA

5. Pauline Marois, "Mondialisation et diversité culturelle — Un instrument international pour préserver la culture," *Le Devoir*, July 25, 2002, http://www.ledevoir.com/non-classe/5903/mondialisation et-diversite-culturelle-un-instrument-international-pour-preserver-la-culture.

6. Article 1(h), Convention on the Protection and Promotion of the Diversity of Cultural Expressions, UNESCO, 2005.

7. Alexandre Malthais, "Cultural exceptions," in *Making Sense of the CETA*, eds. Scott Sinclair, Stuart Trew and Hadrian Mertins-Kirkwood, Canadian Centre for Policy Alternatives, 2014, 49–55.

8. WikiLeaks, "TPP: Country Positions (6 November 2013)," *Second release of secret Trans-Pacific Partnership Agreement documents*, November 13, 2013, https://wikileaks.org/Second-release-of-secret-Trans.html?update.

9. Gilbert Gagné and Antonios Vlassis, "Partenariat transpacifique et exception culturelle : rapports de force," *Culture, commerce et numérique* 9, no. 1, February 2014, http://www.ieim.uqam.ca/IMG/pdf/oif-volume9-numero1fevrier-2014ceim.pdf.

10. Ratification or accession.

11. United States – Import Prohibition of Certain Shrimp and Shrimp Products, Appellate Body Decision, 1998, DS58.

12. For this and all references to the TPP text, see version on New Zealand Ministry of Foreign Affairs and Trade, https://www.mfat.govt.nz/en/about-us/who-we-are/treaty-making-process/trans-pacific-partnership-tpp/text-of-the-trans-pacific-partnership/.

13. Ibid.

14. NAFTA's cultural exception (Article 2106) was carried over from the 1988 Canada–U.S. Free Trade Agreement.

15. See, for example, the Canada–Peru FTA, http://www.international.gc.ca/trade-agreements-accords-commerciaux/agr-acc/peru-perou/preamble-preambule.aspx?lang=eng.

16. Interestingly enough, although it was concluded before the adoption of the UNESCO Convention, the Canada–Costa Rica FTA recognizes "that States have the ability to preserve, develop and implement their cultural policies for the purpose of strengthening cultural diversity."

17. Stephen Clarkson, *Uncle Sam and US: Globalization, Neoconservatism, and the Canadian State* (Toronto: University of Toronto Press, 2002).

18. Garry Neil, "Free trade and deep integration in North America: Saving Canadian culture," in *Whose Canada: Continental Integration, Fortress North America and the Corporate Agenda*, eds. Ricardo Grinspun and Yasmine Shamsie (Montreal: McGill University Press, 2007).

19. It is also curious how Article 29.8 lacks coherence, as there is no elaboration in the description of what "genetic resources" refers to.

20. WIPO, "Traditional knowledge laws: Malaysia," *Traditional Knowledge, Traditional Cultural Expressions & Genetic Resources Laws*, http://www.wipo.

int/tk/en/databases/tklaws/articles/article_0012.html.

21. WIPO, "Glossary," Resources, http://www.wipo.int/tk/en/resources/glossary.html#48.

22. Ibid.

23. Article 4.1, Convention on the Protection and Promotion of the Diversity of Cultural Expressions, UNESCO, 2005.

24. Michael Geist, "The Trans Pacific Partnership and the fight over a cultural exception," blog entry, December 10, 2013, http://www.michaelgeist.ca/2013/12/tpp-cultural-exception/.

25. Michael Geist, "The trouble with the TPP, Day 18: Failure to protect Canadian cultural policy," blog entry, January 27, 2016, http://www.michaelgeist.ca/2016/01/the-trouble-with-the-tpp-day-18-failure-to-protect-canadian-cultural-policy/.

26. For more detail, refer to this short analysis on CETA's cultural exception: Alexandre L. Maltais, "L'Accord économique commercial et général Canada-Union Européenne: Faut-il célébrer l'évocation culturelle?" Institut de recherche en économie contemporaine (IREC), November 2014, http://www.irec.net/upload/File/lettrecommerceno5novembre2014vd.pdf.

CHAPTER 9

1. "Consultations on potential free trade agreement negotiations with Trans-Pacific Partnership members," *Canada Gazette*, December 31, 2011, http://canadagazette.gc.ca/rp-pr/p1/2011/2011-12-31/html/notice-avis-eng.html#d106.

2. Paul Robertson, Government of Canada, "Requests for comments: Canada's expression of interest in proposed Trans-Pacific Partnership Trade Agreement," Comment, http://www.regulations.gov/document?D=USTR-2011-0019-0001.

3. Laura Dawson, "Can Canada join the Trans-Pacific Partnership? Why just wanting it is not enough," C.D. Howe Institute, 2012, www.cdhowe.org/pdf/Commentary_340.pdf.

4. Michael Geist, "The price of admission to the TPP talks revealed: U.S. demanded Canada pass anti-counterfeiting legislation," November 28, 2014, blog post, www.michaelgeist.ca/2014/11/price-admission-tpp-talks-revealed-u-s-demanded-canada-pass-anti-counterfeiting-legislation/.

5. Michael Geist, "How Canada shaped the copyright rules in the EU trade deal," August 21, 2014, blog post, www.michaelgeist.ca/2014/08/canada-shaped-copyright-rules-eu-trade-deal/.

6. "Intellectual Property Policy," *Assessing Economic Impacts of Copyright Reform on Selected users and Consumers*, Industry Canada (link broken on ic.gc.ca).

7. Carolina Rossini and Yana Welinder, "All nations lose with TPP's expansion of copyright terms," *Electronic Frontier Foundation*, August 8, 2012, https://www.eff.org/deeplinks/2012/08/all-nations-lose-tpps-expansion-copyright-terms.

8. New Zealand Foreign Affairs & Trade, "Economic modelling on estimated effect of copyright term extension on New Zealand economy," https://www.tpp.mfat govt.nz/assets/docs/TPP%20-%20Analysis%20of%20 Copyright%20term%20extension,%20explanatory%20cover%20note.pdf.

9. Howard Knopf, "The cost of Canadian copyright term extension capitulation in the TPP — estimates based upon New Zealand Study," *Blog Spot*, November 17, 2015, http://excesscopyright.blogspot.ca/2015/11/the-cost-of-canadian-copyright-term.html.

10. "Copyright concessions may be downside of TPP deal," *The Globe and Mail*, October 23, 2015, http://www.theglobeandmail.com/opinion/editorials/copyright-concessions-may-be-downside-of-tpp-deal/article26939204/.

11. Don LePan, "Copyright, the TPP, and the Canadian election," *Blog Spot*, October 14, 2015, http://donlepan.blogspot.ca/2015/10/copyright-tpp-and-canadian-election.html/.

12. Michael Geist, "Official release of TPP text confirms massive loss to Canadian public domain," November 5, 2015, blog entry, www.michaelgeist.ca/2015/11/official-release-of-tpp-text-confirms-massive-loss-to-canadian-public-domain/.

13. Kimberlee G Weatherall, "Section by section commentary on the TPP final IP chapter published 5 November 2015 – Part 2 – Copyright," 2015, http://works.bepress.com/kimweatherall/32/.

14. WikiLeaks, "Updated secret Trans-Pacific Partnership Agreement (TPP) - IP chapter (second publication)," press release, October 16, 2014, https://wikileaks.org/tpp-ip2/.

15. Trans Atlantic Consumer Dialogue, "Resolution on the terms of protection for copyright and related rights, and measures to expand access to works not exploited by copyright owners," DOC No. IP 10-09, TACD, 2009, http://tacd.org/wp-content/uploads/2013/09/TACD-IP-10-09-Copyright-Terms.pdf.

16. Michael Geist, "The Case for Flexibility in Implementing the WIPO Internet Treaties: An Examination of the Anti-Circumvention Requirements," in ed. Michael Geist, *From "Radical Extremism" to "Balanced Copyright": Canadian Copyright and the Digital Agenda* (Toronto: Irwin Law Inc., 2010), 204, www.irwinlaw.com/sites/default/files/attached/CCDA%2008%20Geist.pdf; also Carys Craig, "Locking Out Lawful Users: Fair Dealing and Anti-Circumvention in Bill C-32," in ed. Michael Geist, *From "Radical Extremism" to "Balanced Copyright": Canadian Copyright and the Digital Agenda* (Toronto: Irwin Law Inc., 2010), 177, www.irwinlaw.com/sites/default/files/attached/CCDA%2007%20Craig.pdf; also Ian Kerr, "Digital Locks and the Automation of Virtue," in ed. Michael Geist, *From "Radical Extremism" to "Balanced Copyright": Canadian Copyright and the Digital Agenda* (Toronto: Irwin Law Inc., 2010), 247, www.irwinlaw.com/sites/default/files/attached/CCDA%2009%20Kerr.pdf; also Jeremy de Beer, "Constitutional Jurisdiction over Paracopyright Laws," in ed. Michael Geist, *From "Radical Extremism" to "Balanced*

Copyright": Canadian Copyright and the Digital Agenda (Toronto: Irwin Law Inc., 2010), 89, www.irwinlaw.com/sites/default/files/attached/Two_01_deBeer.pdf; also Mark Perry, "The Protection of Rights Management Information: Modernization or Cup Half Full?" in ed. Michael Geist, *From "Radical Extremism" to "Balanced Copyright": Canadian Copyright and the Digital Agenda* (Toronto: Irwin Law Inc., 2010), 304, www.irwinlaw.com/sites/default/files/attached/CCDA%2010%20Perry.pdf.

17. David Lametti, "How Virtue Ethics Might Help Erase C-32's Conceptual Incoherence," in ed. Michael Geist, *From "Radical Extremism" to "Balanced Copyright": Canadian Copyright and the Digital Agenda* (Toronto: Irwin Law Inc., 2010), 327, www.irwinlaw.com/sites/default/files/attached/CCDA%2011%20Lametti.pdf.

18. Michael Geist, "The final copyright consultation numbers: No repeat of Bill C-61," April 9, 2010, blog entry, www.michaelgeist.ca/2010/04/copycon-final-numbers.

19. Michael Geist, "Premature capitulation: How Canada caved at the TPP talks in Hawaii," August 17, 2015, blog entry, www.michaelgeist.ca/2015/08/premature-capitulation-how-canada-caved-at-the-tpp-talks-in-hawaii/.

20. "Chapter 22 - Intellectual Property," *Comprehensive Economic and Trade Agreement*, Global Affairs Canada, www.international.gc.ca/trade-agreements-accords-commerciaux/agr-acc/ceta-aecg/text-texte/22.aspx?lang=eng.

21. Ibid.

22. Ibid.

23. Ibid.

24. "Chapter 18 - Intellectual Property, United States Trade Representative," *Trans-Pacific Partnership*, February 4, 2016, https://ustr.gov/sites/default/files/TPP-Final-Text-Intellectual-Property.pdf.

25. Ibid.

26. Michael Geist, "Rightscorp and BMG exploiting copyright notice-and-notice system: Citing false legal information in payment demands," January 8, 2015, blog entry, www.michaelgeist.ca/2015/01/rightscorp-bmg-exploiting-copyright-notice-notice-system-citing-false-legal-information-payment-demands.

27. International Intellectual Property Alliance, *Canada 2015 Special 301 Report on Copyright Protection and Enforcement*, IIPA 301, 2015, http://www.iipawebsite.com/rbc/2015/2015SPEC301CANADA.pdf); also International Intellectual Property Alliance, *Chile 2015 Special 301 Report on Copyright Protection and Enforcement*, IIPA 301, 2015, http://www.iipawebsite.com/rbc/2015/2015SPEC301CHILE.pdf.

28. Annemarie Bridy, "A user-focused commentary on the Trans Pacific Partnership ISP safe harbors," *InfoJustice*, November 23, 2015, http://infojustice.org/archives/35402/.

29. US, Federal Register, *Section 512 Study: Notice and Request for Public Comment*, Copyright Office, 2015, www.federalregister.gov/articles/2015/12/31/2015-32973/section-512-study-notice-and-request-for-public-comment.

30. "Chapter 18, Intellectual Property," *Trans-Pacific Partnership Agreement*, February 4, 2016, https://ustr.gov/sites/default/files/TPP-Final-Text-Intellectual-Property.pdf.

CHAPTER 10

1. *Canada Post Corporation Act*, R.S.C. 1985, c. C-10, s. 5(2)(b). Further to these broad objectives, the act also requires that Canada Post maintain uniform postal rates throughout the country, standards regarding frequency of collection and speed of delivery, and appropriate proximity of postal boxes and post offices.

2. See, e.g., the Liberal Party campaign petition, "Saving home mail delivery," www.liberal.ca/petitions/saving-home-mail-delivery.

3. "Judy Foote 'not ruling out anything' in Canada Post review", *CBC News*, May 5, 2016, www.cbc.ca/1.3565888.

4. Annex 10-B, s. 3 of the Trans-Pacific Partnership (TPP) (www.international.gc.ca/trade-agreements-accords-commerciaux/agr-acc/tpp-ptp/) imposes general restrictions on how the scope of a postal monopoly may be defined (which the *Canada Post Corporation Act* already complies with). This section is only intelligible if states are permitted to have postal monopolies in the first place.

5. Canada Post Corporation, *What's In the Truck: Annual Report, 2015*, 3, www.canadapost.ca/assets/pdf/aboutus/financialreports/2015_ar_complete_en.pdf.

6. Ruosi Zhang, "The liberalization of postal and courier services: ready for delivery," *Opening Markets for Trade in Services Countries and Sectors in Bilateral and WTO Negotiations*, eds. Juan A. Marchetti and Martin Roy (Cambridge: Cambridge University Press, February 2009), 387–88.

7. 2015 Annual Report, *supra*, i.

8. Ibid., 4, 80.

9. *UPS Europe SA v. Commission (Deutsche Post AG intervening)* Case T-175/99, Judgment of March 20, 2002 (Court of First Instance of the European Union).

10. Chile–U.S. Free Trade Agreement, Chapter 11, Annex 11.6.

11. Australia–U.S. Free Trade Agreement, Art. 10.12.3.

12. *Postal Accountability and Enhancement Act*, Pub. L. 109-435, 120 Stat. 3198, 39 U.S.C. §3633(a)(1).

13. United States Trade Representative, *TPP: Made in America*, "Chapter 10: Cross-Border Trade in Services," https://ustr.gov/tpp/.

14. TPP, Annex 10-B, s. 5.

15. TPP, Annex 10-B, s. 6.

16. For a summary of these reviews and investigations, see Scott Sinclair, *The GATS and Canadian Postal Services* (Ottawa: Canadian Centre for Policy Alternatives, March 2001), 26, www.citizen.org/documents/Sinclair%20 POSTAL.pdf); also Jim Grieshaber-Otto and Scott Sinclair, *Return to Sender: The Impact of GATS "Pro-Competitive Regulation" on Postal and Other Public Services* (Canadian Centre for Policy Alternatives, January 28, 2004), 123, www.policyalternatives.ca/publications/reports/return-sender.

17. Siva Somasundram and Iain Sandford, "Regulation of postal services in a changing market environment: lessons from Australia and elsewhere," in *WTO Domestic Regulation and Services Trade: Putting Principles into Practice*, eds. Aik Hoe Lim, Bart De Meester (Cambridge: Cambridge University Press, 2014), 189–90.

18. UPS's claim of abuse of dominance through cross-subsidization under EU competition rules failed in large part due to their inability to identify the specific acts of the postal system that were said to be abusive: see *UPS Europe SA v. Commission, supra* at paras. 59-61.

19. TPP, Art. 17.4.2(d).

20. NAFTA rules prohibit abuse of monopoly positions in non-monopolized markets where they have the effect of adversely affecting the investment of a foreign investor. The TPP rules are framed in terms of negative impacts on trade or investment between parties generally, opening the door to a broader range of complaints than could be raised under NAFTA. *Compare NAFTA*, Art. 1502(3)(d) with *TPP*, s. 17.4.2(d).

21. TPP, Art. 17.6.

22. See TPP, Arts. 17.1, *s.v.* "non-commercial assistance." The argument is as follows: NCA means "assistance to a state-owned enterprise by virtue of that state-owned enterprise's government ownership or control." Purolator is an SOE. Assistance is defined to include "services other than general infrastructure on terms more favourable than those commercially available to that enterprise." "General infrastructure" is not defined, but likely means things like roads and not specialized infrastructure such as used by Canada Post, and so granting Purolator access to it would meet the definition, assuming that it is given on discount or noncommercial basis. The phrase "by virtue of that state-owned enterprise's government ownership and control" is defined to include cases where a party or one of its SOE's "explicitly limits access to the assistance to any of its state-owned enterprises." Since Canada Post is also an SOE, and does not grant access to its infrastructure to companies other than Purolator, the NCA definition would be made out.

23. TPP, Art. 17.6.2(b).

24. See TPP, Art. 10.2.2(a), footnote 1, and Chapter 9, Section B: "Investor-State Dispute Settlement" (Arts. 9.18-9.30).

25. TPP, Articles 9.4, 9.5, 9.6 and 9.7.
26. In the previous chapter to this book, Alexandre Maltais argues Canada's cultural protections are also not as strong as in past FTAs, or the pending (as of publishing) Canada–EU Comprehensive Economic and Trade Agreement.
27. TPP, Annex II (Japan), No. 2.
28. TPP, Annex II (Singapore), No. 21.

INDEX